# EMPOWER
# THE
# PEOPLE

★

# EMPOWER THE PEOPLE

OVERTHROW THE CONSPIRACY

THAT IS STEALING

YOUR MONEY AND FREEDOM

## TONY BROWN

QUILL

WILLIAM MORROW

New York

The Library of Congress has cataloged a previous edition of this title.

Library of Congress Cataloging-in-Publication Data

Brown, Tony, M.S.W.
Empower the people: overthrow the conspiracy
that is stealing your money and freedom / by Tony Brown.
p.     cm.
Includes bibliographical references and index.
ISBN 0-688-15762-9
1. Conspiracies—United States.   2. Elites (Social sciences)—United States.
3. Power (Social sciences)—United States.   4. Upper class—United States.
5. Illuminati—United States.   6. Secret societies—United States.   I. Title.
HV6285.B73   1998
322.4'2'0973—dc21                                        97-36579
                                                              CIP

Paperback ISBN 0-688-16974-0

Printed in the United States of America

First Quill Edition 1999

1  2  3  4  5  6  7  8  9  10

BOOK DESIGN BY JENNIFER ANN DADDIO

www.williammorrow.com

*To my bloodline; my daughter, Taylor; my son, Byron; my grandsons, Remy and Tony, and their unborn. Your legacy.*

# ACKNOWLEDGMENTS

Hitler burned books to destroy the ideas he feared. In our modern American "democracy," the ruling class uses opportunistic professionals, agents, to destroy those who expose America's and the world's rulers and their ruthless commitment to evil. Therefore, I am indebted to anyone, past or present, rich or poor, who has fought or fights the conspiratorial force of darkness.

Most major publishing houses adhere to a status quo policy of serving the ruling class at the expense of the people. To my knowledge, no other major publisher has ever commissioned a book by a Black male dealing with the Conspiracy. In a world in which our major institutions have failed us, it should not pass without notice that William Morrow and Company allowed me—a Black man who believes in God and America—to say so in public.

Black men with proud and strong opinions comprise the lowest rung on the ladder of America's caste system. Consequently they are seldom published. Another caste in the American outcast genre are those who believe in God—because they are the natural enemies of the Conspiracy and its powerful sycophants. They are routinely categorized as fanatical. Another persecuted class is Black people with high self-esteem who reject Anglo-Saxon cultural assimilation, but who understand that they will never enjoy liberty until all White people, as well as other non-Whites, also have it in abundance.

These are the very formidable obstacles that I had to overcome to make this moment a reality. Only God could have given my editor, Paul Bresnick, the intellect to recognize legitimate ideas whose inherent pursuit of the truth makes them commercially viable. Also my greatest appreciation to my agent, Barbara Lowenstein.

In my opinion, this book represents a new literary genre that will make money because it tells the truth, despite the predictable opposition and omission of the Establishment-controlled media and its covert agents. This is a part of the evil I am committed to expose.

The people who stand by me demonstrate why, as the Holy Bible teaches, the days of evil are numbered. Carla Fine, author of *No Time to Say Goodbye: Surviving the Suicide of a Loved One* and a freelance editor, helped me organize my ideas. She was supportive and very professional. My friend and business associate Curtis Green also provided an ongoing source of feedback. Dr. Ronald Fountain, who successfully escaped the academic world with common sense, helped me define the formula for empowerment: $E=CLP+FSI$.

But two Black women, a recurring theme in my life because I was saved at birth by two Black women, contributed the most to make this book possible. Karen Smith, my administrative assistant, literally wrote it (as well as my first one, *Black Lies, White Lies: The Truth According to Tony Brown*) because she typed every word—including twice as much material as made the final cut. Karen served as my biblical consultant as well. Sheryl Cannady, who is the producer, along with her husband, Jim Cannady (who is also the systems operator of *Tony Brown Online*), of *Tony Brown's Journal* on PBS, performed the task of in-house editor.

My words are unable to convey the intensity, commitment, and friendship that Karen and Sheryl demonstrated in bringing this book to the public. Only God can bring friends like these into your life.

It is only fair to admit that this book wrote itself. An out-of-the-box thinker, I never suffered from so-called writer's block or lacked ideas or insight into my subject, that is, the world around me. I went directly to the source of all knowledge. I prayed

*May God grant me the words to speak His thoughts.*

I asked and I received. May the Creator also bless you as you seek your empowerment between these covers.

# CONTENTS

# CONTENTS

## PART TWO: SELF-EMPOWERMENT

# INTRODUCTION

Most Americans sense a danger—a loss of control, an erosion of their standard of living, a social drift. The rich are getting richer, the poor are getting poorer, special interest groups are at each other's throats for ever more scarce resources, and power continues to be consolidated in the hands of a small ruling class. Things have gotten so bad, in fact, that a majority of Americans—74 percent, according to a poll conducted by *George* magazine—believes that the government is involved in a large-scale conspiracy.[1]

And, according to Senator Daniel Moynihan of New York, opinion polls show that 80 percent of Americans believe President John F. Kennedy was assassinated in a United States government conspiracy and that 50 percent of that 80 percent majority believe the CIA was involved or was the mastermind.[2]

In 1996, the Clinton White House leaked to journalists a massive document alleging a right-wing conspiracy among conservative media organizations. In 1998, Hillary Clinton advocated the existence of a "vast conservative conspiracy" that she and President Clinton blame "for rumors about extramarital affairs and for gossip about Clinton's business deals" and grotesque slanders accusing the Clintons of having the former White House Deputy Counsel Vince Foster and Commerce Secretary Ron Brown murdered.[3] Notwithstanding the fact that a faction of right-wing conservatives were delighted that another sex scandal struck Clinton and would form a cabal to steal the White House in a New York minute, there are a few facts that cast doubt on the existence of this conspiracy in the case of a twenty-one-year-old White House intern named Monica Lewinsky, who reportedly accused the president of tawdry behavior.

Democratic Senator Bob Kerrey told the Associated Press[4] that a conspiracy theory to whitewash the Monica Lewinsky sex scandal "doesn't wash." He said, "You can't call *The Washington Post* a right-wing organization. It doesn't work."[5] *Newsweek* broke the story of the reported Lewinsky audiotapes purporting a tryst with Clinton and accusing him of suborning perjury. Attorney General Janet Reno, a Clinton appointee, agreed to expand the inquiry and the president's own FBI supervised the taping of the audiotapes.

Furthermore, it was not a right-winger, but Dick Morris, a former Clinton presidential guru with a foot fetish, who speculated on radio that if President Clinton is cheating on his wife, the reason could be that she is a lesbian (later he said, "I have no evidence she is gay") and ruminated that the president is addicted to phone sex.[6] Unfortunately, the Clintons' self-serving effort at misdirection trivializes the Conspiracy that Bill Clinton's mentor, Professor Carroll Quigley, boasted of belonging to.

In *Empower the People: A 7-Step Plan to Overthrow the Con-*

*spiracy That Is Stealing Your Money and Freedom,* I expose the evil cabal of elitists and money lords that pulls the strings: the Illuminati Ruling Class Conspiracy. This Conspiracy controls our government, steals our income, and usurps our freedom. I trace the history of this Conspiracy and show how it has systematically oppressed and exploited the people of the world.

The Illuminati Ruling Class Conspiracy is not the tony White Anglo-Saxon Protestant (WASP) society of the northeastern United States; that's the legitimate American ruling class elite, the Establishment. The Conspiracy is a criminal empire with religious overtones, while the upper-class WASPs comprise the cultural phenomenon of the Americanized British elite. Yet the Illuminati conspirators have thoroughly infiltrated the Establishment and use the institutional instruments controlled by the upper-class elite—the universities, the government, organized religion—to enslave the people. Thomas C. McAuliffe states in *Debt Bomb and the Savings Pool* that "80 million Americans, fully one third of the nation, are but one paycheck away from being homeless, while the top 1 percent of the population controls 90 percent of the nation's wealth."[7]

It is my mission to lift the veil of secrecy that the Conspiracy counts on for survival. Becoming informed is essential to getting out from under the thrall of this powerful Conspiracy. And in this book, I give you all the information you need for self-empowerment and a seven-step plan for taking back your economic and personal freedom.

An elite insider, Dr. Carroll Quigley, boasted in his book *Tragedy and Hope* that not only is there an "international Anglophile network" conspiracy that is stealing our money and freedom, but he was a proud member of this movement to rule the world.[8] Quigley, President Bill Clinton's Georgetown University mentor, expressed a premeditated contempt for the American middle class and their "petit bourgeois" property rights and Constitutional guarantees.

The apparent purpose of writing such a confrontational confessional was to warn the American people to surrender and accept this dictatorship of the power elite. Professor Quigley, confessed class conspirator, warned us that it is too late to resist the inevitable loss of American democracy and freedom.[9] It would be "tragic" to resist. He implies that there is "hope" for us only if we surrender to the inevitable "instrument" of a totalitarian cabal and serve its evil purposes. Perhaps Bill Clinton took his advice, but this book is a call to arms against evil and the ruling class conspiracy.

The principal purpose of this book is to sound a call to action. Because the Conspiracy for world domination remains unrecognized, it remains unopposed. Wake up, my fellow Americans. It is time to choose between knowledge and ignorance, between freedom and slavery, between Americanism and Conspiracy, between good and evil. We must choose now between remaining the Conspiracy's victims or empowering ourselves by fighting back. If you choose victimization, keep complaining—but keep the Prozac handy. If you choose democracy, revive the spirit of Americanism in your own heart and act to reclaim the God-given human rights of every American.

This book connects some of the dots creating a unique picture of the situation in which America currently finds itself, highlighting some of the conflicting humanistic and moral purposes now at play—for example, the Divinely ordained purpose of true Americanism (as presented in the Declaration of Independence and the Constitution); the esoteric, elitist doctrine of "Illuminism" existing within contemporary Freemasonry; the massive alliance of money and power that exploits the population of the United States; and the emergence of a nation of a new class of "niggers" resulting from the loss of our "unalienable" human rights.

The situation began when the intellectual aristocrats in Europe infiltrated the God-fearing guild of Freemasonry in the eighteenth century at the top and successfully transformed it largely into "Illuminated Freemasonry," technically "Lucife-rian" Illuminated Freemasonry, a pagan religion in the tradition of ancient Babylon's witchcraft mysteries.

## WHAT IS THE DIFFERENCE BETWEEN SATAN AND LUCIFER?

Therefore, the Illuminati's rebirth in 1776 represented a revival of Lucifer's original revolt against the sovereignty of God in Heaven and precipitated a classic struggle between the forces of good and evil in the world—a struggle between faith in God and the hunger for power by an elitist economic royalty that worships the Devil. Only in a mundane sense, however, is the Conspiracy man's struggle against mankind to establish a world-wide totalitarian state, or a one-world government. In a larger sense, it is a battle between God and the Devil for the souls of the people of the world.

However, the idea of a supernatural force of evil in the world is an unfamiliar idea to many people. Even among ordinary Freemasons in the higher occult degrees who have not bought into Illuminati Freemasonry, and especially among secular humanists, there is an adamant denial of "the reality of evil"[10] and a rather hostile attitude toward the biblical religions, especially the absolute dogma of Christianity.

Most of the people I know and most contemporary writers use Lucifer and Satan as interchangeable terms for the Devil. In common Christian usage, Lucifer means "the light bearer" or "the brilliant one." When Lucifer rebelled against God in the Heavens, and God expelled him, Lucifer, the angel of light, became Satan, the adversary of God, the prince of the devils[11] and the great dragon.[12] Satan is now the Devil and the one-third of angels who followed him are his demon army that works to create secret societies, wars, corrupt government, and other vehicles to control the world and oppose God. Satan's demon angels exceed the total population of the earth; they are especially active in political, financial, and religious areas. Satan is ". . . the prince of this world."[13]

However, Satan and Lucifer often have distinctly different meanings in the occult world. Among the Illuminati, for example, "Lucifer is God and the doctrine of Satanism is a heresy. Lucifer is their God of Light. The Christian God (Adonay), they state, is the God of Evil," according to Salem Kirban's book *Satan's Angels Exposed*.[14]

In the context of the political religion that I call Illuminati (Luciferian) Freemasonry, the Devil is invoked through the practice called Theurgy, or White Magic.[15] When the Devil is invoked under the name of Satan, a very popular public practice among rock music bands, it is classified as "Geotry or Black Magic." The Illuminati opposes both Christianity and atheism. Its god is Satan, whom they refuse to acknowledge by his name, preferring instead the appellation of Lucifer.

Therefore, consistent with those definitions, I mean something distinctly different when I refer to the Devil as Lucifer or Satan respectively. And when reading, please make a distinction between ordinary Freemasonry (which is composed of private lodges) or Masonry and the practice of "occult Masonry, the real masonry of the Cabalistic degrees."[16] There are, of course, also Satanists who are Freemasons. This "Luciferian Occultism controls Freemasonry," according to Edith Starr Miller in her classic book *Occult Theocracy*.[17]

During the third century, Luciferian Occultism (Illuminated Freemasonry) was called Gnosticism, and was regarded as a heresy by most Christians. It "blended pagan sex rituals and Mother Goddess worship with elements of New Testament Christianity" and rejected the God Jehovah as an evil demon.[18] Founded by Simon the Magician, it has over the ages, without interruption, down to the present day, periodically changed its mask, but not its beliefs.[19]

Another crucial distinction between the Satanic and Luciferian Devil sects is that Luciferian Occultists never describe their god Lucifer as evil. They deliberately glorify Lucifer "as the principle of good . . . the equal of the God of Christians whom they describe as the principle of evil."[20] On the other hand, Satanists "recognize that their God Satan occupies a position in the supernatural sphere, inferior to that of the Christian deity."[21] Therefore, the god Satan is referred to by his worshipers as the "Spirit of Evil" or "Father and Creator of Crime." Satanists also "accuse the God of the Christians of having betrayed the cause of humanity."[22]

In this eternal struggle, good is still on one end of the spectrum and evil on the other. It all began when Adam and Eve ate the forbidden fruit, the narcotic that opened the mind's eye to the knowledge of good and evil, giving them a false sense of becoming gods through their illuminated reasoning. Since that time in the Garden of Eden, the human race has been in rebellion against God.

A classic battle of good and evil has ensued—a struggle between faith and the hunger for power. This battle took on the proportions of Armageddon in the eighteenth century with the advent of Communism—an Illuminati front. Illuminati Freemason Karl Marx, in his *Communist Manifesto,* outlined a diabolical Illuminati plan to endow the ruling class, through its puppet governments, with absolute power by giving it the means to control people's very survival.

Marx's plan was devilishly elegant: The government should create a central bank with a monopoly over the monetary system. Marx's disciple Lenin tested the concept on the Russian banking system after the revolution of 1917, intentionally causing massive inflation by printing more and more "money" in order "to destroy the people's savings and redistribute the wealth." The middle class was seen as dangerous because it controlled the ownership of property. Therefore, its wealth (property) had to be confiscated. It was in this way wiped out and put completely at the mercy of the government oligarchy—for food, shelter, clothing, work, indeed for life itself.

In the United States, a central bank was created in 1913 by the Illuminati Ruling Class Conspiracy, and it usurped control of the monetary system from our lawfully elected government representatives. This privately owned, profit-making central bank of the United States government, the "Federal" Reserve System (also called the Federal Reserve Bank or simply the Federal Reserve), was granted the legal authority to issue notes of debt as unbacked "money," loan it to the government, and charge the unsuspecting taxpayers interest on the loan. This nifty system of "banking" has had the effect of confiscating the incomes of Americans and gradually transferring them into the accounts of the ruling class. Prior to the creation of the Federal Reserve Bank, there was no national debt. Today, the United States is buried under a $7 trillion mountain of IOUs—making it the world's leading debtor nation.

The Federal Reserve System has been called "the true locus of clandestine power," because it was created unconstitutionally and is responsible to no one. The Chairman of the Federal Reserve is, in effect, America's czar, and his Board of Governors is the clandestine government, answerable to no one but the money lords among the power elite. Article I, Section 8, Paragraph 5 of the Constitution stipulates that only Congress "has the power to coin money and regulate the value thereof." Since it is the President who appoints the Governors and the Chairman of the Federal Reserve, it is a bank of monetary issue that is removed from Congressional control and is therefore unconstitutional.

Furthermore, no President is truly in charge of the central

bank, since each of the members of the Board of Governors serves for fourteen years, and each President appoints only two of the seven members. In addition to wielding other dictatorial powers, the Fed czar dictates policies that manipulate the money supply and the economy in order to make or break a sitting President. Bill Clinton, for example, can be said to have been appointed President in 1996 by czar Alan Greenspan's regulatory manipulation of the money supply to achieve a rosy economic picture before the election. Perhaps Greenspan did not manipulate the economy. But if he had so chosen, there is no opposing power that could have stopped him.

What has the Federal Reserve done for this country? The government has become a tyranny that serves a wealthy and powerful elite, while the people go begging at the doors of the very politicians they vote into office. As the 1997 Congressional hearings on campaign finance have again painfully demonstrated, the government, including the lofty office of the Presidency, has been corrupted by greed to the point of becoming nothing less than an instrument of a Ruling Class Conspiracy.

Even the mainstream media is now forced to confront the possibility, based on an enormous amount of documentation, that a Conspiracy runs America. "This country is in deeper trouble than anyone in mainstream politics or journalism dare imagine," wrote columnist Robert D. Novak.[23] After reviewing a plethora of allegations about criminal activity by President Bill Clinton in Ambrose Evans-Pritchard's book *The Secret Life of Bill Clinton,* Novak's incredulousness seems to have turned into the discovery that a Conspiracy runs the American government. Novak now believes that the "decay in the American body politic" goes beyond "an ethically challenged" President to "corruption that permeates the FBI, the Department of Justice, the federal judiciary, and law enforcement generally. That suggests a malignancy that cannot and will not be excised by Clinton's departure."[24] Novak seems to have finally recognized that a cabal owned the White House before Clinton and will still own it when its next choice replaces him.

Today, top-echelon Illuminists still keep a presence within secret societies, such as the Committee of 300, Freemasonry, the Order, the Group, the Mafia, "The City," the Anglophile Round Table groups' inner core, etc., but they and their "illuminated" operatives for the most part cluster in the academy (universities), the government, financial institutions, the military, the clergy, and most conspicuously, the mass media, as "journalists," whose credo is: "The truth is out there, but don't let anyone know about it."

These are the conspiracy's secret agents, or "spooks," who constantly feed the people the propaganda of elitist hegemony, e.g., Quigley's *Tragedy and Hope.* These "spook agenturs," as I call them, are typically well-bred, exceptionally clever-minded anti-intellectual intellectuals, who trap the American people into worshiping at the altars of statism—the religion of government—by convincing them that the bureaucracy of the state is their only protection from such disasters as economic collapse, international terrorism, and race wars.

Agenturs span the range of demographic groups. Although mostly White and substantially White Anglo-Saxon Protestant, they are also Black, Red, Yellow, and Brown. They include Jews and Gentiles. No matter what their ethnic and racial background, however, they are always affluent, educated, and evil.

Most of these ambitious angels of evil do not consciously recognize themselves as agents of an occult religion and certainly not as members of a conspiracy. But you know the spook agenturs and their Illuminist economic royalty not by their names, but "By their fruits ye shall know them": fruits of elitism, war, poverty, planned unemployment, race warfare, financial panic, etc.

The lower-echelon "illuminated" agents are rarely known to one another, and the high priests in the Illuminati power elite are virtually invisible. The identity of these servants of the forces of evil is irrelevant, anyway. It amounts to a distraction from the task of discovering the Illuminati's structure and methods. Besides, considering what's at stake, the Illuminati's penetration of those groups that most conspiracy theorists identify as the foundation of a worldwide conspiracy of the power elite—the Bilderbergers, the Council on Foreign Relations, and the Trilateral Commission—is a given. These semisecret Round Table organizations are not per se conspiratorial groups, but they have been infiltrated by the agents of a larger international cabal, Illuminati Freemasonry and the "invisible" money lords in "The City," the religious and financial branches of the Illuminati, respectively.

Perhaps the most far-reaching issue before us today is what we plan to do about the Illuminati Ruling Class Conspiracy. The Conspiracy is not impregnable, and we, the people, have the numbers on our side. The main purpose of this book is to help you to arm yourself with a plan to remain free. As Frederick Douglass, the great abolitionist, declared, "Power concedes nothing without a demand." Are you ready to look into the eye of that conspiracy and make a demand? And are you ready to look into your soul and expose the inner conspiracy that exists there? Are you ready to cast off the selfishness and sense of entitlement that has created the fertile soil for the Conspiracy's ascendancy? Are you ready to assume responsibility for yourself and for your community? Those are the questions you need to answer as you read this book and ponder whether you want to follow my seven-point plan for self-empowerment.

The existence of the Order of the Illuminati is a historical fact. I do not raise this issue because I believe in black helicopters or men in black suits. Nor am I a conspiracist. And I do not truck with the paranoid lunatic fringe or take on the victim status that so often accompanies those who have submerged themselves in it. Instead, I have chosen freedom. And I invite you to join me in the fight against the Conspiracy by liberating yourself, your family, and your community.

Jesus knew that His body would be murdered if He told the truth, and John the Baptist knew his enemies would kill him if he told the truth. Both men chose truth over life. They are my heroes, because I learned from them that truth is more important than life. Martin Luther King, Jr., preached his own eulogy and Malcolm X prophesied his own death because they made the same choice. An evil force killed Malcolm and Martin, but the truth grew larger. Truth is the bane of the evil Illuminati's survival—because truth is God.

*Empower the People: A 7-Step Plan to Overthrow the Conspiracy That Is Stealing Your Money and Freedom* shows how David can defeat Goliath. My seven-point plan explains how to beat the ruling class at its own game through personal and community self-empowerment. I detail how Americans can take back their country by having faith in one another and through the use of community-based economies, an independent money system (which is to the Federal Reserve what garlic is to a vampire), direct marketing, bartering, wealth creation, wealth cleansing, intranets, computer networks, and so on. Every individual—and every community of interest—will thrive in a nation that respects every citizen as equal in the eyes of God. I strongly urge that Blacks and Whites abandon the idea of a race war—"Civil War II," as one author describes it—and recognize what and who is subordinating their interests. Then jointly oppose it.

This book demonstrates how to protect yourself from the tragic economic and social consequences of the U.S. government's gradual but massive transfer of the wealth of American citizens to the bankers and investors of the privately owned Federal Reserve System, a process of debauching the currency, but described by our government as a loss of our standard of living. See Chapter 5 for more information. To help you truly understand the situation, I explain some basic rules of economics, especially the principles governing how money and debt operate; and the principle of slavery. The theft of our income and human rights depends on the population's ignorance of those principles.

I offer you a plan for spiritual and economic recovery—for total self-empowerment. I examine the inner and the outer workings of the Conspiracy that steals your money and your right to live life the way you want to live it. Most important, I suggest a way to restore the United States' original system of governance—imbued with the spirit of Americanism—that guaranteed our human rights.

Wake up, America. It's time to choose—conspiracy or empowerment.

PART ONE

# CONSPIRACY

# 1

# THE LOST SPIRIT
# OF AMERICANISM

*We did produce a near perfect Republic. Will they keep it
or will they in the enjoyment of it lose the memory of
freedom? Material abundance without character is the surest
way to destruction.*
—THOMAS JEFFERSON

Although Freemason philosopher Manly Hall sought power through the "seething energies of Lucifer,"[1] rather than from the force of God, he demonstrated excellent powers of observation when he identified the moral imperatives of an idealized Americanism at the heart of the American idea:

"This nation is dedicated to the fulfillment of the Divine Will. To the degree that men realize this and dedicate themselves and their works to this purpose, their land will flourish. To depart from the symbol of this high destiny is to be false to the great trust given as a priceless inheritance."[2]

## THE SHINING CITY ON THE HILL

The founding fathers were explicit about America's humanistic goals in the Declaration of Independence—which mentions the Creator four times. Paradoxically, slavery is a contradiction in a Christian society and the ownership of slaves by its patriotic and virtuous patriarch, George Washington, and Thomas Jefferson—the alleged author of the Declaration of Independence (Benjamin Franklin is the likely author)—is a gross distortion of the moral code inherent in Americanism's stated virtues—then and in the present day. Indeed, the ideals of Americanism are not moral period pieces, and owning slaves in 1660 was not the norm, especially among men who trafficked in the higher meaning of life.

The men who shaped the vision of this nation included John Adams, George Washington, James Madison, Benjamin Franklin, Ethan Allen, Thomas Jefferson, Thomas Paine, and the other patriots who fought for and won independence. Among those patriots were the owners of human property, specifically Washington and Jefferson, who were morally compromised by their personal involvement in the peculiar institution and America's greatest paradox, the enslavement of African people.

On the one hand, Washington and Jefferson authored the modern concept of freedom and of human rights. They created and brilliantly articulated the humanistic virtues of Americanism, which were the essence of those rights. On the other hand, as slaveholders, they demonstrated the ability to isolate these precepts from the whippings, the murders, the denial of freedom, and, in the case of Illuminati Freemason Jefferson, allegedly the enslavement of his own children, born to his wife's half sister. Washington did express a form of contrition as a "lukewarm abolitionist," although he never publicly denounced slavery.[3]

Judging from their lifestyles, Washington and Jefferson never internalized their own bedrock sentiment that "all men are created equal," which lies at the heart of the American idea. They were engulfed by two of the most hateful traits of their own British oppressors: elitism and greed. In Jefferson's case, it may be possible to add hypocrisy, lust, and racism. Ironically, America's inspired documents—the Constitution, the Bill of Rights, and the Declaration of Independence—express the necessity of defending a nation from just such human failure. The founders knew that even a democratic Republic could eventually become corrupted by money and power, exorcise God's authority, and lay claim to being the source of human rights. They therefore made it abundantly clear that our rights as human beings are granted by God and cannot be transferred constitutionally from one transient government to another or taken away altogether. It is the role of our freely elected government to protect and preserve human rights—God's gift to every living soul.

That is the vision of the hymn "America the Beautiful"— a nation of freedom, dignity, and equality in the eyes of God— on which this country was built. It is only a vision, but as the Holy Bible teaches us, "without vision, the people perish." But as I look around me at America at the end of the twentieth century, all I see is an extinguished vision and a people that are perishing.

## A BROKEN COMPACT WITH GOD

God is not mocked. America's first leaders warned that no government that ignores or denies God can be truly American. It will be doomed to ignominious failure if it ever ceases to submit to His will. Well, it has. And I see the signs of failure everywhere. God has been routed from our democratically elected government. Instead of a liberating Divine guidance we are smothered by an evil, oppressive conspiracy. The people are lied to and robbed by the very institutions and leaders they depend on to protect them.

The founding fathers crafted our institutions to protect the nation from the kind of religious oppression that had existed in Europe. By separating church and state, they intended to exclude religious institutions from influencing the government—but they never intended to exclude God from the operations of the state.

Over time, the political class has jettisoned God from the Republic. Or has tried to anyway. That is the main cause of our national demise and a power elite's ascension to absolute control of the country. In fact, in today's America, most people probably believe that their human rights originate with the government and not with God, because of the ruling class's self-serving manipulation of the mandate to separate the affairs of government from religious beliefs.

The degree to which we as a nation have lost sight of our Divine inspiration was made painfully clear when the United States government officially declared in the 1966 United Nations International Covenant on Human Rights that rights can be "determined" by law. This breach of our compact "under God" has had dangerous and far-reaching consequences. The extent to which the government can distance itself from God (not to be confused with religion) is the extent to which the government can avoid its obligation to preserve human rights and can control you and confiscate your wealth.

## THE PRICE WE PAY

Just where is America headed? The public relations circus surrounding the reelection in January 1997 of Republican Newt Gingrich as House Speaker offered two very telling insights into the diminution of Americanism and America's perilous journey into the future. The first was delivered by David Bonior (D-Mich.), a Democratic partisan scold who, basking in Gingrich's ethics problems, warned the political class that every time one of them gets caught abusing the trust of the voters, the message goes out that "lying pays, that cheating works and that wrongdoing goes unpunished."[4] Inadvertently, he might have described the corrupt state of our union.

Then a guilty, beleaguered, and contrite Gingrich made another public relations offering: Improve race relations, fight drugs, and eliminate ignorance, he proposed. His most salient prescription, however, was that to solve the nation's problems, "we need to seek divine guidance in what we are doing."[5] Dr. Gingrich, the former history professor, seemed to be arguing for a return to Americanism, which leads me to conclude that he knows more about the sins of this country's ruling class and the loss of our human rights than he admits.

Gingrich asked his fellow politicians, almost all of whom work for the ruling class, "How do we continue to create one nation, under God, indivisible?"[6] The answer, I think, is to recognize God, not rich, manipulative people, as the key to America's future and thus to restore our inalienable rights. The spectacle of Gingrich offering his contrition for the entire world to witness is evidence of God's power to punish and heal corruption of the soul.

America's history is replete with examples of the inadequacy of human judgment and the weakness of the soul in the face of the temptation of power. Our political leaders, Democrat and

Republican alike, are, with very few exceptions, thoroughly corrupt and habitually disingenuous. Thus, rather than trusting in the promises of politicians, the American people should be seeking Divine guidance and protection *from* the power elite. Placing our faith in God, as America's founders admonished, and not trusting in any man, as the Bible instructs, is our only hope for saving the country from the clutches of the Conspiracy and for avoiding total economic and social destruction.

God and government are not as antithetical as Americans have been deliberately led to believe. On the occasion of his reelection as House Speaker, Gingrich told the country:

> One of the highest values we are going to spend the next two years on is openly dealing with the challenge of meaning that when we say in our declaration [the Declaration of Independence] that we are endowed by our Creator with certain inalienable rights, including life, liberty and the pursuit of happiness, that every child in every neighborhood, of every background is endowed by God. And every time America fails to meet that, we are failing to meet God's test for the country we should be.[7]

"We are endowed by our Creator," Gingrich said, with the basic human rights of life, liberty, and the pursuit of happiness, and whether we can protect these is "God's test for the country we should be."[8] That's precisely the message of the founding fathers. Their vision was not of the morally spoiled country we have become; the America they envisioned is as yet unrealized.

Few would argue that we are yet the country we should be. And this failure is the price we pay for allowing reason to govern over faith and for allowing faith in man and the state, a religion of statism, to take precedence over God.

## THERE ARE NO ACCIDENTS

I do not believe in historical accidents or coincidences. "In politics," President Franklin D. Roosevelt commented, "nothing happens by accident. If it happens, you can bet it was planned that way." In his book *None Dare Call It Conspiracy*, Gary Allen points out that between 1930 and 1970, the United States experienced "32,496 consecutive coincidences" of history, such as wars, depressions, and incidents related to racial and religious hatred. This "stretches the law of averages a bit," Allen rightly asserts. "If we were dealing with the law of averages," he continues, "half of the events affecting our nation's well-being should be good for America. If we were dealing with mere incompetence, our leaders should occasionally make a mistake in our favor."[9]

I do not believe that we have simply drifted away from the founding fathers' vision of America or have accidentally broken our compact with God and lost the spirit of Americanism. A powerful cabal, which I call the Illuminati Ruling Class Conspiracy, has systematically conspired to take control of America and enslave her citizens since the country's very inception.

This kind of talk will get me accused by the Establishment media of operating from a paranoid, militia mentality that sees a conspiracy behind every bush. Ridicule and calumny have always been good weapons against criticism, but truth is its own shield.

My best empirical evidence for the existence of an Illuminati Ruling Class Conspiracy is the condition of this country. After a succession of "hot" and "cold" wars, America is saddled with $7 trillion in debt, making her the number one beggar nation in the world. The government confiscates the citizens' income through burdensome taxes and printing-press inflation, while officially keeping 6 percent of all Americans—or close to 24 percent of the nation's Blacks—unemployed in order to satisfy an unproved theory of controlling price inflation, Nairu (natural inflationary rate of unemployment). It should be called the Nairu Unemployment Plan. In the end, however, it is the absence of civic virtue and the selfishness of *all* Americans that has created the climate necessary for the Conspiracy's ascendancy.

## THE ILLUMINATI RULING CLASS CONSPIRACY

To put it simply, a very small sector of the population, an Anglophile American Establishment, asserts itself over everyone else. This economic and political White Anglo-Saxon Protestant (WASP) elite controls the political process from behind the scenes, and the financial institutions overtly. Its cultural mystique dominates the psyche of the nation, through its control of the banking industry, the media, the business sector, the elite social clubs where they network, the university system, the Round Table groups—such as the Trilateral Commission—and the control they exercise over the aspirations of every bright, ambitious person who wants to achieve prominence in "the system." This includes congressmen and senators, intellectuals, corporate executives, labor leaders, journalists, and so on. Elite WASP America is the ruling class.

In whatever form, the enshrinement and use of WASP culture to define Americanism feeds a deleterious conspiracy of elitist Anglophiles in America. Harvard professor Samuel Huntington, who is the coauthor of *The Crisis of Democracy,* the Trilateral Commission's policy bible, wrote that the 1960s was "the decade of democratic surge and of the reassertion of democratic egalitarianism."[10] Translation: Shut those demanding, noisy Blacks up with Daniel Moynihan's "benign neglect."

Too much democracy has always been a concern for the Trilateralists, which include Clinton's Black good old boy Vernon Jordan.

Randall Robinson, a Black activist and TransAfrica founder, reminded the Black Ruling Class of the "Vernon Jordan disease," a euphemism for Uncle Tom, a Black who betrays other Blacks. According to *The Washington Post,* Robinson said it is a "degenerative disease among blacks in Privilege that results in a loss of memory of what they came to Privilege to accomplish and, further, any memory of the millions camped outside the gate."[11]

Helping Monica Lewinsky, Clinton's twenty-one-year-old self-confessed lover, find a job at a New York firm and away from pesky independent prosecutors in Washington, D.C., was a part of Jordan's role as fixer for Bill Clinton, as well as getting the same company (of which he is a director) to pay Webster Hubbell, Clinton's broke friend and convicted felon, $60,000 "for unspecified services." According to *The New York Times,* "The jobs [Lewinsky and Hubbell], some at Justice [the Justice Department] suspected, were simply vehicles for hush money."[12] And once its agenturs are embroiled in public scandal, even if on its behalf, the ruling class swiftly abandons them.

Even under normal circumstances ethnics are a problem for the Trilateralists. Samuel Huntington, a former member of the National Security Council, has finally figured out the newest threat to American drift: the "excessive influence" of American ethnic groups, amassed since 1989.[13] "If multiculturalism prevails and if the consensus on liberal democracy disintegrates, the United States could join the Soviet Union on the ash heap of history," the WASP-elite Huntington wrote.[14]

The elite Jews want to partner with elite WASPs and run American foreign policy, Huntington is saying. He's saying the same thing in a $2,000 suit that Thomas Chittum, a working-class White advocate of a race war, says in combat boots. Unless

WASPs dominate, this nation can't survive; and it deserves destruction if non-WASPs are allowed among the power elite to democratically shape its policies.

The Anglophile Round Table study groups such as the Council on Foreign Relations and the Trilateral Commission are commonly suspected by students of conspiracy of plotting against the people. The perception that these organizations per se are Illuminati conspiracies results largely from the notorious reputations of some of their founders, such as Illuminists Jacob Schiff and "Colonel" Edward Mandel House of the CFR, and from the naked ambition and gross opportunism of the influence-peddling grandees who inhabit them.

Among this elitist class can be found a critical mass of illuminated "mental spooks," as the Illuminati money lords allegedly refer to their intellectual and immoral sycophants. These opportunists are guaranteed power and money while they literally serve the Devil and his evilarchy's quest for world hegemony. For example, the Rhodes Scholar pool of candidates offers a plethora of choices. President Clinton (who did not graduate) has had many doors to money and power opened for him as a result of these WASP identity politics.

The best thing that can be said for the WASP power elite is that it espouses a superior morality, a basic ethic of fairness and virtue inherited from its Pilgrim culture. However, the morality it exhibits is not at all superior. Although most powerful and wealthy people would not intentionally work to harm the human race, and although conspiracy is too strong a term to be applied to all wealthy and powerful people, nevertheless much of their lifestyle is based on selfish motives. Being rich and powerful does not, of course, in and of itself make one a conspirator, but the social patterns, economic beliefs, and politics of most of the people in this group justify their being called a cabal, camarilla, coterie, oligarchy, or simply, as I prefer, the ruling class. Rich and powerful people tend to conspire to segregate themselves and their wealth among other rich and powerful people. That is how they stay rich and powerful. Money and power marries itself. You cannot argue with the pragmatism. Yet, it can be challenged successfully on moral grounds. And that is the battlefield upon which we should engage the WASP elitists; we should warn them of the danger to themselves of pursuing the beliefs and policies they do, and of the destructive impact of these on the rest of their countrymen.

The ruling class's selfishness and greed feed the obsessive drive for ever more power and hegemony among its members; as a result, though it is a segregated elite, its doors are open to conspiracy within its own ranks. I am convinced that there exists today a rogue faction among this country's self-styled aristocracy. Whether they are formally organized and precisely who they are is beyond the scope of this book. But be assured that an evil force, beyond just the powerful and rich, is driving a conspiracy against humanity.

This international cabal functions in many of the same ways as do religious cabals, and its money lords are conspicuous by their lust for elitism and power. The Illuminists, for example, would never pass up an opportunity to infiltrate the inner circle of the power elite and form their own secret core group within it in order to manipulate and exploit Round Table groups such as the Council on Foreign Relations and the Trilateral Commission, just as they have done since 1776 as the secret Order of the Devil within Freemasonry—thus the name "Illuminati Freemasonry."

At the end of the eighteenth century, on May 1, 1776, a Jesuit priest and professor of canon law at Ingolstadt University in Bavaria, Germany, Adam Weishaupt, created a new church for this Luciferian religion. He recruited a group of university intellectuals and aristocrats, and founded a secret society known as the Order of the Illuminati—"Illuminated Ones"—which would go on to become the modern-day cabal that controls most of the world. The purpose of the Illuminati was to replace religion and faith with a scientific, atheistic "morality"—a political religion—and to allow rational, "illuminated" minds to run the world.

These men considered themselves "the cream of the intelligentsia—the select of the elect—and the only people with the mental capacity, the insight and the resources to govern the world and bring peace."[15] With their elitist concept of the "intellectual superman," these self-appointed saviors of the world could have hardly been called anything but the Order of the Illuminati.

The Order was based on the principle that God does not exist and that human reason is sufficient to understand and improve the world, and achieve immortality. This philosophy of secular humanism also asserted that a favorable outcome justifies any act that may violate moral virtue. To that end, these European aristocrats began to infiltrate the guild of Freemasonry in the eighteenth century, and eventually succeeded in transforming it into "illuminated" Freemasonry.

If this scheme to usurp God's power sounds familiar, it is. Lucifer, the archangel, referred to in the Bible as "son of the morning," became the first Illuminist when he mounted his heavenly revolt. According to Luciferians, the "light bearer" was unjustly cast out of heaven, but, brilliant and proud, he conspired against God and devised the evil doctrine that fosters the arrogant belief that intellectual capacity licenses hegemony over the nonelite. But a few can dominate the majority only by systematically denying the majority their human rights through the use of some form of force. The Illuminati, recognizing that government can be the instrument of such force, methodically works to eliminate God as the moral authority by which government and human rights exist.

This is the impetus for statism in the United States. Americans are being enslaved by the best corruption the ruling class's money can buy. Today, a powerful cabal, the "Illuminati Order," is still at the heart of the Conspiracy.

A hallmark of the Illuminati's religion was its need for absolute secrecy, the purpose of which was to protect it from public exposure and official scrutiny. By infiltrating and controlling other secret societies, such as the Freemasons, the Illuminati became an invisible empire. One can only speculate just how powerful this elitist secret society is today, whether it still has a formal membership, or if it even still exists. I am certain, however, that the purpose of the Illuminati's Luciferian religion—the systematic destruction of democratic governments, morality, and faith in God—is still very much the objective of at least a rogue core group among the world's ruling class. This cabal, I believe, has successfully pulled off a spiritual and material coup d'état against the people of the United States. The observable economic slavery and moral decay that exist today are the fruits of the Conspiracy.

In 1922, Mayor John F. Hylan of New York identified the most arrogant and conspicuous branch of this "invisible government."

> The real menace of our republic is the invisible government which, like a giant octopus, sprawls its slimy length over our city, state and nation. At the head is a small group of banking houses generally referred to as "international bankers." This little coterie of powerful international bankers virtually run our government for their own selfish ends.[16]

In 1913, Congressman Charles Lindbergh, Sr., said that a cabal of Wall Streeters called "the Money Trust" caused the 1907 financial panic.[17] By 1933, President Franklin D. Roosevelt was compelled to admit: "The real truth of the matter is, as you and I know, that a financial element in the large centers has owned the government ever since the days of Andrew Jackson."[18]

The defining moment, however, of the decline of Americanism and a democratic government came on December 23, 1913, when the Federal Reserve Bank was imposed by law on the unsuspecting American people. President Woodrow Wilson ceded control of America to the Illuminati Ruling Class Conspiracy as he opened the gates of the nation to what I call Karl Marx's Trojan Horse. Later, Wilson, in a rare moment of honesty, admitted: "I am a most unhappy man. Unwittingly, I have ruined my country."[19] He was right, if somewhat disingenuous, in his confession.

By 1997, when Americans declared a record number of personal bankruptcies, this so-called central bank had taken a central role in the functioning of the country, not only breeding and spreading panic but managing a system of monetary inflation and national debt that gives rise to ever-increasing human misery. Today, the government is executing a Nairu unemployment policy of deliberately keeping millions of workers permanently unemployed. Aside from the moral implications of that policy, the Federal Reserve also ignores the fact that it is legally bound to aim for a 4 percent unemployment rate.

The government's economic policies have created a very huge class of have-nots, who in turn are now giving birth to a new breed of twenty-first-century "patriots," such as mass murderer Timothy McVeigh. It is only a matter of time before an Ozzie-and-Harriet militia violently confronts the U.S. government. The faces of these home-grown terrorists belong to farmers, aircraft workers, religious teachers, television repairmen, and other otherwise ordinary working Americans—mostly discontented working-poor middle- to low-income White people, who have organized themselves into paramilitary groups to fight the federal government and/or refuse to pay income taxes. This social phenomenon is another inevitable consequence of a loss of faith in our institutions.

We can reasonably speculate that the Illuminati Ruling Class Conspiracy, having gained control of a critical mass of our financial institutions and portions of the U.S. government, is driving the people into a civil war or a race war, whichever comes first. The history of this century gives ample evidence of the Conspiracy's modus operandi: Just look at what the Illuminati, under its various banners of Communism and Fascism during the 1930s and '40s did to Russia, Germany, and the rest of the world. Today, the Conspiracy is creating the same economic climate in America that earlier in this century drove Russia and Germany over the cliff of political disaster into totalitarianism and war. If the past is prologue, we are witnessing an impending twenty-first-century American tragedy.

## PARANOID THINKING

To the extent that I can explain the Illuminati Ruling Class Conspiracy in the context of greed and elitism, good and evil, and the choice between spiritual life and death, I will explore the issues and consequences that derive from it. I will not, however, pursue this discussion as malicious gossip in order to titillate the voyeuristic. Nor will I join the conspiracists' chorus and carpet-bomb entire groups such as Jews, Freemasons, Catholics, or Mormons as branches of the Illuminati. I refuse to sow the seeds of hatred against another individual, group, or even our corrupt federal government.

My ideas will undoubtedly create controversy among various communities of interest. Some anti-Freemasonry Christians will question my defense of some aspects of Freemasonry—for example, the right to a pantheistic choice of gods, including Lucifer. Some will also denigrate my belief in the "pagan" Eastern concepts of reincarnation and karma. At the same time, the anti-religious and the rationalist will label my love of God and acceptance of Jesus Christ as my savior as a silly "superstition."

Illuminati Freemasons will be livid as I "out" them as Luciferian Occultists, who are exploiting Freemasonry to further their evil dogma. And Freemasons—already defensive about the public misperception that confuses Freemasonry with Illuminated Freemasonry, Freemasonry's liberal choice of gods with Illuminati Freemasonry's love of the Devil, and Freemasonry's rejection of Jesus Christ with Illuminated Freemasonry's Luciferian Occultism—will label my lack of regard for their pagan mystery "secrets" and their occult quest for immortality as blasphemous and unenlightened. Those who believe that presidents are royalty, and beyond the law, will bristle at my criticism of Bill Clinton. But I hold to the old-fashioned notion that Presidents should work for the people and their character should be above average.

Some Black Freemasons may feel that I am attempting to turn the Black Christian community against them when I explain that Freemasonry does not believe that Jesus Christ is the Son of God or even that God is necessary for salvation and eternal happiness. American White Freemasons, on the other hand, will find off-putting the exposure of their policies of White supremacy and of sexism in the name of brotherhood, their adherence to a pagan religion, and their legacy as the founding authority for the Ku Klux Klan.

## FRONTING THE JEWS

Historically, emphasis has been placed on blaming the Jews for the Conspiracy. Why have so many Illuminists in the power elite gone to such great lengths over the centuries to falsely blame the Jews for being the Illuminati? The surprising answer seems in part religious and moral envy (see discussion in Chapter 2 on British Israelism) and the practical need to eliminate a potential challenge to WASP hegemony. The anti-Jewish savants and the fair-haired "intellectuals" who believe that *The Protocols of the Learned Elders of Zion* is a blueprint for a Jewish conspiracy to control the world will cast me as another prominent Black beaten down by Jewish financial pressure. They will claim that that is the reason why I believe the Jews have been scapegoated by Illuminati Gentile Freemasonic disinformation, as a decoy, as was successfully accomplished in the eighteenth century with a subversive irreligious sect of JINO (Jews in Name Only) Jews named after Jacob Frank. The Frankists, who believed that purity could "be achieved through sin,"[20] were originally known as the Haskala movement. It was the name given the early Jewish liberals who later were known as the Jewish Reform movement.[21] Its early leader was Moses Mendelssohn, a Freemason, who inspired Adam Weishaupt, the founder of the Illuminati.[22] As a result of being Illuminists and anti-Jewish, the Frankist-Reform Jews were ripe for exploitation.

The original *Protocols*, which were written in French, were stolen from a Masonic lodge in Paris in 1884 and then taken to Russia, where they were translated into Russian in 1903.[23] They were later edited and published in a Russian newspaper, by a "noted and militant anti-Semite," as *The Jewish Peril*. In the 1930s and 1940s, they were used by the Nazis to justify their campaign of genocide against the Jews.[24]

The most prominent Frankist and the spokesman for the Communists was a German Jew, Levi Mordechai, who had changed his name to Karl Marx. Sponsored by the Illuminati, he published the *Communist Manifesto* in 1848. The Gentile-controlled Illuminati also carefully placed Jews in positions of public prominence during 1848 to lead the violent Communist upheavals that occurred all over Europe. These bloody uprisings were used by the Illuminati as confirmation that the *Protocols'* alleged Jewish promise of mass slaughter had come to fruition. According to Daniel, in *Scarlet and the Beast:* "Gentile Freemasonry successfully fronted the Jews . . . since most of the leaders in all the Revolutionary posts were Jews, the Russians blamed the Jews for Bolshevism. No one knew at that time that they were fronts for anti-Semitic Gentile Orient Freemasonry."[25] "Orient" is a Masonic code word for Lucifer.

The condemnation of all Jews as anarchists and Illuminists hell-bent on dominating the world followed the 1848 uprisings. This climate triggered a spate of anti-Jewish conspiracy books that eventually would help produce Adolf Hitler and his occult religion of Nazism, which cited the *Protocols* as proof of a Jewish plot to control the world.

In a word, the Illuminati had manipulated its Frankist-Reform Jewish clients. The terror caused all over Europe by this self-hating Jewish sect set the stage for the genocide of Jews nearly a century later. The liberal, subversive Frankist was the perfect scapegoat: Almost enthusiastic in his anti-Semitism, he was further blinded by his hedonistic excesses; the Frankists indulged in sex orgies and a licentious lifestyle, and were committed to the destruction of both Judaism and Christianity.

Taking note of the violently anti-Jewish reaction the Frankists had triggered, Jewish Orthodox rabbis compared the Berlin Frankist leaders to "the whore of Samson" and, mindful of Samson's punishment by God at the hand of the Philistines, "prophesied a Jewish holocaust 150 years before the advent of Hitler and Nazi Germany."[26] The worldly instrument of the deeply "prophetic insights and foresights of the rabbis," who said that the Jews' destruction would come from Berlin, would be the Gentile Illuminati Freemasons' *Protocols*.

It is also extremely unlikely, as John Daniel relates, that 197 Jewish delegates at a Zionist conference comprising the entire spectrum of Jewish thought from orthodoxy to anarchy could discuss, debate, and then agree on "a detailed conspiracy for world domination."[27] The *Protocols* contained the alleged proceedings of twenty-four lengthy sessions, detailing the conspiracy. Many Jews are smart, but not that smart. And no group that contentious and diverse could agree on and write up that much material in three days of meetings.

No, the Jews were framed by the same Gentiles whom Jesus admonished and called " 'the synagogue of Satan' which say they are Jews, and are not, but do lie."[28] Daniel believes that "Freemasonry is Christ's prophesied 'synagogue of Satan'"[29] and points to its own rituals as evidence. He cites Warren Weston's book *Father of Lies,* which reveals how the Jewish Cabala was used to develop the Scottish Rite's thirty-three degrees and the fact that "the ten separate interpretations for each degree" originate from "the ten emanations of the Cabalistic god."[30]

*Sion* is a French word for "Zion." The Priory of Sion is a revival of the old Babylonian witchcraft religion in a modern disguise within British Illuminati Freemasonry. Some go so far as to say it's the "synagogue of Satan," the imposter Jews about whom Jesus warned. The Priory of Sion's kings believe they are really Jews who are descended from an illicit union between Jesus and Mary Magdalene. The authors of *Holy Blood, Holy Grail* and *Scarlet and the Beast* make an excellent case that *The Protocols of the Learned Elders of Zion* is a document written by the "representatives of Sion of the 33rd Degree." Thus, *Protocols* is very likely a forged document from the Thirty-third-Degree Supreme Council of the Rite of Mizraim, a front for the Priory of Sion, which set the Jews up for mass destruction.[31]

Evidence of Masonic culpability also comes from the *Chicago Daily News* edition of June 23, 1920, which reported that Empress Alexandra, wife of Czar Nicholas II, wrote on April 7, 1918: "Nicholas read to us the protocols of the free mason."[32] Daniel describes the *Protocols* as a "vicious attempt by anti-Semitic gentile Freemasonry to destroy the Jews."[33] For example, the exclusively WASP Templar Anglophiles in The Order at Yale's Skull and Bones call outsiders "Gentiles" and, like Gentile Freemasons, including the Priory of Sion kings, call themselves Jewish, notwithstanding their indigenous anti-Jewish WASP cultural identification. And the Ku Klux Klan was created by Scottish Rite Masonry, which is the author of its anti-Jewish, anti-Catholic, anti-Black ideology of hatred.

Regardless of these arguments and my beliefs, Jews like the New York man who labeled me "anti-Semitic" because I criticized Federal Reserve Chairman Alan Greenspan's monetary and fiscal policies will see red at the very mention of even Court Jews (*Hofjuden*) such as Jacob Schiff, Paul Warburg, and Nathan Rothschild in connection with the Illuminati Ruling Class Conspiracy.

While the Rothschild and other Illuminati Jewish banking families cooperated with the Anglophile Illuminati dynastic families, the ventures were neither controlled by Jews nor a Jewish conspiracy.[34] People who comprise the Illuminati have no national loyalty and control fortunes or the minds of millions in organizations such as Freemasonry, which also spreads their religious dogma. The JINO (Jews in Name Only) Jews in the Illuminati have perfected the use of disinformation in the form of accusations of "anti-Semitism" to deflect any attack away from the Illuminati Ruling Class Conspiracy's nefarious activities.

The danger of believing in a Jewish plot was driven home to me by a Black man in Indianapolis on June 8, 1997, while I was still writing this book. During the question-and-answer period following a speech I had given, he amicably posed a series of questions on various aspects of conspiracy thought. He then asked for my confirmation of the theory that B'nai B'rith was a Jewish Masonic order that controlled the Illuminati. I responded that I had never heard that theory before. He braced his body as if shoved by an invisible force. And when in response to another Jew-baiting question, I voiced my views on *The Protocols of the Learned Elders of Zion,* the questioner turned ugly and accused me of covering for a Jewish conspiracy that controls the world.

I have never covered for any conspiracy, or belonged to any secret society, but I am proud to be a member of Alpha Phi Alpha fraternity, whose membership list is open to the public and whose goals are "manly deeds, scholarship and love for all mankind." That's the only "secret" that I learned, and we sing it in public. In my previous book, *Black Lies, White Lies: The Truth According to Tony Brown,* I explain the African origin of ancient Greece and state that if any group has a claim on being Greek, it is Africans of the Diaspora.[35] An ignorance of history, fueled by their envy of the achievements of successful members of their own group, has led some Blacks to a pursuit of ethnic self-immolation.

Later that night, when I returned to New York from Indianapolis, I found a reference to the B'nai B'rith as the "Independent Order of B'nai B'rith (Jewish Masonry)" in a book by Edith Starr Miller, the anti-Jewish author of *Occult Theocrasy,* published in 1933. During this era, when anti-Jewish conspiracy books were very popular because of the publication of *The Protocols of the Learned Elders of Zion* in the 1920s, Miller, who believed that the Ordo Templi Orientis (OTO) ultrasecret lodge was the Illuminati's interlocking directorate between English and French Masonry,[36] stated:

> There is little doubt now that the B'nai B'rith seems to be the supreme body, shaping and directing, for the attainment of its own ends, the policies, whatever they may be, of all Freemasonry beginning with the Grand Lodge of England, The Grand Orient and Scottish Rites, and ending in the O.T.O. [Order of Oriental Templars].[37]

Having been accused only hours before of being a conspirator myself, I was particularly sensitive to accusations as sweeping as this one. An especially rabid anti-Jewish sentiment was driving the widespread rumors that the Jewish House of Rothschild's financial empire controlled the governments of Europe and that Jews were never loyal to national interests, only to a plan to subjugate the world to "Messianic" Jewry. Miller's B'nai B'rith characterization seemed to fit that conspiracy genre.

Furthermore, I thought, it was inconceivable that a Gentile, predominantly WASP Illuminati Freemasonry and an unwieldy group of international esoteric organizations would submit to any single leadership—especially a Jewish one. Then, of course, there is the testimony of Professor Carroll Quigley, an avowed insider of the Illuminati's organization, who described the conspiracy as "an Anglophile network."[38] I interpret that to mean that its ranks include few, if any, Jews, other than the JINOs.

B'nai B'rith means "Sons of the Covenant," and it is an exclusively Jewish Masonic society. The Independent Order of B'nai B'rith (IOBB) was founded in 1843 by New York Reform Jews of German descent. The Frankist Jews were recognized as the Jewish Reform Movement during that era. According to Rabbi Marvin S. Antleman, author of *To Eliminate the Opiate,* although the Frankists were outwardly religious, they clung to their "cherished" goals—"the annihilation" of all religions and "a general revolution" that would tear down the existing order and allow for the rebuilding of a new order. In his 1974 book, Antleman called Frankists "anti-Semitic" and said that it was "obligatory for every pious Jew to search and expose them."[39] In the early twentieth century, B'nai B'rith founded the Anti-Defamation League, the American Jewish Congress, and Federations of Jewish Charities.

According to conspiracy theorists, a major player in the Reform Movement was Freemason Jacob Schiff, the man accused of being sent to America to gain control of the U.S. money system by creating a central bank and to create racial strife between Blacks and Whites. According to Rabbi Marvin Antleman, Frankist Reform Jews in the illuminated Masonic lodges exploited Blacks "for their own ends."[40] The NAACP was founded by Schiff and his Rothschild coconspirators for this Hegelian purpose, according to Myron Fagan (a racist) on a tape entitled "Illuminati."

I can't confirm either Fagan's or Antleman's allegations, but it is a fact that White Gentiles and Jews, mostly Socialists, did become the acknowledged leadership of the Black community when they started both the NAACP and the Urban League. In 1918, Joel Spingarn, a JINO assimilationist, was one of a long line of white NAACP presidents. He was reportedly chosen by the Lehman financial dynasty to run the NAACP as an adjunct for leftist causes, some of which hurt Blacks. As I reported in *Black Lies, White Lies,*[41] Spingarn ran a spy network against Blacks for the Military Intelligence Division, as part of a government conspiracy. He exploited his position at the NAACP and turned over the membership list to the Army intelligence unit.

Only one Black was on the NAACP staff when it was founded in 1909, Dr. W.E.B. Du Bois, a Freemason who had studied at the University of Berlin when the political philosophy of Hegelian dialectics was sweeping Germany. Du Bois's job at the White-led NAACP was as propaganda minister and his major targets were Black self-help advocates, especially Booker T. Washington and Marcus Garvey. The elitist Du Bois and his White Masonic allies wiped out all organized Black resistance to illuminated Communism (a philosophy that Du Bois would embrace openly later in life).

The Black community is a planned failure. The Illuminati programmed Blacks to avoid self-empowerment. See my book *Black Lies, White Lies: The Truth According to Tony Brown* for the details of the anti-Black conspiracy that I formerly believed was motivated by liberal racism. It's *much* deeper than that.

The incident in Indianapolis reminded me of a *Village Voice* article I had read a few years before that accused Indiana of breeding "weird, violent people," such as Jim Jones and Charles Manson.[42] But it is not any particular place, group, or race that breeds violence; it is fear and suspicion. Without a plan to sublimate these hostile emotions into a sensible, productive outlet, we only produce more Timothy McVeighs, who not only have "internalized the fires" of Waco, Texas, but had gasoline thrown on them by conspiracy theory lunatics.

The people whose bible is *The Turner Diaries* have concluded that the world would be a better place without Jews. They have also decided to reinstate slavery for the Blacks they don't kill in the twenty-first century, vowing to "take back America for the White race." They miss the point. The entire population, in fact, is being enslaved.

Things are bad enough as they are. Our situation does not need to be inflamed. We need solutions. We need to know how to defeat the Illuminati Ruling Class Conspiracy by defeating the need to be superior—the Illuminists within ourselves—first. That is why I am not hostile toward any group. I am a proponent of the truth. Unfortunately, members of communities of interest tend to reject the truth unless it flatters their causes and predisposed beliefs. I am sure it will be the same with this book as I cross the controversial minefield I have mapped out—as I cross the Rubicon of truth.

# 2

# THE RULING CLASS

*Again I tell you, it is easier for a camel to go through the eye of a*
*needle than for a rich man to enter the kingdom of God.*
—MATTHEW 19:24

Abraham Lincoln described the essence of slavery as the principle of "you work, I'll eat." This drive to live off the sweat of
others has animated the world's power elite since time imme-
morial. But is the ruling class automatically a conspiracy?

The working definition of conspiracy is a "plot" or "secret
agreement." There is nothing secret about the ruling class's desire for money and power. No conspiracy. The tendency of the
ruling class and its institutions toward elitism, however, does
create fertile ground for the growth of conspiracy. I believe that
the Illuminati has successfully taken control of the institutions
of America's ruling class Establishment and is using them to
advance its conspiracy against God.

The Illuminati Ruling Class Conspiracy has thus subsumed
the system. That creates quite a predicament, since you cannot

arrest the system, and the system is not going to arrest itself. To take America back and restore her Divine purpose, we will have to work within the boundaries of the Establishment to create our own reality, identity, purpose, and destiny. It is essential, therefore, that we recognize and understand the differences between the moral values of the ruling class—with its essentially Christian humanitarianism—and the Luciferian goals of the Illuminati Ruling Class Conspiracy.

## IMPERIAL ROOTS

The apple does not fall far from the tree, as the saying goes. In this instance a more appropriate trusim may be: "He who lies down with dogs shall rise with fleas." So to understand the nature of America's ruling class, we must turn to the nation's history as a colony of the British Empire. I was reminded of this necessity by Professor Carroll Quigley, Bill Clinton's mentor at the Georgetown University School of Foreign Service. In an act of modern-day conspiratorial candor, Dr. Quigley, who has admitted to having spent most of his life "close to it and many of its instruments," described the "Conspiracy" as the "Anglophile network which we may identify as the Round Table Groups."[1] He thus pointed the way toward recognizing the connection between America's ruling class and its Old World English progenitors and the growth of the Conspiracy in this country.

Quigley, a proud conspiratorist, explains how money lord J. P. Morgan used German Hegelianism to manipulate both the Republicans and the Democrats in the early twentieth century. This includes financial support for the extreme left of the political spectrum and the Communist Party itself.[2] The American WASP Establishment ruling class and the twenty or thirty families of its inner circle, The Order of Anglophile Pilgrims (my designation), persist in this multipartisan practice to this day.

## WASP Mystique

Emanating from Quigley's book is an understanding of the extensive use of the Hegelian dialectical process and the taxpayers' own money to pit subpopulation groups, especially Blacks and Whites, against one another. The purpose of this contrived competition is to destroy national unity and foster dependence on a system of statism. The state is, in reality, the elitist WASP oligarchy, whose culture automatically becomes the American norm.

According to the authors of *The WASP Mystique,* Dr. Richard Robertiello, a psychiatrist, and Diana Hoguet, "For WASPs there is a persistent need to be morally superior. . . . Dependence is humiliating" for these upper-class WASPs, who "have the usual amount of prejudice towards Blacks, Hispanics, Italians, Poles and Irish."[3] But since these groups don't threaten their moral or financial superiority, they don't matter. "The major target of WASP prejudice clearly is and always was . . . Jews."[4]

The English-based WASP culture also infuses American culture with its sexual norms, Robertiello and Hoguet state. "What is the English way of making love? The French way is oral; the Greek way is anal. The English way involves spanking, strappings and being victimized, shamed and humiliated by punitive authorities such as headmasters or headmistresses. . . . These fantasies . . . are often eroticised" and observed in other ethnic groups, but "they seem particularly common to WASPs."[5]

A retired Army colonel who confessed to being a part of the Conspiracy until he retired in 1966 told author A. Ralph Epperson that the alleged involvement of the Rothschilds is disseminated "by the very conspiracy that was," Epperson believes, "semi-concealing its activities."[6] Epperson also believes that

Professor Quigley's book *Tragedy and Hope* was, in fact, a deliberate disclosure of the Conspiracy that Quigley so admired, because he was allowed to "review their private papers."[7] According to Quigley's exposé, "an international Anglophile network" is basically controlled by the English economic power elite, which is working in "cooperation with the Communists."[8]

The English Anglophile homeland, as usual, is a good example. In the early 1950s, British spies at the top echelons of the British Security Service—Kim Philby, Donald MacLean, Guy Burgess, and Sir Anthony Blunt—were KGB agents. I suspect that, among other things, they stole United States nuclear secrets for the Russians. Prior to his defection to Russia, Philby served in Washington with the CIA and the FBI in close proximity to Thirty-third-Degree Freemason J. Edgar Hoover, who established a special FBI Masonic lodge. The KGB used Freemasonry to seriously penetrate British intelligence and, possibly, the CIA and the FBI. When Philby first came under suspicion, Hoover promptly cleared him of being a Soviet agent.[9]

In 1963, Philby was promoted to the rank of general in the Russian KGB. Years later, it was learned that as a Soviet agent, Philby's intelligence control had been not the Russians, but Queen Elizabeth's confidant, Sir Anthony Blunt, for Britain's royal court.[10]

Such a scheme is much too sophisticated and diabolical for the average person to ever grasp and there are so many layers of power that giving up the Rothschilds, whom no one can touch anyway, gives us something to write about for the next twenty years (at which time, we'll probably get another morsel). Most important, exposing a dynasty as powerful as the Rothschilds makes the point once again that "even the wealthy Rothschilds and Warburgs were pawns. . . . Jews were used, then abused as scapegoats."[11]

It is indeed an enigma within a conspiracy. The Conspiracy's very complexity engenders fear. And the fear is enough to stop any serious threat to its power. The media conveniently ignore the existence of the Anglophilic conspiracy altogether.

Quigley's book, I believe, had that desired effect. After Quigley's exposure of the Conspiracy in 1966, there has been no diminution in its power or a public demand to end it. If Quigley's book, which expressed the Conspiracy's utter contempt for the ordinary person, was a test of the will of the people, the Illuminati Ruling Class Conspiracy has nothing to worry about. Gaining control of the world is just a matter of time.

## THE ORDER, THE MASON LINK, AND THE ENGLISH

In his speech in 1992 at the Democratic Party's national convention, in which he accepted his party's nomination for the Presidency, Freemason Bill Clinton praised and "clarified" confessed Illuminist Carroll Quigley's message that the English-led conspiracy against freedom in the world was a *fait accompli* and all who stood in its path would invariably be destroyed, but all who cooperated could buy a place of peace in a New World Order of totalitarian rule. Thus the title of Quigley's book, *Tragedy and Hope* (tragedy for those who oppose tyrannical statism, and hope for those who surrender and become Illuminati shills). Freemason Clinton's "clarification" is a typical oblique Masonic message.

According to information obtained from a break-in at the Bones Temple[12] at Yale, the Skull and Bones "Society" is actually a Skull and Bones "Chapter" and is, some believe, Chapter 322 of the Order of the Illuminati in Germany. In 1996, in my opinion, George Bush's public service was retired because The Order put the Establishment's money and media horses behind the fawning Arkansas spook. It was Clinton's turn to lie, cheat, and steal from the people and, of course, to safeguard the interests of the power elite. It was his turn to steer the nation toward a new synthesis along Hegelian lines where only statism (the rule of the ruling class) can bring peace from the conflict and pain that the power elite itself intentionally inflicts on the people. It was also Bill Clinton's turn to lead the government's affirmative action conspiracy against Black America.

"And as a Rhodes Scholar, Clinton is an Anglophile," John Daniel wrote in *Scarlet and the Beast*. He is "a puppet of English Freemasonry."[13]

In *Partners in Power*, Roger Morris quotes "a former government official who claims to have seen the files long since destroyed" that established Clinton's role as a full-fledged CIA "asset."[14] Morris says that his "ties go all the way back to Oxford and come forward from there " to include his alleged complicity as governor of Arkansas with the CIA in trafficking guns and drugs through the infamous Mena, Arkansas, airport.

According to Morris, compensation from the CIA to the future President as a full-fledged "asset" ranged "from cash payments to help with the local draft boards and even promised deferments" to more general promises of furtive connections to power to advance future career goals.[15] Aware that the Rhodes and Fulbright Anglophiles will be "important folks someday," the CIA knows "the advantages of helping out," explained a former CIA officer.[16]

*Compromised,* by Terry Reed, a former CIA asset, and John Cummings, is a book that alleges that years later Bill Clinton as governor of Arkansas was still an asset for the CIA and sought the agency's support in his bid for the Presidency. Reed, who claimed to have participated in a clandestine meeting in Arkansas with Reagan White House officials, who were also CIA officers working directly under Vice President George Bush and Governor Bill Clinton, recalls the following statement by CIA Director William Casey's surrogate to the ambitious Clinton:

> Bill, you are Mr. Casey's fair-haired boy. But you do have competition for the job you seek. We would never put all

our eggs in one basket. You and your state have been our greatest asset. The beauty of this, as you know, is that you're a Democrat, and with our ability to influence both parties, this country can get beyond partisan gridlock. Mr. Casey wanted me to pass on to you that unless you fuck up and do something stupid, you're No. 1 on the short list for a shot at the job you've always wanted.[17]

In this way, the WASP Establishment perpetuates itself. America's WASP elite, "The Eastern Establishment," is named for the English Freemasons who in 1813 established secret subversive lodges in the northeastern United States (New "England") in England's perennial war to overthrow the United States government. The Masons immediately gained control of the American economy, and subsequently the country.

## PRESIDENT CLINTON AND BRITISH ISRAELISM

Clinton's status as a Rhodes Scholar who was recruited by Quigley at Georgetown to further the British motherland's imperialism assured the completion of his "Anglophilic education at Oxford."[18] Quigley, the insider, exposed "the English Masonic conspiracy of Cecil Rhodes to take back the United States through subversive politicians educated at Oxford by British Masonic professors."[19]

The economic royalty operating from the Ruling Class Conspiracy's headquarters in the heart of "The City," London's financial district, is able to infiltrate and manipulate the U.S. media, government, foundations, universities, and business sector through some of those American "scholars" who have been inculcated with the doctrine of "British Israelism," the ideological foundation for Anglo-Saxon imperialism under a one-world government.

In the late nineteenth century, Cecil Rhodes, the Rhodes

Scholar's imperial patron, devised a social philosophy that is based on a racist and fascist interpretation of the Holy Bible. He enshrined his doctrine of British Israelism at Oxford University in order to instill in his White American mental spooks a political bias toward British imperialism and racism and to reinforce their attachment to their Anglo-Saxon roots. According to British Israelism, as explained in *Our Israelitism Origin* by C. F. Smyth (1840), the White English-speaking people of England and the United States are the descendants of the House of Israel's Northern Kingdom; the Jews inhabited the Southern Kingdom.

The alleged Anglo-Israelis trace their migration from Africa to Europe—the tribe of Dan becoming the Danes, the Scythians settling in Scotland, and the Sons of Isaac (the Sacac) evolving into the Saxons. The English bought the Bethel Stone, which Jacob had used as a pillow, and it is now in Westminster Abbey and is used in the crowning of the English monarchy. Who, perhaps, were the Canaanites, or the Black Guelphs, as Europe's Black nobility was called (see the discussion of these later in this chapter).

Whoever they are, Rhodes believed that the Anglo-Saxons were God's chosen people, destined to rule the world; they reached their highest level of development in the British royalty, who were proof of White supremacy and who ruled by "divine right," keeping Jesus' seat warm until He would return to rule over His earthly kingdom. The Rhodes Scholars have for the past century, wittingly and unwittingly, disseminated Rhodes's doctrine of Anglo Israelism, and in so doing have played their part in the theft of the Jews' religion and its use as the basis of a fascist and racist interpretation of the Bible. The ideas of the Ku Klux Klan and even of Hitler derive ultimately from Rhodes's theory of British Israelism.

Fortunately, the Bible supports the traditional Christian viewpoint that Jesus rules today in the hearts of His believers.

"Free" (as in Freemason) Christian churches, following the teachings of British Israelism, believe that the Devil is sovereign in the world today and that Jesus will return to earth where He will establish His kingdom after He defeats the forces of evil at the Battle of Armageddon. British Israelism believes that Jesus will rule from the earthly throne which the so-called chosen English-speaking Anglo-Saxons now inhabit.

From his training as a "British Race Patriot," as Cecil Rhodes called the Rhodes Scholars, or Rhodes White supremacists, as I call them, Clinton headed to Yale, home of The Order, Yale Skull and Bones branch, the seat of the power elite conspiracy in America and the Anglo twin of The Group, the wellborn, in England.

"Bones" men are "Knights" at Yale and "Patriarchs" afterward, among others, managing Anglophile fortunes at Brown Brothers Harriman investment firm; publishing the *National Review;* creating *Doonesbury;* and promoting other Bones men to positions of authority from its White House base. It is a fact that our President and his Anglophile Vice President, Al Gore, are steering the United States into more indebtedness to the English merchant bankers (which includes Brown Brothers Harriman), stockholders of our central bank. The policies of the White House Rhodes Scholar have served the House of Windsor dynasty, the royalty of England, well.

The American Revolution was an anticolonial war for independence that was sparked to a great extent by the colonies' resistance to continued British economic control. And although it was a civil war that replaced monarchy with a republic, it was not a clear-cut class war. Both the Patriots and the British Loyalists had support among all classes and economic groups. The Declaration of Independence signed on July 4, 1776, therefore, did not mark the beginning of a whole new society but the start of the evolution of an old society under new conditions.

In this light, it is not surprising that even men as intimately involved in the creation of this new society as George Washington, Thomas Jefferson, Alexander Hamilton, James Madison, and John Adams held on to some of the values of the old society. "There is a natural aristocracy among men," Jefferson wrote to Adams, for example. "The grounds of this are virtue and talents." The people, Jefferson firmly believed, would elect to be ruled by such "natural" aristocrats. Little wonder that he, along with most of the founding fathers, tolerated slavery in the new United States. They were shaped by the world they lived in and, like many great biblical figures, were humanly flawed.

In Jefferson's belief that the "natural aristocracy" was destined to rule the United States, we see the founding principle of America's ruling class. We also see the evolution of British elitism into American elitism—or possibly not evolution at all, but deliberate adaptation. (See Chapter 3 for a discussion of John Quincy Adams's accusation that Jefferson was an Illuminati spy.) In today's society, only that which is WASP is deemed truly American.

The brainwashed Irish-Catholic Patrick Buchanan worries incessantly about the United States maintaining "European" (WASP) cultural hegemony, essentially British character traits. And the erstwhile WASP Episcopalian Secretary of State, Madeleine Albright, only recently discovered by reading *The Washington Post* that she's a Jew. These examples, and many others like them, demonstrate the desire of many non-WASPs to become identified as WASPs. According to Dr. Robertiello, Jews more than any other non-WASP groups—Polish, Irish, Asians, Black, Hispanics, etc.—"emulate the WASPs" but all non-WASP groups are drowning their cultures to some degree to achieve the WASP mystique. The worship of WASP acceptance is the British legacy among non-WASPs in America, including Hispanics and Blacks like Randall Kennedy at Harvard who crave White validation and openly assault the concepts of Black unity and self-help. Even WASPs love WASP culture so much that the quest to be a better WASP never ends, according to the authors of *The WASP Mystique.*

## GREED UNION

"In 1775," wrote Eustace Mullins, "the colonists of America declared their independence from Great Britain, and subsequently won their freedom by the American Revolution. Although they achieved political freedom, financial independence proved to be a more difficult matter."[20] The American colonies won the shooting war, but a powerful economic and psychological connection remained between the two Anglophile countries.

That connection was forged on the high seas of international trade. "In America as in Europe, pretty much everything was deemed fair in the pursuit of profits," explains Karl E. Meyer in a recent *New York Times* editorial "The Opium War's Secret History." "Along with the slave trade, the traffic in opium was the dirty underside of an evolving global trading economy."[21]

The British East India Company, the family business of the royals and Britain's aristocracy, began trading opium in China in 1715. It was not until the end of the eighteenth century, however, that the British Crown, faced with financial disaster resulting from its efforts to retain the American colonies and the loss of the colonial revenues, as well as with a huge trade deficit with China, began to view opium as an important commodity.

Adam Smith, the free-enterprise icon and author of the 1776 classic *The Wealth of Nations,* was a propagandist for the British East India Company. He made a case for the expansion of the opium ("the produce") trade, in the context of his free-trade philosophy.[22] In 1783, Lord Shelburne, the British prime minister who negotiated the peace with the American colonies, acted on Smith's advice to expand the opium trade. He reorganized the British East India Company and "made it the central instrument of loot" for a bankrupt British Empire.[23] Shelburne's plan, according to some, was to use opium profits to overthrow the United States government.

F. S. Turner's 1876 book *British Opium Policy* details the British monarchy's deep involvement in the opium trade, a crime that targeted the Chinese specifically in the nineteenth century and that allegedly targets America today. The monarchy's history as a drug supplier dates from that time. It murdered the people of China with drugs and then laundered the enormous profits it made in so doing in special banks it chartered in Hong Kong, an island it took, along with $28 million in silver, from the Chinese with opium and guns.

"The British Empire has prospered on piracy, slavery and the drug traffic," Eustace Mullins asserts in his book *The World Order: Our Secret Rulers*.[24] In the first edition of Lyndon La-Rouche's book *Dope, Inc.*, subtitled *Britain's Opium War Against the United States,* LaRouche accused the British government of creating "the modern international drug traffic."[25] Successive United States governments have conducted an elaborate cover-up of what LaRouche claims is the newest drug offensive against the American people by the People's Republic of China.[26]

By 1787, British opium merchants—scions of elitist families such as the Jardines, Mathesons, Sassoons, Japhets, Dents, and others—had grown enormously wealthy by almost destroying China's mandarin class and the country with their "black dirt." Governmental structures, law enforcement, and the moral fiber of China broke down under the awesome weight of this insidious poison. One British trafficker commented that "there is not the least reason to fear that she [China] will become a military power of any importance, as the habit [opium addiction] saps the energies and vitality of the nation."[27]

The British Crown, which held a virtual monopoly on the China opium trade through the British East India Company, granted franchises to its American allies in Boston, New York, and Philadelphia. In 1816, John Jacob Astor of New York, for instance, was the first "American" rewarded with an opium route for his services as a British intelligence agent and for providing funds that helped Aaron Burr escape after he killed Alexander Hamilton.[28] Astor was an American sycophant to English banking interests that were in the formative stages of attempting to take control of America. Other American friends of the British were also granted franchises as drug traffickers—just as 125 years after Astor, Charles "Lucky" Luciano and the Mafia were rewarded by the U.S. and British intelligence establishments with a drug franchise in the Black community for fighting Communists on the docks in New York and Germans in Italy. Karl Meyer in *The New York Times* describes how the opium trade turned red-blooded Americans into blue-blooded aristocrats.

> In 1823 a 24-year-old Yankee, Warren Delano, sailed to Canton, where he did so well that within seven years he was a senior partner in Russell & Company [a Boston clipper-ship concern].
>
> Writing home, Delano said he could not pretend to justify the opium trade on moral grounds, "but as a merchant I insist it has been . . . fair, honorable and legitimate," and no more objectionable than the importation of wines and spirits to the U.S.[29]

The American drug-pusher "aristocracy" was led by the "Boston Brahmin" families—the Hathaways, Perkinses, and Forbeses—who jointly owned Russell & Company.[30] The opium and slave trades established the fortunes of all of Boston's merchant families: the Cabots, Lodges, Cunninghams, Appletons, Bacons, Russells, Coolidges, Parkmans, Shaws, Codmans, Boylstons, and Runnewells.[31] Significantly, it was again the British East India Company that granted American blue bloods "a monopoly in the slave trade in 1833."[32]

These are the Pilgrim families that are vulnerable to a class-action lawsuit for reparation payments to Americanized Africans for slavery. Although the Rothschild family and the Lehmans, Jewish German bankers, made their entry into the United States through the pre–Civil War slave trade, slavery was primarily a WASP institution.[33] For many blue-blooded families, the African slave trade and the drug trade are the sources of their enormous fortunes, blood money.

> Warren Delano returned to America rich, and in 1851 settled in Newburgh, N.Y. There he eventually gave his daughter Sara in marriage to a well-born neighbor, James Roosevelt, the father of Franklin Roosevelt. The old China trader was closed-mouthed about opium, as were his partners in Russell & Company. It is not clear how much F.D.R. knew about this source of his grandfather's wealth.[34]

The Delano-Roosevelt bloodline is typical of today's truly powerful WASP ruling class Establishment. This power elite comprises about three hundred "old money" families in an interlocking alliance of marriages and businesses, especially in the financial centers, that are linked with equally powerful individuals, families, and groups in Britain and around the world.

## THE "PILGRIMS"

Upper-class American WASPs identify as a British culture, but there is no sentiment for an anti-God cabal such as the Illuminati Ruling Class Conspiracy. Besides, there are too many layers in the international Anglophile conspiracy for anyone to really distinguish drug money from old money.

For our purposes here, we are not talking about the average WASP of Middle America from among the 49.6 million English-descended and the 49.2 million German-descended WASPs, the ethnic majority of the country.[35] Rather, I am referring only to the upper class of American WASPs, a minority of all WASPs, who cluster around the cities of the North Atlantic and New England and feel morally superior, according to Dr. Richard Robertiello, coauthor of *The Wasp Mystique*.

This ruling class created "the WASP mystique"—the cultural and moral standards that make the American WASPs the "most distinguishable minority of them all,"[36] by comparison to which all other American ancestry is considered virtually non-American. Nevertheless, employing the strategy of playing by the ruling class's rules is counterproductive for non-WASPs, even though those rules are the national standards for becoming a part of the socioeconomic elite.

American WASPs comprise the ruling class precisely because, after a tough start as demeaned dissidents and immigrants, they "got to the top fast by an accident of history, not inherent worth. So-called minorities should try to keep this in mind."[37] In other words, WASPs were the group that first achieved economic and social dominance, which they then perpetuated by creating an exclusive, not inclusive, social order. Each social milieu conditions, or programs, its inhabitants in specific cultural ways to achieve economic success and social acceptance. According to *The WASP Mystique:* "WASPs get their reward for being copies of one another, for suppressing their unique individual feelings and behaving in a predictable group fashion. To stand out, to be exhibitionistic, is to break the rules of conformity and invite punishment or public shunning."[38]

The upper-class WASPs' psychological nationality is an identification with Europe. Specifically, WASPs copy their English counterparts. It is the attitude toward culture that distinguishes the WASP ethnicity from other Americans. Their ethnic conditioning drives them to pursue moral superiority[39] and the pursuit of tradition and affiliation with other WASPs. This culture does not pressure its members for achievement, a trait that is so conspicuous among Jews and Asians.

In 1897, the relationship between British and American ruling class Establishments was formalized with the founding of the secret International Pilgrim Society. The "Pilgrims" were (and continue to be) the inner circle of the power elite, hardwired into "The City"—the international financial oligarchy's sovereign world state located in the financial district of London. The society's founding was animated by the millions that Cecil Rhodes left to it and his imperialistic White supremacist vision of a world order, including a recaptured, recolonized United States. William Allen White, a Pilgrim propagandist, articulated the society's purpose with chilling clarity: "It is the destiny of the pure Aryan Anglo-Saxon race to dominate the world and kill off or else reduce to servile status all other inferior races."[40]

After Rhodes died in 1902, the Rhodes Foundation's fortune of $150 million ensured that the Pilgrims would continue "to work towards eventual British rule of all the world" and implement the "provisions in his will designed to bring the United States among the countries 'possessed by Great Britain.' "[41]

Among the Pilgrims, the greed and thirst for power of the British and American ruling classes began to acquire a direction and an infrastructure. Money and its attendant influence were consolidated in the hands of the very few—the elite of the elite—for the purpose of advancing WASP economic and political control of the world. E. C. Knuth describes a 1915 Pilgrim gala in New York as a gathering of the inner circle of the power elite, two years after the Anglophile ruling class took over America's finances through the creation of the Federal Reserve.

The magic number of 400, once the symbol of reigning wealth and privilege, appears here in a new role. Men of millions here sway the destiny, the life or death of their fellow citizens, with an organization which is subversive to the spirit and the letter of the Constitution of the United States, an organization of which not one in one thousand of their fellow citizens has ever heard. The purpose of these men is completely interwoven with the dependence of their own invariably great fortunes on the operations of "The City," citadel of International Finance. Not only do these men collectively exert a planned influence of immense weight in utter secrecy, but they operate with the support of the immense funds provided by Cecil Rhodes and Andrew Carnegie.[42]

In 1908, Senator Robert M. La Follette stated that only one hundred men controlled the business interests of America. After being bitterly denounced, La Follette offered evidence from a series of interlocking directorates that proved that fewer than twelve men were in control of America and that "in the last analysis, the houses of Rockefeller and Morgan were the real kings of America."[43]

If the Rockefellers and the Morgans were America's business royalty, what did that make Lord Nathan Rothschild of the British House of Rothschild, who financed the Rockefeller empire and who owned J. P. Morgan lock, stock, and barrel? Chauncey M. Depew, the revered founder of the Pilgrims, in his autobiography, *My Memories of Eighty Years,* circa 1924, recalls a conversation in which the same Lord Rothschild "offered Puerto Rico and the Philippine Islands to the United States."[44] I would say that an English Freemason aristocrat who makes offers like that believes that he rules the world.

## THE DIANA FILE

I don't believe it's unreasonable to suspect the English royalty of doing in the twentieth century what it did in the nineteenth century. Nor do I find it out of the realm of probability, given the English aristocracy's history and evil nature, literally Luciferian Occultism, to suspect a planned MI-6 (British Intelligence Military Intelligence Division 6) assassination of Princess Diana.

MI-6 performs "dirty tricks" around the world. "Officially, MI-6 does not exist, its budget comes out of the Queen's purse and 'private funds.' "[45] A former member of British MI-6, John Coleman, says that three hundred families run America and one hundred families run England; they are "intertwined" through marriage, business, the Black nobility, and the religion of Freemasonry.[46] This power controls every government and the finances of the world, as well as the drug trade. This cabal is "under the control of the British monarch, in this case, Elizabeth II."[47]

Diana's affair and near marriage to an African and a Muslim, and her reported pregnancy by him, could have sunk "The Firm," as the billionaire Windsors are known. A non-White man as the future King of England's stepfather is unthinkable to this ruthless dynasty. *Newsweek* magazine observed that "British tastemakers" did not approve of the romance of the African Muslim with "the mother of their future king." Some of "the British elite have always had it in for Mohamed Al Fayed, Dodi Fayed's billionaire father."[48]

Paris police confirmed that "a white Fiat Uno . . . played a key role" in the fatal crash of Dodi Fayed's Mercedes in a tunnel. Officials said that "shattered plastic from the taillight of a Fiat were found near a pillar the Mercedes hit. Also traces of paint, possibly from another car were found on the Mercedes' wreckage," *USA Today* reported.[49] It seems that someone other than the paparazzi was there in the tunnel at the time of the crash. In fact, eight of ten witnesses said they heard two crashes that suggested a collision between the Fiat and the Mercedes.[50]

In an article entitled "The Diana File," *Newsweek* reported that photographs prove that "six cars passed the wreck before traffic was stopped. That would make it possible for the Fiat to stop, recover, and drive on. So why haven't the occupants come forward?"[51] The Fiat carried additional paparazzi, *Newsweek* theorized. Instead, it could have carried MI-6 assassins. The motive for the occupants of this mystery car remaining silent is not fear of punitive awards because they are not the custom or law in France.

Prior to the police findings, Fayed's family reported a "mystery car driving in front of Princess Diana's Mercedes" the afternoon before the crash.[52] A Fayed bodyguard told London's *Mail* that a Black Peugeot swerved in front of Diana and Dodi's car, "buzzing around like hornets trying to zoom in front to split the back-up car from the Mercedes."[53]

Diana was a threat to the Illuminati dynasty. The British intelligence spooks have killed millions before on behalf of Her Majesty.

Remember "007"? He's a composite fiction based on agents who are licensed killers in an alleged assassination bureau called Permindex, under the control of British Special Operations Executives (SOE), which allegedly specializes in political assassinations of heads of state and other notables. Sir William Stevenson, Britain's World War II James Bond and behind-the-scenes founder of the CIA, left behind in the CIA a "British SOE fifth column embedded deeply into the American intelligence community," writes Lyndon LaRouche in *Dope, Inc.*[54]

LaRouche believes that SOE's Permindex killed President John F. Kennedy because he "dared to violate the special relationship" with the British Crown. Reportedly, CIA agent Clay Shaw, who was tried for the murder of President John Kennedy, ran Permindex out of the Trade Mart Center in New Orleans.[55]

Why would extinguishing the life of one idealistic, love-struck woman cause these "pest control" agents to hesitate any more than they would before snuffing out a head of state? The Windsors, even on their best behavior, had to be forced by public pressure to express grief for "the People's Princess" whom they had abused so wantonly in life. Fearing to have a Black (even Africans in the part of Africa called the Middle East prefer to call Fayed an Egyptian) involved in the modern affairs of British royalty is an extreme irony, since the House of Windsor's foundation is "the Black nobility."

## THE BLACK NOBILITY

Europe's Black nobility, claims author Eustace Mullins in *The Curse of Canaan,* originated with Noah and his second son, Ham, on the Ark during the Flood. Violating God's command to abstain from sex while on the Ark, Ham engaged in sexual intercourse with the witch Naamah—"a pre-Adamite," his father's aunt, and a Black woman—and began a "mixed race" that, because it was not of "pure stock," was nonthinking and therefore, by virtue of being Black, lacked the "rigid moral code of the Adamites."[56] Moses, according to Mullins, would make the same mistake and marry a Cushite (Black) woman.

In support of this White supremacist theory, Mullins goes on to say that Canaan, the Black son of Ham, "being of mixed blood . . . probably committed a homosexual act on his grandfather," Noah, after the Flood. Mullins is undeterred by the fact that the Bible makes no such claim. Instead, he cites unnamed "scholars" who believe the curse on all Canaanites, descendants of Canaan, results from that degrading act.[57]

Mullins believes in the supremacy of the "people of Shem," whose descendants, he claims, are not the Jews but the Anglo-Saxons; the Jews, he says, are descended from the Chazars, an ancient people of Canaanite-Turkish mixture. Today's Sephardim Jews, Mullins says, derive from the thirty-one cursed Black tribes of Canaanites of Judea and Samaria. "The 'Semites' are really the 'anti-Semites' or Canaanites, the heirs of the Curse of Canaan . . . ; the true Semites are the fair-haired warriors who built one great civilization after another." Mullins's main point seems to be that Jews are Black and evil.[58]

Despite the fact that Mullins's book places God, the Holy Bible, Christianity, and history in the service of rabid White racism and prejudice against modern Jews, the story of the Black nobility of Europe that emerges in *The Curse of Canaan* belies Mullins's prejudices and seems to be the truth. The one positive contribution made by Mullins's work is its delineation of the lineage of today's White ruling class in Europe, especially of the royal family of England. And despite the book's intolerant moorings, I also recommend it as a source for detailed information on the Devil-worshiping pagan Black Cushites and Black Canaanites who, according to Mullins, changed their identity to become the Phoenicians after 1200 B.C., and became Europe's royalty.

The Canaanites-turned-Phoenicians (Phoenicia derives from the Greek word for "purple") monopolized the production of purple dye, the rare color that is favored by the ruling class and royalty in Europe. In *The Phoenician Origin of the Britons, Scots, and Anglo-Saxons,* L. A. Waddell explains that Julius Caesar wrote about clans of nonagricultural people who "painted their skin blue with a plant-based dye and were called 'Picts' or 'Blue Legs' " and practiced incest openly.[59]

The Canaanites-turned-Phoenicians remained an evil, sex-crazed witchcraft cult that hated God and burned their firstborn in offerings to their demon gods, Mullins maintains. Ashtoreth, one of their Egyptian female gods, survived in European rites as Astra or Ostara, a male god. According to Mullins: "In this form, he became the patron god of the Nazi movement in Germany."[60] Using a secret code to identify themselves, the Canaanites established Carthage in 900 B.C. and called themselves Punics. After three Punic Wars, Rome finally defeated Carthage's leader, Hannibal (the traditional name today for mulattoes), and enslaved the Canaanite-Carthaginians in 201 B.C.[61]

However, by A.D. 466, the enterprising Canaanite-Phoenicians founded the city of Venice (Phoenicia) and controlled the commerce of the Mediterranean region, the heart of the commercial world. "Like some new form of plague," the deceptive Black worshipers of Baal, now called Venetians, dominated banking and forcefully intermarried into the old nobility, Mullins asserts.[62]

> From the year 1711, this group became known throughout Europe as "the black nobility," because they were of Canaanite origin, as contrasted to the fair-skinned nobility of the people of Shem. The black nobility gradually infiltrated the noble families of Europe; today, they constitute most of the surviving European royalty.[63]

By now these wicked, cursed Canaanites, the descendants of Cush and Nimrod, were being called Guelphs, the Black Guelphs, or "the Black nobility." (The word "Guelph," according to *Webster's Third New International Dictionary,* is associated with the German ducal family of Welf, which today is probably known as the House of Brunswick, the House of Hanover, or the House of Windsor—all or which belong to the royal family of England.) Regarding this process of assimilation, Mullins cites several examples. For instance, Peter, the Italian Count of Savoy, became England's Earl of Richmond through the marriage of his niece to King Henry III. Before he died in 1268, Peter Savoy "brought in other members of the black nobility to marry English noblemen. . . . Peter's younger brother, Boniface, was appointed Archbishop of Canterbury."[64] According to Mullins:

The founders of the European dynasties which lasted into the twentieth century were Rupert, Count of Nassau, who died in 1124, and Christian, Count of Oldenbourg, who died in 1167. From Rupert came the Hesse-Darmstadt line, the Hesse-Cassel line, the Dukes of Luxembourg, the Battenborgs, the Prince of Orange and Nassau, and the Kings of the Netherlands. From Christian came the Kings of Denmark and Norway, the Schleswig-Holstein line, and the Hanovers, who became the Kings of Great Britain from 1717 to the present time. Also of the black nobility were the Dukes of Normandy, the Angevins and the Plantagenets, who became the Tudor and Stuart Kings of England, the Saxe-Coburgs, and the Wittlebachs. The Hanover line was always deeply involved with Freemasonry. The Hanovers become Kings of England in 1717. That same year, the first Grand Lodge was established in England.[65]

In this way, the occult Babylonian witchcraft religion practiced by the Canaanites was institutionalized among the royalty and aristocrats as Freemasonry and the descendants of the ancient Canaanite fused into the bloodlines of the Hanovers, Angevins, and Plantagenets, and other royal families of Europe. From Rupert's Hesse-Cassel line comes England's Queen Elizabeth's husband, Philip Mountbatten, son of the former King George of Greece, "whose family name of Battenberg was conferred by his great-grandfather Alexander, son of the Duke of Hesse. He is related . . . through the Cassels to Meyer Rothschild, the founder of the Jewish banking firm."[66] The Canaanite gene pool, whose phenotype is now Caucasian, has finally triumphed. As Mullins writes: "The House of Windsor is the world's preeminent family of reigning monarchs today. They represent the final triumph of the Guelph faction, or black nobility, the culmination of the Canaanite drive for power."[67]

The implications of this history are staggering. It repudiates Hilter's myth of the pure Aryan and the concept of Aryan Anglo-Saxon superiority and Mullins's own premise, because if the royalty of Europe is superior, it is a racially "mixed" superiority. It also means, in a word, that the racists among the European and American ruling class elitists are self-hating Blacks, based on the prevailing sociological and cultural definition of race (one drop of "Black" blood makes one 100 percent "Black").

The late President Franklin Delano Roosevelt and the Roosevelt dynasty, through intermarriage with the Astors, the Biddles, the Drexels, and the Pauls, have a common ancestry with England's royal family, the Windsor dynasty. FDR was Queen Elizabeth's third cousin. He was also related to twelve Presidents of the United States: George Washington, John Adams, John Quincy Adams, Martin Van Buren, James Madison, William Henry Harrison, Zachary Taylor, Andrew Johnson, Ulysses S. Grant, Benjamin Harrison, William Howard Taft, and Theodore Roosevelt. General Robert E. Lee was a fifth cousin of Theodore Roosevelt's mother.[68]

Typically, Black in the United States refers genetically to an admixture of "races" (gene pools), and there is no such thing as a "pure" Black or White race. If the figure cited in "Finds Touch of Africa in 28 Million Whites,"[69] a 1958 Associated Press story, is accurate, it means that a minimum of 21 percent of the "White" population of the United States share an African ancestry. So, once again, intolerance and elitism are exposed as evil beliefs for which there is no empirical evidence, and which can lead to national self-destruction. Europe's nobility may not be cursed, but it is definitely descended from Canaan.

Inadvertently, Mullins reveals the fallacy of his theory of Anglo-Saxon supremacy with his own facts. Similarly, any group that promotes itself as a racially superior ruling class must ultimately arrive at the same conclusion. None of today's blue-blooded American descendants of Europeans who share the elite WASPs' "usual amount of prejudice towards Blacks"[70] can withstand the scrutiny of history. In short, racists among the power elite are always vulnerable to the truth: There is only one race, a human race.

Furthermore, God has blessed poor Black people as much as the White power elite. Many Blacks fail to realize this fact because they have been brainwashed. It is the Devil, not God, who has rewarded the slave traders and drug trafficking families in the power elite with money and the illusion of power. Whether they are the "Black nobility" or the "White nobility," they are deceived souls on the fast track to eternal damnation. They should enjoy their time on earth because it will be hell after that. Don't forget that camel and that needle.

When Lyndon LaRouche, a Grand Orient Freemason, according to author John Daniel, first charged the Queen of England with drug trafficking several years ago, I thought it was preposterous, and I was susceptible to the media lampooning of him as a kook. However, his extremely controversial background, his criminal record, even the charge that he is a Communist agent for French Grand Orient Freemasonry assigned to destroy its rival, English Freemasonry, as well as the government of the United States, do not diminish the fact that he has one of the best intelligence-gathering operations in the world.

Even his enemies concede that he was the only one in the mid-1980s who predicted that evil conspirators in the Illuminati cabal were planning the disintegration of the Soviet Union. LaRouche's people have reportedly infiltrated and maintained high-level contacts with the CIA, among other sensitive intelligence agencies, and the Ronald Reagan administration when Reagan was President. LaRouche has also allegedly penetrated the British oligarchy, which, in my opinion, means he is peeking in on the Illuminati's inner core. Whatever his motives or his biases, many of the facts in his book *Dope, Inc.,* are irrefutable, especially the history of England's drug aristocracy—and its occult background.

Ben Hecht wrote that "the British love freedom almost as much as they love depriving people of it."[71] Because of the Crown's history of imperialism, that view is shared by many students of history. I cannot prove, other than by circumstantial evidence, that there is an Illuminati Ruling Class Conspiracy. But I can make a strong case for the greed, selfishness, and destructiveness of British imperialism; the drug epidemic caused by British Opium Wars against China; Britain's role as the world's major drug trafficker; and the adoption of the Babylonian witchcraft religions, which include the use of drugs and sex orgies, among many key players in the British aristocracy.

## ILLUMINATED SUPREMACY

While the British people have proved to be among the most tenacious and the bravest, especially during World War II, its aristocracy has not. No country's leadership, including that of Nazi Germany, has committed more evil in the world than England's. One reason is the Luciferian Occult tradition of the oligarchy that has always made it an agent of the Antichrist. "The British Empire has prospered on piracy, slavery and the drug traffic," Eustace Mullins asserts in his book *The World Order: Our Secret Rulers*.[72] The history of the British Empire is the history of human corruption.

"Misery followed the Union Jack across the seas and across the centuries. The world was its outhouse, however civilized it appeared at home," wrote columnist Sidney Zion.[73] At home the oligarchy that exported opium, White supremacy, and the evil of elitism to the four corners of the globe was steeped in Devil worship and its notion of illuminated supremacy.

## A Political Religion

Although Lyndon LaRouche, and anyone who dares quote him, has been ridiculed by the media for exposing the aristocratic English cancer on world history, its tradition of evil and occult Illuminism is a fact.

> The sinister element that sets the British oligarchy apart from the popular image of the mafia family is its unshakable belief that it alone is fit to rule the world—the view reflected in Cecil Rhodes's 1877 Testament. Their religion is not the Anglican Christianity they publicly profess, but a hodgepodge of paganism, including satanic cults such as Theosophy and Rosicrucianism. The central, syncretic ideology of the oligarchy's inner cult life is the revived Egyptian drug cult, the myth of Isis and Osiris, the same anti-Christian cult that ran the Roman Empire. And like the ancient Isis-worshipping Egyptian dynasties, the British ruling family networks have maintained power for centuries by keeping the secrets of their intrigues within the family.
>
> The Cult of Isis, dredged up in modern format, was the official ideology of leading British politicians, financiers, and literary figures during the previous century. The Isis cult also formed the core of Lord Palmerston's Scottish Rite of Freemasonry. Its great public exponent was the colonial secretary during the Second Opium War, Edward Bulwer-Lytton, who is the author of *The Last Days of Pompeii,* which first popularized the Isis cult, and the mentor of Cecil Rhodes's whole generation of British imperialists.[74]

Edward VIII, energetic supporter of Hitler, was crowned both King of England and Grand Master of English Freemasonry in

1936. Daniel says that "the Windsors were fascinated by the Fuehrer." King Edward promoted Nazism and British aristocrats joined the Nazi Party in droves.[75]

The philosophy of Great Britain's ruling class is a mirror image of the basic doctrine of the Illuminati Order. And like the Illuminati, the ruling class adheres to a political religion. For example, it is very difficult to know where the imperialism of the Illuminists Cecil Rhodes, Lord Rothschild, and their Oxford buddies ends and their Circle of Initiates' cult worship of the sun-sex god Osiris (Lucifer) begins. These aristocrats, who would later rise to great prominence in world affairs, committed their lives to a religiopolitical Illuminati Order that would use psychoactive drugs for profit and Hegelian social control of the populations of the world—especially the United States.

The mystery religions worship nature, specifically the sun. To the initiated, Osiris is a name for the sun god, as is Nimrod. Both names are used interchangeably for Lucifer and are also used in a larger sense to identify the phallus or the male "generative principle" (the symbol "G" in Masonry, which symbolizes its sun god) because the sun's rays (the phallus) penetrate the earth (Isis, the feminine principle) and create new life. Thirty-third-Degree Mason Lord Alfred Milner shaped Cecil Rhodes's vision of British Race Patriots into American Rhodes Scholar counterparts. Freemasonry, which was evident among Rhodes, Milner, Rothschild, and the rest of the Oxford brotherhood, "is a revival of the Old Religion," which is in fact the "ancient mysteries."[76] In a word, witchcraft.

## AMERICA'S RULING CLASS AND THE OCCULT

The "All-Seeing Eye" of "Osiris, the Creator," sun and sex god and the "Solar Eye . . . the symbol of the Arabian god of Jethro, the black father-in-law of Moses,"[77] was placed on the one-dollar bill in 1935 by two Thirty-second-Degree Masons,

President Franklin Delano Roosevelt and Henry Wallace, Roosevelt's Secretary of Agriculture.[78] Another Mason, Secretary of the Treasury Henry Morgenthau, Jr., carried out their orders. Wallace, later the Communist Party candidate for President, became an associate of a Russian occultist and once quoted "cabalistic" references for "the descent of America into the depths of purifying fires."[79] The emblems on the Seal of the United States and Wallace's "descent of America," especially with his quasi-Illuminist Communist background, have been interpreted to mean the destruction of the United States—occultly speaking.

There is even a secret cult of the All-Seeing Eye that worships an unknown god and is a pre-Christian pagan model of a secret society that also wants to destroy Christianity. You can experience its elaborate system of veiled allegories and secret symbols by visiting one of its three public temples in the United States: "namely, the Meditation Rooms in the United Nations and at Wainwright House, Rye, New York, and the Prayer Room in the United States Capitol."[80] The link here is between the European Rosicrucian occultists who influenced Wallace and are the driving force behind the "Seeing Eye" cult in America today.

## THE RULING CLASS BUREAUCRACY

"Fifty men have run America," bootlegger and robber baron Joseph Kennedy once said, "and that's a high figure."[81] He probably meant fifty WASP men, because as an Irish Catholic, he was an ethnic outsider. For America's ruling class is limited to the WASP elite of Anglo-Americans, who, along with their cousins the Anglo-Americanized Germans, consider themselves the "natural aristocracy." To ensure that the people continue to believe in their superiority and elect to be ruled by the elite among them, these illuminated "aristocrats" have created a bureaucracy that educates and employs clever, ambitious people who are hungry for status and money. Cecil Rhodes, for instance, in his will, committed the Rhodes Scholarships to "creating in American students an attachment to the country from which they originally sprang"—read the WASP ruling class.[82] At this very moment, the spirit of WASP supremacist Rhodes and the Pilgrims is guiding the United States in the person of Rhodes Scholar Clinton.

The Skull and Bones Chapter 322 senior society at Yale, of which former President George Bush is a member, is another example of the apparatus that helps perpetuate the American version of the imperialistic British ruling class. The ultrasecret fraternity is a powerful vehicle for the elite WASP families that exists because, in the words of Rose Kennedy, some people have the need for "a power beyond the power of money."[83]

Professor Quigley's description of the conspiratorial "international Anglophile network . . . which we may identify as the Round Table Groups,"[84] again gives us a clue as to the shape of the ruling class bureaucracy. He identified a "power structure between London and New York which penetrated deeply into university life, the press and the practice of foreign policy."[85] Bill Clinton found Quigley, who worked inside the Conspiracy for two years, "fascinating, electrifying, brilliant."[86]

Even some conspiracy theorists concede, though, that the usual suspects, especially the Council on Foreign Relations and the Trilateral Commission, have a membership of mostly ambitious people who are eager for opportunity and professional advancement. This is the only explanation I can find for the presence on the Trilateral Commission of Black people such as columnist Carl Rowan, Director of the U.S. Information Agency in the Freemason Lyndon Johnson administration; Vernon Jordan, lawyer and close friend of the Freemason Bill Clinton administration; politician Andrew Young, Ambassador to the United Nations in the Freemason Jimmy Carter administration; and William T. Coleman, Secretary of Transportation in the Freemason Gerald Ford administration.

All of the Black Trilateralist insiders have proved themselves invaluable to the ruling class by shaping Black opinion and channeling the energies of the Black civil rights movement into the service of their respective presidential administrations. Former Trilateralist Rowan, for example, is a professional propagandist who, among other things, deflects the blame for Martin Luther King, Jr.'s murder in the direction of the FBI, away from his former ruling class patron, Lyndon Johnson, who has now been identified by King's family as the prime suspect for the person who ordered King's assassination. Trilateralist Young, for his part, successfully led the effort that delivered the Black community's support for Trilateralist Jimmy Carter in the 1976 presidential election. The Black base enabled the unknown Southern ex-governor to dominate the Democratic primaries after a pre-primaries poll standing of a paltry 4 percent.

David Rockefeller—in defending himself against the charge of being "cabalist in chief" and his Trilateral Commission against the accusation of being, as he put it, "a nefarious plot by an Eastern establishment of businessmen in the service of multinational corporations, who will do almost anything, including going into cahoots with the Kremlin [Communists], for the sake of financial gain"—said the Commission's membership was broad-based, including "research institute directors" and a "hefty West Coast branch."[87]

Rockefeller, the most conspicuous member of the ruling class, told the Los Angeles World Affairs Council that there was nothing unusual in President Jimmy Carter's appointing no fewer than twenty-five out of the seventy-five American members of the Trilateral Commission to the highest posts in his administration. Rockefeller's explanation for the presence of Trilateralists in the positions of, among others, Vice President, Secretary of State, Secretary of Defense, and of course Chairman of the Federal Reserve Board was that these were simply "the most outstanding citizens."[88]

Bill Moyers brilliantly captured the mind-set of the ruling class when he described Rockefeller's attitude about the elite's control of the global economy as "just another day's work."[89] Thomas Jefferson's "natural aristocrats" are alive and well, and ruling today's America. Elitism drives America's and England's power elite in a frightening Anglophile alliance.

## TRILATERAL PRESIDENTS

Former Senator Barry Goldwater described the Trilateral Commission as "the vehicle for multinational consolidation of the commercial banking interests by seizing control of the political government of the United States.[90] For the last quarter century, at least, the Commission has in fact run the Presidency.

During the 1976 presidential campaign, Hamilton Jordan, Carter's future White House Chief of Staff, declared; "If after the inauguration you find Cyrus Vance as Secretary of State and Zbigniew Brzezinski as head of national security, then I would say that we failed. And I'd quit."[91]

They did fail, and Trilateralists Vance and Brzezinski ran the Carter administration. Much of Carter's domestic and all of his foreign policies came directly from the Trilateral Commission. According to the *Los Angeles Times,* the President's response to foreign policy initiatives was "Has Brzezinski (former director of the Trilateral Commission) seen this?"[92]

Hamilton Jordan, for his part, quickly learned to play ruling class politics, tucked his tail between his legs, shut up, and went to work for the Trilateralists.

Trilateralist Vernon Jordan, the former head of the National Urban League and now a Washington lobbyist-lawyer, was given credit by the Trilateralist Secretary of Commerce Mickey

Kantor for having "anointed" Trilateralist Clinton.[93] In 1991, Jordan walked Rhodes Scholar Clinton—a "Slick Willie," wheeler-dealer, precandidate for President of the United States—right through the front door of the annual conference of the Bilderberg group, whose every member is also a member of the Council on Foreign Relations and/or the Trilateral Commission. The conference, held in Germany, was according to Kantor, "a coming-out party" for Clinton, at which, I suspect, he probably made globalist promises in exchange for international money.[94]

Bill Clinton's international-money habit has continued in office. As a sitting President of the United States, he has directly profited from a blatant relationship with a possible intelligence agent of the People's Republic of China.

John Huang, ostensibly Deputy Secretary of Commerce but in fact a fund-raiser for Clinton and the Democratic Party, is known to have met face-to-face with the Preisdent at least fifteen times—and to have been at the White House on at least ninety occasions—between 1993 and his public exposure in 1997. Huang had previously worked for the Indonesian Lippo Group, a banking and real estate conglomerate that is full partners with a foreign firm that is an alleged front for Chinese military intelligence. Mysteriously, this ruling class agent received "a top-secret security clearance six months before starting his government job—without the usual full background security check."[95]

In his position at the Commerce Department, Huang received weekly classified intelligence briefings from the CIA and bimonthly briefings from the intelligence liaison officer for Commerce. There is a distinct possibility that he was passing on sensitive information to his associates. He often made three calls to his former employer on the same days of the briefings and several other calls within a few days of the briefings. Not only were the national security and economic interests of the United States compromised, but President Bill Clinton and his associates indirectly received millions of dollars from a Chinese espionage front.

On one occasion, after a $100,000 "campaign contribution" from the Chinese government to the Democratic Party, the President obediently flip-flopped on his 1992 campaign pledge and granted Most Favored Nation trade status to the human-rights-challenged Communist government of China. This gave the Chinese government billions of dollars in profits and large-scale technology transfers that it can ultimately use to produce weapons of mass destruction—to be deployed someday, perhaps, against Americans.[96] It is no surprise that the United States has an enormous trade deficit with China.

The ruling class bureaucracy consisting of President Bill Clinton and his administration, the U.S. intelligence community, the Communist government of China, an international banking group, a Communist espionage front, and the mainstream American media—which ignored the situation as long as it could—has successfully robbed Americans of their money and their freedom, to say nothing of their trust.

## THE CLINTON CONSPIRACIES

Ambrose Evans-Pritchard's 1997 book, *The Secret Life of Bill Clinton,* tells, according to a *Wall Street Journal* story by Quin Hillyer, an "implausible tale" of government complicity of "some of the wildest tales from the land of Clintonphobia . . . : the death of Vincent Foster; the murder of a security executive in Little Rock; two Arkansas teenagers dismembered by a train; the drugs-and-sex escapades of Mr. Clinton's friend Dan Lasater; drug running at the airport in Mena, Ark.; and other peculiarities."[97] But with the possible exception of the case of the death of Vince Foster, Hillyer is wrong to describe the factual reporting in Evans-Pritchard's book as "Clintonphobia." While the *Journal* cites Evans-Pritchard's "airtight case" that the FBI and the Bureau of Alcohol, Tobacco and Firearms knew in advance who was "collaborating with Timothy McVeigh in the Oklahoma City bombings," it maintains that it has nothing to do with Clinton's "proximate influence."[98]

This "airtight case" of government complicity is relevant because a mass murder of Americans has occurred and the FBI's own undercover informers, two neo-Nazis in Elohim, Oklahoma, were identified by the ATF's covert agent as plotters of America's worst terrorist tragedy, along with Timothy McVeigh and Terry Nichols.[99] Evans-Pritchard also proved that in the two years of interviewing twenty thousand witnesses, the FBI never interviewed these two suspects[100] or a Nazi informant who allegedly made contact with the Nation of Islam and militant Hispanic and American Indian groups[101] (probably with other FBI moles in each group) to unite against the government.

Why can one journalist unearth what the entire federal government cannot find? Even when their own covert agent had already told them? Is this conspiracy time or is this conspiracy time? And the *Journal* writer can't figure out the implications of this information for the Presidency.

If I am asked to blindly believe in Clinton's innocence, why does the *Journal* find it "implausible" that since twenty-eight "people connected some way to Bill Clinton met an untimely death,"[102] others are wondering out loud if he draws lightning, or something? Under such circumstances, it would be "implausible" not to suspect Clinton of knowing something about the deaths of this many of his associates, laundering drug money out of the Mena airport in Arkansas for Oliver North, and multiple cases of using his government-derived power to bribe and/ or subordinate women sexually. Is *The Wall Street Journal* pulling my "plausible" leg and why did Quin Hillyer not factually refute Evans-Pritchard's allegations point by point?

The mainstream and wannabe mainstream media pundits are afraid to rationally confront the charges and the facts. They fear what they might find out about their mythical America and themselves, by investigating a Ruling Class Conspiracy. The chances of Clinton ever coming to justice are about the same as one of the elitist Clintonites apologizing to a working-class White woman, Paula Jones, for calling her "a trailer park whore" because she publicly charged that Bill Clinton demanded oral sex when she was in his Arkansas government.[103] In the most digusting example of slander and class bias against Paula Jones, James Carville, one of President Clinton's best friends, reportedly said: "Drag a hundred dollars through a trailer park and there's no telling what you'll find."[104] Carville can now say that dragging $700,000 through a trailer park didn't work because Paula Jones turned down a $700,000 out-of-court settlement to drop her case. She did not display the moral relativism of the Clintonites when she placed integrity and the rule of law above opportunism. But there's no telling what the people of the United States will finally find out about their president when he goes on trial for sexual harassment. Without a doubt, there will be the more salacious charges by a former Miss Arkansas that Bill Clinton "liked to cavort around wearing her black nightdress" and Paula Jones's testimony that when he dropped his pants to expose an erection, he also revealed "a half-inch wide mole"—the alleged famous "distinguishing characteristic" of Clinton's phallic anatomy.[105]

## FORNIGATE: SERIAL SEX

Bill Clinton is, by his own admission in a deposition in the Paula Jones case, a liar and a philanderer. In addition to these revelations, after a decade of adamant denials, there is the peculiar satisfaction of his appetites for cunnilingus and fellatio, per Gennifer Flowers and now Monica Lewinsky, but his wife seems very comfortable with it all, fueling further rumors. The President's alleged sexual escapades with Catherine Cornelius, who is reportedly his cousin and a former White House aide, was linked by "ex-White House official David Watkins publicly and by other presidential staffers privately," a New York *Daily News* article, "Bill's Cousin Kissing Kin?" reported.[106]

Other than his cousin, the most salacious charge of Oval-oral sex, and a state job for Arkansas sex for Gennifer Flowers, there are charges from various sources of sexual relationships with Kathleen Willey, a former Clinton administration employee; Sheila David Lawrence, widow of a former ambassador to Switzerland (she denies it); an assortment of women from Arkansas; and, according to Lewinsky, five other White House employees.

Critical of the deleterious effect that the mountain of Clinton scandals is having on his party, the top House Democrat, Congressman Richard Gephardt, said the Democrats needed "a movement for values— and not a money machine."[107] A senior Clinton aide replied that Gephardt had once again chosen "politics over principle."[108] Gephardt, intimidated, folded like a tent.

One would have to stop breathing not to smell the perversity in such a cheap shot against one of the few genuine Democrats left in the Democratic Party. The fact that President Clinton has aided the Chinese Communist government's "all-out offensive to infiltrate America's political, military, and security apparatus, while penetrating the United States economy in unprecedented and hitherto unnoticed ways," according to Kenneth R. Timmerman in his article "While America Sleeps," was lost.[109]

In addition to receiving the head of China's state-owned arms company, Poly Technologies, into the White House for coffee, says Timmerman, the path had been strewn by months of old-fashioned influence peddling with donations to the Democratic National Committee and Clinton's legal defense fund from state-owned Bank of China wire transfers "to Clinton crony Yah Lin Trie."[110] Timmerman summarizes Clinton's performance as an "appalling record by any standard,"[111] and goes on:

> So far the President of the United States has accepted campaign contributions from mainland Chinese donors, sponsored questionable investments for them in the United States, approved the sale of sophisticated technology to the Chinese military, failed to enforce U.S. laws when the Chinese sell cruise missiles to Iran by sanctioning the Chinese firms involved, welcomed the most notorious Chinese arms dealer into the White House, and encouraged the man's firm to raise money in U.S. capital markets.[112]

In an allegorical depiction of the emerging Clinton legacy, *Newsweek* magazine, sister publication of the Clinton-friendly *Washington Post,* published a cartoon by Marlette: a picture of the Lincoln Memorial next to a picture of the Jefferson Memorial next to the picture of a partially unzipped zipper atop a monument foundation, above the words: "Clinton Memorial."[113] I honestly hate to say this, but the real victim of this sociopath's tenure as President will be future American governments, which will face an increasingly difficult task in winning the confidence of the people.

After the Paula Jones trial, the focus may shift to the "apparent gunshot wound" that was found in the late Ron Brown's skull, according to Dr. Steve Cogswell, an Air Force colonel and deputy medical examiner with the Armed Forces Institute of Pathology.[114] Questions about the former Secretary of Commerce's death and the bizarre investigation of the plane crash in which he and others died—missing black boxes, the flight data recorder, three fired generals, and a Croatian chief maintenance engineer at the airport who committed suicide just before his interrogation on the crash, in a culture where suicides are very rare—may lead to a plethora of new questions.[115]

I certainly am not blaming the President or anyone else of murder, but I do feel unsettled by the numerous seeming coincidences. As a former psychiatric social worker, however, I do feel more comfortable discussing sociopathic (psychopathic) personality disorders. (For a clinical discussion of the subject, I suggest *Without Conscience* by Dr. Robert Hare,[116] and for material from the pages of Clinton's life that are applicable to sociopathic behavior, I recommend *One More Link* by Michael Kellett.)[117] Since Clinton hit the national scene in 1992, I have suspected that he has a sociopathic personality disorder, characterized by Sigmund Freud as a stunted superego (conscience), which makes antisocial behavior normal and moral behavior unnecessary. This is also the psychological prototype for an Illuminati agent.

Clinton's behavior is characterized by recklessness; his drive for power and his sexual impulses seem one and the same; there are also his defiant lying in the case of Gennifer Flowers; his alleged bizarre belief that the Bible sanctions oral sex because it is not sex; his sociopathic union of arrangement with a political partner as wife; his alleged compulsive drive to punish women with his power; and his "I dare you to catch me" pattern of philandering. The Monica Lewinsky charges fit this personality pattern.

Dr. Hare says that in addition to being "slick,"[118] liars, and fast talkers, sociopaths are unable to alter their behavior even when caught.

Psychopaths are social predators who charm, manipulate, and ruthlessly plow their way through life, leaving a broad trail of broken hearts, shattered expectations, and empty wallets. Completely lacking in conscience and in feelings for others, they selfishly take what they want and do as they please, violating social norms and expectations without the slightest sense of guilt or regret.[119]

Clinton's conduct in office and the revelations of Senate committee hearings into campaign-finance abuses have been sobering reminders of the corrupting influence of the ruling class bureaucracy. Traditionally, the bureaucracy appoints a "special commission" to investigate its own corruption and to write an obscure report that, if the situation demands, vilifies a dispensable errand boy—e.g., Daniel Ellsberg, Oliver North, Jonathan Pollard. No one in the ruling class is ever even mentioned, much less punished, of course, confirming Lord Acton's adage: "Power corrupts, and absolute power corrupts absolutely."

## THE "CAPITALIST" VERSUS "COMMUNIST" SCAM

Conspicuous in the Clinton-Huang connection is the working alliance of the ruling class crony Capitalists and mongrelized Marxists, who exploit the American and Chinese people and manipulate the United States government. These ostensible enemies, Capitalists and Communists, in reality, are partners in the same business: violating the civil rights of their respective people for the purpose of promoting their own self-interest. Together these ruling class elites comprise an interlocking power network of each nation's most powerful families and their cohorts—including big business and cooperative government agencies.

The "Communists," the American people have been told since World War II, threaten our way of life. The truth is that when it is expedient, factions of the Illuminati Ruling Class Conspiracy identify themselves as both "Communist (Marxist)" or "Capitalist." However, you can reach both of them at the same address. Only their victims are truly committed to mutual

Hegelian destruction: Blacks versus Whites, men versus women, conservatives versus liberals, have-nots versus haves, etc.

## ESTABLISHMENT DOES NOT EQUAL CONSPIRACY

It is critical that we do not confuse the ruling class Anglophile Establishment or its semisecret class of professional opportunists with the ultrasecret Illuminati Ruling Class Conspiracy and its ruthless secret army of mental spooks in the influence-peddling class that routinely rationalizes murder as a "noble" action of the state, as enunciated by one illuminated Rhodes Scholar George Stephanopoulos. Both hegemonic powers, of course, bear great similarities in that they manipulate our lives to their own advantage. But although it is often impossible to know where one ends and the other begins, we must distinguish the legitimate, albeit immoral, objectives of the Establishment from the outright demonic objectives of the Conspiracy.

The guilt-by-association approach to uncovering members of the Conspiracy is counterproductive. Labeling every famous or successful person in the world as a conspirator only succeeds in producing disinformation. In casting a net this wide, you are bound to catch some conspirators, along with a plethora of spook advisers, opinion-makers, and sycophant agenturs. In the process, though, you do real damage to the truth and to the reputations of the majority who are only guilty of being success-ful opportunists.

The membership of the Council on Foreign Relations and the Trilateral Commission, the two groups primarily suspected of harboring Illuminati activity, are not secret nor are their meetings clandestine. In the case of the Council on Foreign Relations, their membership is simply too large for clandestine decisions. However, some of The Order's "Patriarchs" are members and they work in secret; some could well be Illuminists or American operatives working for the innermost sanctum of the Conspiracy. Undoubtedly, there is a secret core group within the inner circle of each Round Table group that represents the Illuminati Ruling Class Conspiracy.

The U.S. Labor Party's claim that every single member of the Trilateral Commission is slavishly following "the Rockefellers as a 'cover' for a 'British conspiracy' " only helps to confuse America's ruling class Establishment with the Illuminati Ruling Class Conspiracy.[120] As hard as it is for some to understand, "spooks" like the Henry Kissingers and newly emerging elitist power brokers, such as Trilateralist Vernon Jordan, do not control things. They carry messages and negotiate on behalf of the people who do. Their main function is to shape public opinion for the ruling class.

"The truth about the nature and the power of the elite is not some secret which men of affairs know but will not tell," explains C. Wright Mills in *The Power Elite*. "Such men hold quite different theories about their own roles in the sequence of event and decision. Often they are uncertain about their roles."[121]

## THE "INVISIBLE ONES"

Wars. The worldwide distribution of narcotics. Global control of governments. All of these things are being coordinated—and all at the same time. Neither the large and unwieldy membership of the Council on Foreign Relations nor the Trilateral Commission, with their quasi-openness and high visibility, could ever pull this off. The Illuminati Conspiracy—the Luciferian religion of evil intellectual zealots—is fully capable of controlling these man-made plagues that ever increasingly confront our world today, and is motivated to do so. This is accomplished by small cells of secret rogue groups within just about every influential organization in the world, including the CFR and, the Trilateral Commission. The jury is out on the Royal Institute of International Affairs in London.

True, Round Table groups such as these are involved in a "conspiracy" (a venal but not diabolical one) to accrue all of the money and power they can for their members, as is true of most other enterprises. But I do not believe that their motive is to destroy the world as we know it or collect souls for the Devil. Neither is their cunning ability to staff various presidential administrations with their members de facto evidence that they are conspiring to enslave the world's population.

The Illuminati's religious convictions and obsessive secrecy are missing in the typical suspect from the Round Table groups. Most of these excessively ambitious sycophants are just not evil enough. A good intellectual rationalist like Freemason Henry Kissinger is a much better choice. Kissinger's "role in global drug-trafficking," according to Lyndon LaRouche, "squelched all mention of the P.R.C. [People's Republic of China] as a drug source. . . . At several points, Kissinger specifically intervened to protect the P.R.C. against charges that the Communists were the major source of heroin flooding Vietnam, and U.S. cities."[122]

Beyond a shadow of a doubt, the "Invisible Ones," heads of our invisible government as the Illuminati rulers are called, screen each new crop of the ambitious class—those young men and women who have gone down the traditional career path of private schools, followed preferably by Harvard, Princeton, Columbia, or the CIA's favorites, Yale and Williams, and whose conduct demonstrates that they have renounced virtue for roles as agenturs. Those who go on to graduate school at England's Oxford for a two-year indoctrination as Rhodes "scholars" are selected for high-level posts in the academy, investment banking establishments, prominent law firms, or brokerage houses.[123] But no matter how far they get in the ruling class establishment, agenturs and mental spooks is all they can ever be. Their blood, you might say, is not blue.

## KILLING SAVES LIVES; EVIL IS GOOD

"Why We Should Kill Saddam," a recent *Newsweek* article by George Stephanopoulos,[124] is typical of the structural immoralism indigenous to the horde of elite trained seals from Cecil Rhodes's Oxford brainwashing cult who followed another of their kind into the White House and now control the United States. In another era, another group of intellectual influence peddlers of the Illumined class, led by Robert McNamara, who played the spook agentur role that Stephanopoulos is now playing, recruited 365,000 low-IQ American teenagers into the Vietnam War to disproportionately fill the high-risk combat units—after he knew the United States could not win the war. Mental spooks like McNamara and Stephanopoulos seem to be trained to think in immoral, perverted terms.

Stephanopoulos boasts of discussing the idea of murdering Saddam Hussein, a dangerous despot who was sly enough in 1991 to record a U.S. State Department official encouraging him to invade Kuwait, in the Oval Office. The diminutive hawk is now simultaneously shopping his murderous proposal from the newly created Establishment platform as a *Newsweek* "contributor," a commentator at the ABC television network, and as a teacher at Columbia University, one of the intelligence community's favorite haunts.

What he is testing on the public through this impressive array of institutional support—the mainstream media, the academy, the Clinton administration, and, without a doubt, the CIA—is immorality. Stephanopoulos, the Hegelian, says in *Newsweek*, "What is unlawful . . . is not necessarily immoral."[125] That's why "killing" Saddam is the "moral course."[126] He deployed the historical lessons of Cicero and invoked Grecian pagan rituals to press his jaded view that it is "not only necessary, but noble" to murder whenever the state (his handlers in the power elite) finds it expedient. "Assassination . . . is the least random act of war. Relaxing the moral norm against it is a . . . justifiable price to pay," to God, I suppose he means, because, he believes, "killing can be a humanitarian act that saves far more lives than it risks."[127] Support the intelligence community and Clinton in this immoral effort, he implores in his transparent ruse to manipulate the population.

Ambition has clouded this opportunist's judgment. Saddam Hussein already has mole units inside the United States and he has enough chemical and biological ingredients to kill every human on the planet. Do you for one second doubt this madman's resolve to have already put into place a plan to use this lethal combination on a population center in the event of his assassination? The Clinton spin doctor of *Newsweek*, ABC, and Columbia wants a nation to surrender its morality and risk a venal retaliation to sanction this Establishment murder of a man who very likely is an ally of the same power elite that now wants him dead. Hussein was also a butcher with a biological and chemical arsenal when the power elite's former agents, George Bush and Colin Powell, did not follow him into Baghdad during the Persian Gulf War in 1991 and kill him. At that time, they wanted him to remain in power with his military arsenal intact. The ruling class's politics have obviously changed and it now wants the American people to sanction the new immorality, which does show some signs of catching on among a gullible public.

Stephanopoulos's "ideals" as a member of the Cecil Rhodes cult, according to Carroll Quigley, Stephanopoulos's mentor's mentor, "could be carried out best by a secret society of men devoted to a common cause. The [Rhodes] scholarships were merely a facade to conceal the secret society, or, more accurately, they were to be one of the instruments by which the members of the secret society could carry out his purpose."[128] The Clinton spin doctors' "noble" idea of murder under reasonable conditions also seems to have found a home among the White Skinheads, emboldened by their hatred and frustrated by their economic impotence, who were charged with a series of murders of Blacks in Denver.[129] One confessed Skinhead murderer admitted that he did not know the difference between right and wrong. Neither, it can be speculated, do the intellectual spooks for hire from Oxford and Yale.

## Who Heads the Illuminati?

I believe, contrary to the conventional wisdom of conspiracy theorists, that it is impossible to prove membership in today's Illuminati. There are others, however, who differ. John Daniel believes that the Illuminati Conspiracy is housed today in the Lucis (Latin for Lucifer) Trust, formerly Lucifer Publishing of New York.[130] In 1982, Daniel claims, its leader, Freemason Robert McNamara, Secretary of Defense in the John F. Kennedy administration and past president of the World Bank, who, Daniel writes, on nights when he is not "bathing in moonbeams," reads himself to sleep on Madame Helena Petrovna Blavatsky and her protégée Annie Besant of the Theosophical Society, Luciferian occult leaders from Britain at the turn of this century.[131] Among other prominent members of Lucis Trust, according to Daniel, are Walter Cronkite, Ted Turner, and Henry Lausen, former Supreme Grand Commander of the Supreme Council, Southern Jurisdiction of Scottish Rite Freemasonry.[132]

Whether McNamara heads the Illuminati or tucks himself in at night with Luciferian tales of baby ritual sacrifices or genocide, he is an agent of the people who are the Illuminati, wittingly or unwittingly. He's an Establishment elitist whose crimes against humanity include 50,000 dead, 300,000 wounded, and 500,000 heroin-addicted Americans—mostly teenagers who were sacrificed in Vietnam by him and his mental spook cronies at the White House, the Pentagon, and the CIA.

How did McNamara wield power? After he told Lyndon Johnson that the Vietnam War was unwinnable, as Secretary of Defense, McNamara devised a triage plan aimed at Black young men from the ghettos and White youths from the rural poor areas. They were called the "Moron Corps" because of their low IQ scores. Myra MacPherson offers a graphic depiction in a *Washington Monthly* article, "McNamara's 'Other' Crimes: The Stories You Haven't Heard," of the class warfare and death that was inflicted on 354,000 young men who volunteered to better their lives. They were in reality insurance against "the lily-white" college students losing their deferments.[133] The poor boys of the "Moron Corps" were placed in combat in higher numbers and they died in higher numbers.[134]

McNamara also knew of the toxicity of the chemical Agent Orange, but remained silent as the United States government sprayed it on its own troops in Vietnam, MacPherson explained. The faces of the Illuminati could not look much worse than McNamara's, of whom Herb DeBose, a Black first lieutenant in Vietnam said: "I think McNamara should be shot."[135] If most people really understood the Illuminati Ruling Class Conspiracy, they would also want its economic royalty and their mental spooks shot.

I also have the minority view that the constant speculation about the identities of individual conspirators—such as the indiscriminate finger-pointing at the Rockefellers and incriminating the Jews—is nothing more than empty titillation.

Since only members of the intellectual and ruling classes can effectively carry out a conspiracy to control the world, the possible candidates are not unduly difficult to divine. I know that this universe of ruling class suspects is restricted to the power elite. For example, the international cabal of Class A stockholders of the Federal Reserve System are very likely suspects.

According to Professor Quigley, families with the best banking traditions around the time the Federal Reserve Bank was established were "Protestant of Swiss origin . . . or Jews of German origin."[136] Thus, the Illuminati of the early twentieth century also consisted of German bankers such as Freemason Jacob Schiff, Mayer Amschel Rothschild, and Freemason Paul Warburg—all House Jews of English Illuminati Freemasonry. Freemason Thomas Jefferson, another Illuminist, protected Freemason Adam Weishaupt, Illuminati founder, and was widely suspected of promoting British interests over America's, even as President of the United States.

But even if we could identify the Illuminists today, the system under which we live would never bring them to justice because the system is substantially corrupt. A pungent odor coming out of the White House leads directly, for anyone who will read *The Secret Life of Bill Clinton,* to a systemic corruption of the federal government. And that's only the tip of the Illuminati Conspiracy iceberg. My Illuminati Ruling Class Conspiracy theory forestalls the need for a search for individual conspirators' identities. I know *who* they are; they are the evil people in the ruling class. My approach is to understand *what institution* holds the key to the ruling class's control of the population. Then we can focus on breaking its structure and restoring freedom in America.

# 3

# THE ILLUMINATI
# RULING CLASS
# CONSPIRACY

*For we wrestle not against flesh and blood, but against*
*principalities, against powers, against the rulers of the darkness*
*of this world, against the spiritual wickedness in high places.*
—EPHESIANS 6:12

According to Edith Starr Miller's *Occult Theocrasy:* "The term 'Illuminism' used in the 18th century is replaced by the wide term Freemasonry which embraces all the existent secret societies."[1] I refer to the same evil camarilla as the Illuminati Ruling Class Conspiracy and its Luciferian occult political religion as Illuminati Freemasonry. It is the pantheistic Masonic religion that holds together the evilarchy's diverse components—the economic money lords, the royal families, the crony Capitalists, the Communists, the clergy from all religions. Illuminati Freemasonry also guarantees the cabal's perpetuation from one generation to the next. Remember the adage "The family that prays together, stays together." This is true even when the family prays to the Devil.

A man I would call the Grand Dragon of Illuminati Freemasonry, Albert Pike, explained in the Masonic bible, *Morals and Dogma,* that "everything grand in the religious dreams of the Illuminati . . . is borrowed from the *Kaballah.*"[2] This means, one writer believes, that because Freemasonry originated in the Kaballah, "it accomplishes its devious purposes through the even more secret organization of the Illuminati, the inner circle which controls the six million Freemasons of the world."

Illuminati Freemasons, Masons who worship the Devil and work for his control of the world, comprise the secret core group of approximately 300 Thirty-third-Degree Masons within the inner circle of about 5,000 Thirty-third-Degree Masons that controls the world's 6 million Freemasons—97 percent of whom have never read the Illuminati leader Albert Pike, the Luciferian founder of the Ku Klux Klan, and are unaware that a Black man named Nimrod is the god and founder of their fraternity.

The Illuminati Ruling Class Conspiracy is not simply a group of egomaniacal, internationalist elitists. If it were held together solely by secret fraternities, exclusive clubs, and Round Table groups, the Conspiracy would have died out long ago. The unbroken authority of this cabal cannot be explained merely by the thirst for money and power of the privileged families to which its members belong. The evil force that is plotting to rule the world is much more than the sum of individual political and financial ambitions.

"The only secret in the world is the history you don't know," former United States President Harry S. Truman sagely advised. That statement is particularly significant, as you will see, coming as it does from a Thirty-third-Degree Mason. It certainly was true for me about three hundred or so books ago, before I started the research for this book. I was not only ignorant of the true nature of evil in this world but also unaware of how brainwashed my understanding of history was. Taught to assume that evil has very little to do with our everyday life, I was bedeviled by questions about the Illuminati Ruling Class Conspiracy: What is its fundamental motivation? What inspires its rich and powerful members to attempt to dominate the world? How does an evilarchy of economic royalty continue from generation to generation?

My suspicions of evil deeds in high places were ignited by a seemingly innocuous statement made by Benjamin Disraeli, Prime Minister of Great Britain at the end of the nineteenth century. This member of the British nobility, novelist, and statesman wrote: "The world is ruled by very different personages from what is imagined by those who are not behind the scenes."[3] Disraeli may have simply been referring to the human frailty of the ruling class, but his words reminded me of the paradoxical truth that the greatest trick the Devil ever pulled off was to convince the world that he does not exist.

I awoke to the fact that the Order of the Illuminati—the evil soul of the Conspiracy—is the most powerful, albeit secret, religion on earth. The Illuminati's god is Lucifer. Its dogma serves the same religious purpose as does the faith of any pious family, and is passed down from one generation to another. The Illuminati's evil quest is for confirmation of intellectual—"illuminated"—superiority.

It cannot be empirically proved that an Illuminati Order per se still exists today. Nevertheless, I oppose it, as an evil religious doctrine, on the basis of a similar supposition found in the Bible: "Have nothing to do with the fruitless deeds of darkness, but rather expose them."[4]

## SLAVES TO REASON

The eighteenth century was known as the Age of Reason, of rational "Enlightenment." With the advent of the natural sciences, some among the educated elite came to believe that faith was a blind superstition and that reason alone could decipher the mysteries of creation. God, in this context, becomes, at best, a quaint anachronism, and, at worst, "the opiate of the masses," according to latter-day Illuminati rationalist Karl Marx.

The impulse to "believe and belong," however, is a powerful part of human nature, as Theodore J. Fortsmann, a cofounder of Empower America and Cato Institute board member, points out in "Statism: The Opiate of the Elites." "And when men cease to believe in God, they will not believe in nothing, they will believe in anything."[5]

Fortsmann goes on to quote Paul Johnson's *Intellectuals* to describe the deluded elitists of the "Enlightenment."

For the first time in human history . . . men arose to assert that they could diagnose the ills of society and cure them with their own unaided intellects: more, that they could devise formulae whereby not merely the structure of society but the fundamental habits of human beings could be transformed. . . . [These] were not servants and interpreters of the gods but substitutes.[6]

In the Judeo-Christian tradition, It was Lucifer, "the shining one,"[7] "the bright" angel "full of wisdom"[8] who in his arrogance first presumed to equate himself with God. It is his spirit that "now worketh in the children of disobedience,"[9] who were tempted by his promise made to our mother Eve: "Your eyes shall be opened, and ye shall be as gods, knowing good and evil."[10]

God said to Lucifer before expelling him from heaven: "Thou hast corrupted thy wisdom by reason of thy brightness."[11] So it was with the "bright" European elitists of the eighteenth century. They were so blinded by the light of their own intellects, they rejected God, thus putting themselves in league with Lucifer.

## ILLUMINATED FREEMASONRY

Although the larger media elites ridicule the subject of the Illuminati Order as a myth and dismiss its relevance to achieve political correctness and absolve themselves of the responsibility to report the facts, the facts about its origins and subsequent growth were revealed by Dr. John Robison, distinguished professor at the University of Edinburgh in Scotland. Robison, himself an outstanding intellectual, witnessed firsthand the workings of the Illuminati and published his findings under the ponderous title *Proofs of a Conspiracy against all the Religions and Governments of Europe, carried on by secret meetings of Free Masons, Illuminati and Reading Societies, collected from good authorities by the Author Professor of natural Philosophy and Secretary of the Royal Society of Edinburgh.*

Known today simply as *Proofs of a Conspiracy,* Robison's book was first published in 1798. (The shop of the printer was promptly destroyed by fire.) In it, the author explained Weishaupt's diabolical brainchild and other systems of Illuminism that had existed as far back as ancient times. Citing the Illuminati Order's internal documents discovered by the Bavarian authorities in 1783, Robison also explained why rumors of its demise were premature.

Robison details Weishaupt's infiltration of "a remarkable Lodge of the Eclectic Masonry . . . called The Lodge Theodore of Good Counsel."[12] Lodge Theodore was "erected" in what today is Munich, Germany.

Refining gradually on the simple British Masonry, the Lodge had formed a system of practical morality, which it asserted to be the aim of genuine Masonry, saying, that a true Mason, and a man of upright heart and active virtue, are synonymous characters, and that the great

aim of Freemasonry is to promote the happiness of mankind by every mean in our power.[13]

The secretive nature of Masonic lodges allowed Weishaupt
to create a secret Illuminati organization within the lodge. The
doctrine of this inner sanctum was diametrically opposed to that
of Lodge Theodore. Under cover of Masonry's secrets and its
teachings of "active virtue," Weishaupt spread the evil elitist
dogma of "arrogant self-conceit of the mentally superior who
feel that they should be running the world and everyone in it."[14]
The Illuminati founder explained his purpose as follows:

If only the aim is achieved, it does not matter under what
cover it takes place, and a cover is always necessary. For
in concealment lies a great part of our strength. For this
reason we must cover ourselves with the name of another society. The lodges that are under Freemasonry
are in the meantime the most suitable cloak for our high
purpose, because the world is already accustomed to expect nothing great from them which merits attention.
As in the spiritual Orders of the Roman Church, religion
was, alas! only a pretense, so must our Order also in a
nobler way try to conceal itself behind a learned society
or something of the kind. A society concealed in this
manner cannot be worked against. We shall be shrouded
in impenetrable darkness from spies and emissaries of
other societies.[15]

Weishaupt thus *"grafted it* [the Illuminati] . . . *onto Freemasonry—like a fungus"* (emphasis in original).[16] What he grafted
was a philosophy based on the assumption that the masses who
believed in God were superstitious fools and that the "illuminated ones" were chosen to rule over them. (Remember Illuminist Thomas Jefferson's "natural aristocracy"?) This elitist

philosophy caught on immediately among the intellectual and patrician classes—i.e., the lawyers, doctors, clergy, as well as other aristocrats, and especially, the university professors. Through the vehicle of Freemasonry, the doctrine that reason was a force superior to superstitious faith in a weak God spread across Europe like wildfire.

By 1782, the Illuminati "had grown to over three million members worldwide and was in control of the lodges throughout Europe."[17] That same year, Freemasonry surrendered in disgrace, when it officially recognized the Illuminati Masonic Order in Wilhelmsbad, Germany, according to author David L. Carrico.[18] In *Adam Weishaupt: A Human Devil*, Gerald B. Winrod explains:

> Secret societies, sometimes founded upon high ideals and lofty precepts, are frequently prostituted by men of evil genius who get control of them for their own private gain and selfish use. Because there is always an element of mystery associated with a lodge, it becomes a convenient cloak and an ideal means for secret operations, when taken over by subversive influences.[19]

To a Christian world, Weishaupt taught that "Freemasonry is hidden Christianity." To his minions, he elucidated that he could explain Masonic symbols in such a way as to give the appearance of Christianity.[20] "In the way in which I explain Christianity no one need to be ashamed to be a Christian, for I leave the name and substitute for it Reason,"[21] confessed the man who, in effect, destroyed the Christian basis for Freemasonry. To that end, the Illuminati lodges were used as "underground breeding places of crime, anarchy, atheism and violence."[22]

After the bloody French Revolution, many Freemasons recognized the damage that the revolution-minded Illuminati had done to their fraternity, especially in France, Britain, and Germany. The Duke of Brunswick, the Grand Master of German Masonry, issued a manifesto in 1794, warning that "European Masonry had been completely perverted by the new sect, the Illuminati."[23] He blamed the "Illuminated Masonic Order" for "casting odium on religion" and undermining the foundations of Freemasonry "to the point of complete overthrow."[24]

"Illuminated lodges" all over Europe replaced God with the reason of Lucifer and sunk Freemasonry into a sea of revolution, deception, and the Weishauptian principle: "The end justifies the means." In other words, "any moral law may be transgressed to promote" the group's objectives of worldwide revolution and subversion, later called Communism, and the destruction of belief in God.[25]

Weishaupt, who was one of the profoundest conspirators in history, explained that the Masonic lodge should be regarded as the Illuminati's "nursery garden," a place to gradually seduce Christian Masons into committing their lives to the service of Lucifer. "To some of these Masons we shall not at once reveal that we have something more than the Masons have," he proclaimed. "All those who are not suited to the work shall remain in the Masonic Lodge and advance in that without knowing anything of the further system."[26] When Weishaupt and his elitist followers infiltrated the lodges and formed secret inner circles, they would only recruit Masons who were known to be internationalists and atheists.[27]

Weishaupt provided a structure for the Illuminati and taught that only "by degrees—going from lower Nursery degrees of *Preparation, Novice, Mineral* and *Illuminatus Minor* to the higher 'Mysteries' of *Priest, Regent, Magus* and *Rex*—could the initiated learn the true mysteries and purposes of the Order" (emphasis in original).[28] The same system is operative today. Illuminati Freemasons are constantly looking for the elitist and arrogant among Freemasons in the lower craft degrees, those who are "enlightened" enough to believe that through revealed knowledge they can become "as gods."

Over 97 percent of Masons never go beyond the first three—out of thirty-three—degrees of Freemasonry. Nor is all of Freemasonry necessarily Illuminati Freemasonry. In confronting the Illuminati Ruling Class Conspiracy, however, it is crucial that we understand Freemasonry's historical role as a vehicle for the Illuminati Luciferian religion.

## THE ILLUMINATED STATES OF AMERICA

English and French Freemasonry formed a "crucial alliance" in America in 1776.[29] Many of the nation's founders were Masons, including George Washington, Paul Revere, Ben Franklin, Thomas Jefferson, John Adams, and all of the participants in the Boston Tea Party. Washington, however, was an inactive Mason who showed no sign of being committed to the brotherhood's cause. According to John Daniel, Franklin and Jefferson "were the men most responsible for bringing the Illuminati to America."[30]

Jefferson, who did not worship the Christian God, was a student and ardent defender of Adam Weishaupt. In fact, Jefferson was accused by a brother Mason, John Quincy Adams, of "using Masonic lodges for subversive purpose" (of the Illuminati).[31] Jefferson was as duplicitous about his religious and political convictions as he was about his rumored sexual relationship with Sally Hemmings, his black slave and the half sister of his wife, whom he allegedly impregnated for the first time when she was a teenager, and who bore him "at least four children, possibly six," according to researcher Pearl M. Graham.[32]

Many historians are livid at the long-standing rumor that Jefferson has Black descendants and one White Jefferson descendant calls the claim a "moral impossibility," given Jefferson's strident opposition to miscegenation.[33] We may soon know if Jefferson was the hypocrite that John Quincy Adams and many others say he was, and if he had Black children, when the results of DNA testing at Oxford University are released. Eighteen Blacks who claim to be Jefferson descendants have submitted blood samples.[34] Hemmings and five children, allegedly by Jefferson, remained enslaved at Monticello.

Franklin was very close to the violent and Luciferian roots of atheistic French Orient Freemasonry, which was one reason for his popularity in France. "In the veiled language of Masonry," John Daniel points out, "Orient actually means Lucifer."[35] Franklin, however, was also a Rosicrucian (British) and probably was a double agent for the rival English and French Illuminati Masons.[36]

The Continental Congress of 1776 selected Benjamin Franklin, Thomas Jefferson, and John Adams—all three Masons—to design a seal for the United States. John Daniel believes that Franklin brought the Illuminati seal—along with a plan to control America—to the United States after a probable meeting with Adam Weishaupt in Paris.

The Illuminati had brought together the two competing Masonries, the Sion in Britain and the Templars in France. According to this theory, both placed their mark, including the mark of the Beast, on the American seal, in a statement of joint ownership. The British Priory of Sion Freemasons, who believe that Jesus had children by Mary Magdalene and their descendants are the nobility of France, staked out control of the U.S. credit system and future central bank. The French Orient Knights Templar assumed control of America's anti-God, secular-humanist, welfare-statist evolution, for the singular purpose of substituting "the Masonic phallic religion" for Christianity.

Symbols and their placement are of great significance to Freemasonry. They reveal the "Secret Doctrine" of the

Priory of Sion. The thirteen Templar stars arranged to shape Sion's six-pointed star sent a clear message to the initiated few that Sion and the Templar were united in founding the United States of America. The sacred symbols of Sion and the Temple, united in one design peering through the glory cloud hovering above the Great American Eagle, signifies that both Sion and the Temple oversee the direction of our nation.[37]

What we consider as the reverse and obverse sides of the Seal of the United States (see dollar bill), according to Daniel, is a stamp of ownership of French and British Freemasonry respectively.

> The left side of the Great Seal is spiritual. The All-Seeing Eye hovering above the unfinished pyramid represents the Priory of Sion overseeing the Templar task of building a universal New World Order.
>
> The right side of the Great Seal is political. The 13-starred hexagram hovering above the Flying Eagle represents the union of Sion and the Temple brought about by the revived Roman empire.[38]

Illuminist Franklin, the double agent for French and British Masonry, convinced Jefferson and Adams that the Roman numeral MDCCLXXVI (1776) on the base of the unfinished pyramid represented America's year of independence and probably the year the Illuminati was founded, and that the thirteen layers of brick signified the thirteen colonies. The committee added the thirteen stripes on the eagle's breast-shield, thirteen berries and thirteen leaves in the eagle's talon, thirteen arrows and thirteen letters in E PLURIBUS UNUM.

In reality, the thirteen stars above the eagle's head in a "glory cloud" form a six-pointed star, or hexagram, in symbolic arrangement of thirteen pentagrams. The hexagram is the coat of arms of the British Priory of Sion Masons, and the thirteen pentagrams represent the French Knights Templar Masons.

The Illuminati seal, therefore, represents the British and French Masonries. The French Templars are associated with the thirteen steps of the unfinished pyramid and the thirteen letters in ANNUIT COEPTIS. The British, the Sion, are represented by "the All-Seeing Eye of the Illuminati, which is the Eye of Lucifer."[39] And above and below this Devil symbol and the pyramid are arranged the words ANNUIT OCEPTIS NOVUS ORDO SECLORUM, Latin for "Announcing the Birth of a New Secular Order," the Masonic concept of pantheism and secular humanism.

But it's those Roman numerals MDCCLXXVI at the base of the pyramid—the 1776 birth year of the Illuminati and the United States—that give every citizen of the Republic that was organized "under God" the Devil's identification number, 666. That "is the only date that arranges the Roman numerals in the exact order spoken of by John in Revelation 13:18: 'and his number is Six hundred threescore and six' (600 + 60 + 6 = 666)."[40] This involves triangle symbology that is observable in the Thirty-third-Degree Mason pin, or Jewel, which includes a serpent eating its own tail and three interlaced triangles that, once separated, reveal 666.

By separating the three triangles and arranging the nine Roman numerals into groups of threes, but adding only the numbers at the base of the triangles, the mark of the Beast reveals itself. Group I, D (500) and C (100), equal 600; Group II, L (50) and X (10), equal 60; and Group III, V (5) and I (1), equal 6. The Roman numerals total 1776 exoterically and 666 (600 + 60 + 6) esoterically. A good place to study all of this is in Volume I of John Daniel's *Scarlet and the Beast* or Warren Weston's *Father of Lies*.

President Franklin D. Roosevelt—scion of America's opium trade and then Thirty-second-Degree Mason—placed the Illuminati seal on the U.S. one-dollar bill in 1934, fulfilling John's prophecy in Revelation:

> And he causeth all, both small and great, rich and poor, free and bond, to receive a mark in their right hand, or in their foreheads:
>
> And that no man might buy and sell, save he that had the mark, or the name of the beast, or the number of his name.[41]

The universal currency, the United States dollar, now ensures that "the mark of the Beast is in the palm of our hand."[42]

The founding fathers made other significant contributions to the rise of the Illuminati Ruling Class Conspiracy in the United States. For instance, after Alexander Hamilton relinquished the privilege of choosing the location of the nation's capital to Thomas Jefferson, in exchange for the privilege of founding a central bank (the First Bank of the United States), Jefferson located the capital in what is now the District of Columbia, and its streets were laid out, according to Ed Decker's *Freemasonry: Satan's Door to America,* to form Masonic symbols. When you visit Washington, D.C., Decker suggests, bring a street map of the downtown area and face the Capitol from the Mall. Visualizing the Capitol as the top of a compass, Pennsylvania Avenue as the left leg, and Maryland Avenue as the right leg, you will observe the following Masonic symbols: the Square, the Compass, the Rule, the Pentagram, the Pentagon, and the Octagon. In fact, an octagonal pattern, representing the French Masonic Templar splayed cross, encompasses both the White House and the Capitol building. Decker offers a guided tour of our Masonic capital city.

> The Square is found in the usual Masonic position with intersection of Canal St. and Louisiana Ave. The left leg of the Compass stands on the Jefferson Memorial. The

circle drive and short streets behind the Capitol form the head and ears of what Satanists call the *Goat of Mendes* or Goat's head.

On top (to the north) of the White House is an inverted 5-pointed star, or Pentagram. The point is facing South in true occult fashion. It sits within the intersections of Connecticut and Vermont Avenues north to Dupont and Logan Circles, with Rhode Island and Massachusetts going to Washington Circle to the West and Mt. Vernon Square on the East.

The center of the pentagram is 16th St. where, thirteen blocks due north of the very center of the White House, the Masonic House of the Temple sits at the top of this occult iceberg.

The Washington Monument stands in perfect line to the intersecting point of the form of the Masonic square, stretching from the House of the Temple to the Capitol building. Within the hypotenuse of that right triangle sit many of the headquarters buildings for the most powerful departments of government, such as the Justice Dept., U.S. Senate and the Internal Revenue Service.

Every key Federal building from the White House to the Capitol Building has had a cornerstone laid in a Masonic ritual and had specific Masonic paraphernalia placed in each one.

The Washington Monument actually represents the *Phallic Principle* upon which Speculative Masonry is based. From above, the monument and its circular drive form the esoteric Masonic "Point within a circle." The Reflecting Pool bears its shadowed image, with the illusion duplicated in the Lincoln Memorial. [Emphasis in original][43]

I hope you are beginning to realize the extent to which Illuminati Freemasonry—a minuscule number, perhaps three hundred, of all Masons and about ten thousand Illuminati cover organizations form the core of the Illuminati Ruling Class Conspiracy—control the world and your life.

## POLITICAL RELIGION

Lyndon LaRouche's research into the drug trade, the British aristocracy, and occult societies has led him to the same conclusions as mine about the cultic nature and longevity of an international Anglophile conspiracy. LaRouche is a convicted felon and is widely considered to be a reactionary extremist—even worse by his enemies. He has also been accused of being anti-Jewish and anti-Israel. The upshot of all this is that although LaRouche has done extensive research on the history of international conspiracies, he is shunned as a source by many writers out of fear of being accused of sharing his views regarding the English aristocracy's traditions of drug trafficking and occult Illuminism. Aside from all of that, I find some of his research to be impeccable. For example, according to LaRouche:

> The sinister element that sets the British oligarchy apart from the popular image of the mafia family is its unshakable belief that it alone is fit to rule the world—the view reflected in Cecil Rhodes's 1877 Testament. Their religion is not the Anglican Christianity they publicly profess, but a hodgepodge of paganism, including satanic cults such as Theosophy and Rosicrucianism. The central, syncretic ideology of the oligarchy's inner cult life is the revived Egyptian drug cult, the myth of Isis and Osiris, the same anti-Christian cult that ran the Roman Empire. And like the ancient Isis-worshipping Egyptian dynasties, the British ruling family networks have main-

tained power for centuries by keeping the secrets of their intrigues within the family.

The Cult of Isis, dredged up in modern format, was the official ideology of leading British politicians, financiers, and literary figures during the previous century. The Isis cult also formed the core of Lord Palmerston's Scottish Rite of Freemasonry. Its great public exponent was the colonial secretary during the Second Opium War, Edward Bulwer-Lytton, who is the author of *The Last Days of Pompeii,* which first popularized the Isis cult, and the mentor of Cecil Rhodes's whole generation of British imperialists.[44]

In other words, the philosophy of Great Britain's ruling class is practically identical to the basic doctrine of the Illuminati. However, it is very difficult to know where the imperialism of Illuminists Cecil Rhodes and other Oxford coconspirators ends and their Circle of Initiates cult's worship of the sun-sex god Osiris (Lucifer) begins. There is no clear dividing line between the two.

The official ideology of the British aristocracy in the nineteenth century derived from a revived Egyptian drug and sex cult with its myth of the mother sun-goddess Isis and her consort the sun god Osiris, and its anti-Christian legacy absorbed from ancient Rome. This Babylonian mystery religion provided English Masonry with its racist, imperialistic rationales.[45]

Moreover, according to John Daniel, "as homosexuality was practiced in mystery religions, the worship of the phallus became a ceremonial rite,"[46] phallus worship is centered around the myth of Osiris and Isis and the worship of the sun. The original names of these deities (prior to the destruction of the Tower of Babel) were Nimrod and Semiramis, respectively. Nimrod became known by many names in various lands: Ninus, Bel, Belus, Baal, etc.

All mystery religions worship Lucifer or Satan, which "is the secret of ancient mystery Babylon and remains the secret of Freemasonry," says John Daniel.[47] The proof of this, he says, is that the leader of the Scottish Rite Masonry today "always wears the Baphomet, a universal symbol of Lucifer/Satan."[48]

The ancient pagans also believed that Semiramis was both the mother and wife of Nimrod, and that she was impregnated by a ray of light from the sun (or Nimrod/Osiris). Nimrod was also known as the light bearer or Lucifer. The ancients also believed that Semiramis (Isis) was the morning or Eastern star, known by some as the Lucifer star. Many of the wives of Masons belong to an auxiliary secret society named the Eastern Star. Cecil Rhodes's Illuminati tradition began as an Isis cult.

These "natural aristocrats" or "British Race Patriots" from Oxford, led by Freemasons Cecil Rhodes, Alfred Milner, and Lord Nathan Mayer Rothschild, played pivotal roles in history. They committed their lives to the political religion of the Illuminati that preaches social control, exploitation, and destruction of the will of the people by the elite.

Lord Edward Bulwer-Lytton, a close friend of Disraeli, was Viceroy of India during Britain's imperialistic heyday at the end of the nineteenth century. His true interest was in producing a race of supermen through the use of magic to induce an evolutionary process in the human brain. Maurice Vidal Portman, an English orientalist and politician, who had founded the Grand Lamaistic Order of Light, was Bulwer-Lytton's intimate friend and associate. While Oxford professor John Ruskin, a protégé of Lord Bulwer-Lytton's, became the mentor of Cecil Rhodes, the future diamond mogul, and his imperialist friends, who in 1891 formed the secret society named the Circle of Initiates.[49] This cult's Illuminati religiopolitical emphasis distinguished its plans for globalist hegemony from those of the traditional elitist study groups and from the imperialism of its day. The Circle later changed its name to the benign-sounding Royal Institute for International Affairs.

Beginning around this time, we find a shift in the Illuminati's approach, involving an expansion from the Masonic lodges into the academy and Round Table groups. The new strategy employed was to enlist young scholars and indoctrinate them with the materialistic doctrine of globalism (and its corollary, imperialism). It was assumed that the young Bill Clintons and other members of the Rhodes Scholar elitist brigade would eventually become presidents, senators, and mayors, and would hold other strategic positions of "power and influence in the various opinion making and power wielding agencies of the world and so achieve their aims."[50] This is a Fabian concept borrowed from Socialism, a long-range strategy based on "the doctrine of the inevitability of gradualism."[51]

The other side of the Illuminati's Janus-faced political religion—with its dogma of a one-world society under its control—is Communism (born in 1848). Illuminati Communism's Pied Piper Karl Marx followed German philosopher Georg W. F. Hegel's "attempt to marry God and government at the altar of philosophy: 'The Universal is to be found in the State,' he said, and 'the State is the Divine Idea as it exists on earth. . . . We must therefore worship the State as the manifestation of the Divine on earth.' "[52] In other words, the state is God on earth and it is to be worshiped. That is statism. But the Devil-loving Marx would have none of the spiritual God stuff, so he converted the Hegelian system of political thought into material determinism. Property—money or land—became the objects of seizure by the "Divine State." He kept Hegel's concept of statist divinity and pronounced socialism as "the Functional equivalent of religion."[53]

Thus "statism has become 'the spirit of spiritless conditions' and the opiate, not of the masses, but of the elites."[54] The Illuminati political religion of statism still appeals to the "self-conceit of half-baked intellectuals . . . educators, writers, philosophers, publishers, and clergymen."[55] Its modern workplace is likely to be "the great subsidized universities, tax-free foundations, mass media communication systems, government bureaus such as the State Department," and a plethora of study groups.[56] Nowhere is the implementation of this "Communist" idea more advanced today than in the "Capitalist" United States. Whether it's called Communist or Capitalist, it's spelled Illuminati statism.

# 4

# THE THREAT OF
# SECRET SOCIETIES AND
# PAGANISM AT WORK

*Come out of her, my people, that ye be not partakers of her sins, and*
*that ye receive not of her plagues.*
—REVELATION 18:4

The Roman Catholic Church has been right all along. Secret societies are detrimental to a nation—especially to its soul. Their very nature exposes upstanding citizens to the devices of a pathological few, who invariably become a corrupting force in well-intentioned organizations. The drive for secrecy springs from an evil impulse. And secrecy provides elitism with a veneer of respectability and breeds deception.

The secrets of the ancient Babylonian mystery school have been passed down through the ages in clandestine societies such as Freemasonry, which, since its birth in England in 1717, has evolved from a creed that was essentially Christian to one that is now pantheistic and/or atheistic-Luciferian. The intellectual and aristocratic classes in Europe traditionally have looked down upon blind faith in God as merely superstition and antithetical to reason. The idea of a loving God who cares equally for all His children threatens elitists, which is why members of the secret Illuminati Order of Elites hate the worship of God. Illuminists have increasingly infiltrated Freemasonry in the nineteenth and twentieth centuries and clandestinely created a cult of Devil worshipers within it.

William Guy Carr, like a handful of other authors who study the occult, is convinced that "there is plenty of documentary evidence to prove that Pike [Albert Pike, America's most famous Masonic Leader], like [Adam] Weishaupt, was head of the Luciferian Priesthood [the Order of the Illuminati] in his day."[1] Albert Pike (1809–1891), who was a brilliant scholar, a confederate general in the Civil War, and the founder of the Ku Klux Klan, is the *capo de tutti capi* of American Freemasonry.

Despite Pike's undisputed record as an Illuminati Freemason, militant foe of Christianity, worshiper of the Devil, and terrorist (as head of the KKK), the average American Mason does not embrace the Masonic fraternity because of him; in fact, many have never heard of Albert Pike. The truth is that the overwhelming majority of Freemasons are harmless, know very little about Freemasonry, and have probably never heard of Illuminati Freemasonry—or the Illuminati. Furthermore, most Masons will know more about Freemasonry after they read this chapter than they will ever be taught at the lodges.

The rank and file in the Blue Lodges, the first three degrees, do not read books by Masonic scholars such as Pike, J. D. Buck, Arthur E. Waite, and Manly P. Hall. Many Masons are creatures of opportunity, not seekers of knowledge, occult or otherwise. Yet they are associated with the acknowledged Devil worshipers and conspirators who are among Masonry's most elite group. The prototype that Professor Weishaupt's Illuminati Masonic Order created in the eighteenth century when it infiltrated Freemasonry allows members of other occult orders to "work within Freemasonry often times without the knowledge of the actual leaders of the lodge."[2]

"Freemasonry is truly an organization that deceives good men," David Carrico writes in *The Dark Side of Freemasonry*. "Many honorable men who are in the lodge actually believe that they belong to a Christian fraternal organization, and nothing could be further from the truth. . . . There is most assuredly more to Freemasonry than most Freemasons realize."[3] In the first degree, a Christian "is kissing Jesus goodby at the altar of Baal,"[4] reveals Jim Shaw, a former Thirty-third-Degree Mason who has renounced Freemasonry.

In tacit agreement, Masonry's greatest philosopher, Manly P. Hall, explains that Freemasonry is only looking for a few good men to become Illuminists in the "inner brotherhood" of Lucifer. The chosen few Royal Arch Masons are taught "the meaning of the secret word" in the "Supreme Degree," says Masonic scholar Arthur Edward Waite.[5] According to Thirty-third-Degree Mason Jim Shaw, who defected to Christianity and coauthored *The Deadly Deception,* an exposé of Freemasonry, Masons learn that

> the name of their god combines part of the sacred name of Yahweh, or Jehovah, with Baal, or Bel, the pagan god ancient Israel was warned not to touch, and with On, representing Osiris, the Egyptian sun god [the god of sex and fertility], or Om, the generic Hindu name for their gods. In their most secret moment of ritual, they [Masons] declare that the name of God is YA-BEL-ON or JE-BUL-ON . . . the supreme name of their god always combines the first sounds in Jehovah or Yahweh with Baal or Bel and On or Om (*Aum*).[6]

The name "Jabulon," comprised of Jehovah, the God of the Bible, Baal or Bel (Cush), and On (pronounced Aum), which somtimes is also known as Nimrod or Osiris, the Egyptian sun-sex god of fertility, "is apparently an acronym meant to symbol-ize the Masonic acceptance of a separate and easily identifiable God of Masonry."[7] Baal, a term for master, was also the name of Ham's son, a pagan deity named Cush. Cush's son, Nimrod, another Black man, is the sun god in every language in the world. He was a Devil worshiper who founded the Kingdom of Babylon and Freemasonry. He also led the rebellion against God at Babel.

The "seething energies of Lucifer" that Manly Hall and Illu-minati Masons promise the innocents is described throughout Masonic writings, rituals, and lectures as being somehow related to "the lost word," the name of God, Jabulon. According to Tom McKenney, author of *Please Tell Me:* "Masonry's position is that God's 'true' nature was once known to a select, elite [group of pagans] who happily worshipped the phallus" until the stupid and narrow-minded Christians got rid of the Illumi-nated Ones and "the Word" was lost with them.[8]

McKenney explains the Masonic occult belief that "if any-one knows the true name of a spirit, one then possesses that spirit's power and can control that spirit." Imagine what the occultists, especially those who practice witchcraft, think they could do if they "could know the lost name of God, Himself."[9] Indeed, they "could take over and become the God of the uni-verse," they believe. "This was Lucifer's big mistake, and intelli-gent people the world over are going to great expense and effort trying to repeat it," Tom McKenney adds in his *Please Tell Me.* "And for grown men, with brain enough to memorize all that childish, catechetic drivel, to take it seriously can only be de-scribed as (please forgive me if this seems harsh) stupid!"[10]

A spirited defense of Freemasonry against the charge of Devil worship is made by John J. Robinson, a non-Mason, al-beit a sympathizer, in *Born in Blood,* in which he explains that Masonry is not a Christian organization and that each member chooses his own god. One curious feature, however, of Robinson's book is that, perhaps as the result of an oversight, he never mentions Albert Pike, American Masonry's greatest hero and chief Illuminati leader of the nineteenth century. That is a most conspicuous omission, akin to writing a history of the United States and never mentioning George Washington.

Regardless of Robinson's protests to the contrary, a group of Illuminati agentur occultists control Freemasonry, and Illuminati Freemasonry is the crucial ecclesiastical branch of the Illuminati Ruling Class Conspiracy. It is this religious order that guarantees the perpetuation of Illuminati family dynasties in the power elite. Occult Freemasonry is the church of the Illuminati. Only a pantheistic mystery religion such as Freemasonry could hold Christian clergy, Jews, Communists, royalty, merchant bankers, and other power elites together in unity and secrecy generation after generation. These are the members of "the Hidden Hand," the Illuminati inner core that is concealed, according to John Daniel, "within the highest degree of Freemasonry, the 33rd degree Supreme Council."[11]

Illuminati Freemasons, according to author William Guy Carr in *Pawns in the Game*, "introduce the worship of Satan in the lower degrees . . . and then initiate selected individuals to the FULL SECRET that Lucifer is God."[12] Members of the Masonic rank and file, the so-called Blue Degrees, are considered "imperfect initiates" and are never instructed by the Masonic Illuminati evilarchy in the nuances of the Luciferian ideology. During the 1870s, the Sovereign Pontiff of Universal Freemasonry, Albert Pike, was also the "Head of the Illuminati."[13]

In the Grand Orient lodges that were organized by Weishaupt as "the secret headquarters of the Illuminati" and Pike's New and Reformed Palladian Rite of overt Devil worshipers, "not even the 32nd and 33rd degree Masons know what's going on."[14] Cardinal Caro y Rodriquez of Santiago, Chile, revealed in his book, *The Mystery of Freemasonry Unveiled,* that "not one Mason in one hundred, below the 32nd degree, even suspects the Illuminati are in control."[15]

I identify three groups in Freemasonry: (1) the majority who are in the first three degrees, of which the ultimate one is the Master Mason (these are the philosophical innocents, more interested in a better job than curling up at night with a book by Albert Pike); (2) the financially well-off who are philosophically interested and ambitious enough professionally to buy and earn the degrees after Master Mason—men like Jim Shaw, a Thirty-third-Degree Mason who was never approached to become a Devil devotee or to do anything that he thought was immoral; and (3) the Illuminati Freemason Luciferian Occultists in the upper degrees and various occult orders, who are ever on the lookout for those inclined to and opportunistic enough to sell their souls to the Devil. In fact, Freemasonry serves as a kind of affirmative action program for most White men, a secret preference system that favors them over women, non-Whites, and non-Masons—"the profane"—for jobs, business opportunities, and political appointments.

Black Masons also quietly network among themselves, trading on their insider status for advantage over non-Masons. When the late Robert Johnson was the Executive Editor of *Jet* magazine, he often boasted about how the publisher, Freemason John A. Johnson, had single-handedly used the magazine to make Freemason Jesse Jackson the premier leader of Black America. As a non-Mason and a critic of Jesse Jackson, I have not been mentioned at all, or very rarely, over the last twenty years in Johnson's magazines. I have finally had to agree with most observers that I have been declared persona non grata at *Jet, Ebony,* and other Johnson publications. After this book comes out, the ban on mentioning me will probably be lifted long enough for attacks by a plethora of Freemason Black elitists and a few non-Masonic sycophants eager to win favor with powerful Masons who can help their careers or promote their ambitions.

Some of the White Masons who oppose affirmative action preference for Blacks and other ethnic groups and deride the practice as "reverse discrimination" are the greatest offenders of fairness. Besides its appeal to the Mason's pocketbook, Freemason-style affirmative action preference engenders a sense of elitism and reinforces for him society's WASP mystique. The men in the lodge are not evil, but they are manipulated by an evil force. But the Masonic good-old-boys network violates the law of the land.

## THE LIGHT OF TRUTH SHINES ON MASONRY

In writing *Illustrations of Masonry by One of the Fraternity Who has Devoted Thirty Years to the Subject: Captain W. Morgan's Exposition of Freemasonry,* Morgan literally signed his own death warrant. He suffered a crisis of conscience about what as a Christian he considered the immorality of Freemasonry and exposed its rituals, signs, grips, and emblems. Less than a month after his book was published in 1826, Morgan was kidnapped from the village of Batavia, New York, and murdered by three Masons who had been selected by drawing lots after lodge leaders had condemned him to death.

Ironically, the Weishauptian Gestapo tactic of murder, intended to silence potential future Morgans and intimidate the entire brotherhood, backfired. Approximately 45,000 of the 50,000 Masons in America resigned from their lodges in anger. The disingenuous Masons who remained loyal to the murderers desperately published two false editions of Morgan's book in an unsuccessful attempt to confuse the issue. Many of the more prominent Masons who defected read the secret Masonic rituals into court records to make the knowledge public as an act of defiance.

An Anti-Mason political party sprang up, with Congressman John Quincy Adams, a former President of the United States, among its leaders. Adams asked Masons to quit the fraternity and non-Masons not to join such a barbarous cult. Freemasonry's coarse oath, which included a statement of willingness to commit murder, among other immoral acts, Adams argued, was unconscionable.

Mainly because of Morgan's murder, anything you want to know about Masonry can today be found somewhere in a book, including the Thirty-third-Degree ceremonies, which, according to Warren Weston's book, *Father of Lies,* makes the Mason a "Sovereign Pontiff of the Synagogue of Satan."[16] See Chapter 5 for a discussion of the Thirty-third Degree ("the Order is the Great Avenger") oath to destroy, in a "war to the death and without quarter," government, private property, and biblical religions.[17]

Jacob Schiff and Paul Warburg, German bankers, and the man who pulled the strings, Sir Nathan Rothschild of England, were all Freemasons. As members of the Grand Orient lodge, a notoriously antireligious one, Schiff and Warburg were Thirty-third-Degree Masons. According to the Thirty-third-Degree initiation ceremony, "the Order is the Great Avenger," whose target is "government . . . the right to own private property; and the concept that man is to live by God's moral absolutes."[18] Religion is "but philosophies evolved by men" and it is one of the assassins on whom we have sworn to wreak vengeance, enemies against whom we have declared war to the death and without quarter, the Thirty-third-Degree Mason swears as he is enlisted as an "avenger" against government, property, and the right to worship God in an organized religion.

As Thirty-third-Degree Masons, Schiff and Warburg, and probably Rothschild, were definitely JINO (Jews in Name

Only) Jews. In fact, they represented family empires of *Hofju-den* (Court Jews) "who have served the British monarch . . . for generations. These families have a centuries-long unbroken tradition of attaching themselves to the predominant noble houses of Europe,"[19] specifically around the British. "The Hof-juden have less than nothing to do with the Jewish people, their well-being and aspirations for themselves and their prosperity. These families' only relation to the Jews has been to periodically call down persecution upon them, and then to excuse their own role in it by their surnames,"[20] Lyndon LaRouche reports. In my opinion, *Hofjuden* Schiff, Warburg, Rothschild, and Karl Marx were Illuminati Freemasons, first and foremost.

The honorific "Avenger" Thirty-third Degree, "the degree that cannot be earned or bought," is conferred by the Supreme Council of the Thirty-third Degree at Masonry's House of the Temple headquarters in Washington, D.C.[21] According to the Reverend Jim Shaw, the following Thirty-third-Degree Masons were present at his ceremony: a Billy Graham imposter; J. Edgar Hoover, FBI tyrant and bigot; Gerald Ford, former U.S. President and suspected Warren Commission fixer; and Prince Bern-hardt of the Netherlands, a former SS officer of Hitler's Third Reich and alleged founder of the Bilderbergers, a suspected front for English Freemasonry's Round Table groups.[22]

Perhaps because so many notable people are Thirty-third-Degree Masons, certain exotic rumors have sprung up over the years. In all fairness, however, if you have ever heard that Thirty-third-degree Masons are required to travel secretly to Saudi Arbia to partake of Jesus Christ's wisdom by viewing His pre-served remains or that they are required to murder someone preselected by Masonic police and judges, or any other such rumors, please dump them on the same trash heap that you have the rumor that there is a computer chip hard-wired into the Prince of Wales's buttocks.

In fact, Shaw now views the climax of his twenty-five-year

search for meaning as a top-of-the-line Mason with a sense of ennui and regret for promises unfulfilled.

> Well, there it is. This absurd, disarticulated mixture of silly contradiction, pagan blasphemy and unfulfilled promise is all they get. They are not "Princes of the Royal Secret," and aren't even sure what the secret is! . . . Here they are at the final destination, the 32nd Degree, and they find out that it isn't the final destination! In fact, they learn that not only must they press on and reach the final destination on their own, they don't even know what that destination is! After spending all this money and effort to reach "the Light," they are told they still are not there, that they must search farther and find it on their own. And they still don't really know what it is!
>
> And these victimized men, "ever learning, and never able to come to the knowledge of the truth," don't even realize that they are the victims. How very sad.[23]

As an occult religion, Masonry conveys its belief system through symbols and allegory. The symbols are not used to illustrate a lesson; the symbol is the lesson. Even words become symbols in Freemasonry. This approach to salvation is in conflict with the biblical religions, which rely almost exclusively on the written and revealed word of God. Therefore, there is an inherent conflict between Christianity and Freemasonry.

When a Mason is also a Christian, the question inevitably arises, "Can a Christian be a Mason?" The New Testament teaches Christians that no one can reach heaven or immortality without Jesus Christ. The pagan "symbols" and doctrine of Masonry ignore the importance of Jesus Christ and forbid the use of His name in the lodge. This is the basic doctrine of Freemasonry. And Illuminati Freemasons are Masons who believe in Lucifer and support the Conspiracy to rule the world in his honor. However, for the ordinary Mason and the Mason who preaches the art of conspiracy, the focus is on the esoteric aspects of the ancient Babylonian mysteries.

So why do so many Masons profess to be Christians? Either (1) they have been misled into believing that Masonry is a Christian religion (the First-Degree initiation ritual displays the Holy Bible on the altar to support the false Masonic claim that Jesus, "the Carpenter," was a Mason); (2) they believe that Masonry is not a religion (as Masonic leaders insist); (3) they have never studied Masonry's doctrines (97 percent have not); or (4) they are duplicitous and find the status of being a Christian to have practical value in the world of politics and business, while also finding Masonry's secret affirmative action program of inestimable economic value.

Christianity and Masonry are incompatible because Christians believe that paganism is the tool of the Devil, who is eternally at war with the Gospel of Christ. The Bible alerts believers to the identity of the spirit of the Devil or the Antichrist in Ephesians 6:12: "For we wrestle not against flesh and blood, but against principalities, against powers, against the rulers of the darkness of this world, against spiritual wickedness in high places."

You probably know the Masonic symbol of omniscience as "the All-Seeing Eye" on the Great Seal of the United States and the one-dollar bill. It is, according to the greatest American Masonic authority, Albert Pike, "the emblem of Osiris, the Creator." When Masons call God "the Great Architect of the Universe," they are actually referring not to the God of Christians, but to Osiris or Nimrod, the sun god and Masonry's spiritual ancestor. Christians are rarely knowledgeable enough about occult orders to suspect that this is not "the eye of God" or pantheistically suspicious enough to ask, "Which god?"

In addition to communicating meaning and allegory, pagan symbols are used as tactical decoys against nosy outsiders and neophyte insiders. Pike, in his Masonic tour de force, *Morals and Dogma*, explains how Masonry "*conceals* its secrets." The "truth" (such as "The Word" or "Ja-Bul-On") is also "concealed" from those Masons, in Pike's words, "who deserve to be misled," the so-called Blue Lodge Masons, who comprise 95 to 97 percent of the 2.5 million American Masonic fraternity. They are "deliberately deceived as to the true meaning of the symbols," writes McKenney in *Please Tell Me*.[24]

Books such as this one are routinely branded as "anti-Mason" by some in the craft's hierarchy who want these facts to remain out of the public's eye and the Masonic-illiterate Christians in the Blue Lodges who are fearful of admitting they have been duped or confronting an inevitable spiritual crisis. It is part of a subtle campaign to discourage any serious study of Freemasonry. There is every reason to suspect that on the average, Masons do not study what they have sworn a bloodcurdling oath to uphold. Be assured, however, that the hierarchy of Freemasonry will read this book and attack it, but not in their roles as Masons.

Typical Masons also realize the danger to themselves and their families—financial ruin, trouble with the police and the courts, loss of jobs and reputations, character assassination, and, in rare instances, the loss of lives. During my research for this book, I saw an abundance of fear and confusion among Masons when exposed to the scheme that has taken a large part of their lives. Typically, their reaction was not confrontational. It was mostly ambivalent—a mixture of fear that they would expose themselves as dupes and an equal fear that they needed to know the truth in order to put their lives in order. I could almost smell the fear in all of them, which proves they are sincere and good men who have been spiritually swindled. By design, Freemasonry is a philosophical Tower of Babel. And, by design, there is no consensus as to what Freemasonry really means. The men in the Blue Lodges, the first three degrees of the Scottish

Rite and the York Rite, are watched carefully over the years by the unseen eyes of the priests and rulers of the brotherhood to determine which of ten "truths" of Freemasonry is appropriate in their training process. John Daniel explains the scheme in *Scarlet and the Beast:*

> For example, if the initiate is a clergyman, he will be taught a spiritual interpretation, whereas one aspiring to be a politician will be taught a political interpretation. If the initiate is a Jew, Hindu or Christian, he will be taught an interpretation compatible with his particular religion. And if the initiate is a communist, he will be taught an interpretation different from that of a democrat.
>
> There are ten interpretations of Freemasonry. And once the Mason arrives at the 33rd degree, the interpretation he has been taught remains with him for life. Therefore, the Hierarchy in Freemasonry (the 33rd degree Supreme Council—approximately 5,000 in all) are not of one mind as to the true interpretation of Freemasonry.[25]

But there is a consistent theme, albeit subtle. According to Warren Weston, in his *Father of Lies:*

> Whether a Mason realizes it or not, from the first degree of initiation to the 11th, the Supreme Council considers the initiate a slave of Lucifer. From the 12th to the 22nd degrees, the initiate works towards becoming a pontiff of Lucifer. And from the 23rd to the 33rd degrees, his goal is to become a sovereign of Lucifer.[26]

One of the ten paths of "truth" in the scheme is explicitly a Luciferian interpretation. In *The Ideal Initiate,* Freemason

Oswald Wirth warns that the penalty "for taking the Masonic oath is selling one's soul to the Devil"[27] and warns those who do not that "the Evil one will not be tricked . . . and there is no escape" from the covenant.[28]

Moses, in fact, simply "unveiled or revealed" what Cush and Nimrod, Masonry's founder, had already taught in the Babylonian mystery religions, the Twenty-third-Degree Mason learns.[29] The early Christians, too, the Mason is taught, acquired "greater perfection, those primitive truths" that had been passed from the Egyptians to the Jews, preserved by the monastic cult of the Essenes and institutionalized in "the Mysteries."[30]

The three-hundred-pound Pike, whose idea of a good time was to "straddle [naked] a phallic throne in the woods, accompanied by a gang of prostitutes,"[31] in two-day orgies of sex, food, and liquor, mentored an inner circle of top members of the Supreme Council on Luciferianism and became the most powerful Mason in the world when he delivered Masonry's new Luciferian Doctrine to its ruling body on July 14, 1889. Pike removed all doubt about Freemasonry's role as an instrument of the Devil or "the Masonic religion" of Luciferian Occultism when he addressed the world's twenty-three Supreme Councils of Scottish Rites in Paris.

That which we must say to the crowd is—We worship a God, but it is the God that one adores without superstition.

To you, Sovereign Grand Inspectors General, we say this, that you may repeat it to the Brethren of the 32nd, 31st and 30th degrees—The Masonic religion should be, by all of us initiates of the high degrees, maintained in the purity of the Luciferian doctrine.

If Lucifer were not God, would Adonay (The God of the Christians) whose deeds prove his cruelty, perfidy, and hatred of man, barbarism and repulsion for science, would Adonay and his priests, calumniate him?

Yes, Lucifer is God, and unfortunately Adonay is also God. For the eternal law is that there is no light without shade, no beauty without ugliness, no white without black, for the absolute can only exist as two Gods: darkness being necessary to light to serve as its foil as the pedestal is necessary to the statue, and the brake to the locomotive. . . .

Thus, the doctrine of Satanism is a heresy; and the true and pure philosophic religion is the belief in Lucifer, the equal of Adonay; but Lucifer, God of Light and God of Good, is struggling for humanity against Adonay, the God of Darkness and Evil.[32]

The hierarchy of English Freemasonry and American Freemasonry joined atheistic French Grand Orient Freemasonry in its declaration that "God is dead!" and raised the banner of Baphomet (the Great Deceiver's Luciferian name) at this Paris meeting. The purpose of the meeting, notwithstanding Pike's exhortations that Freemasonry should run its own brothels to support a Luciferian lifestyle, was to unite spiritually Masons throughout the world around Devil worship and Hegelian dialectics to control societies.

This decision was precipitated by a period of exhaustive introspective scholarly research by English Freemasonry into its legacy as a mystery religion. According to Daniel, the prominent Masonic scholars had already concluded prior to Pike's declaration of Devil worship that: (1) ancient pagan religions worshiped Lucifer; (2) the Babylonian priesthood used drugs and sex to control the population; and (3) human sacrifice was used for population control.[33] These aristocratic scholars, among whom were higher-ups of the Anglican Church, offered to assist any Masonic group in integrating these discoveries into their activities, according to Nigel Davies's *Human Sacrifices in History and Today*.[34]

Notwithstanding his apparent reverence for Lucifer and his widespread reputation as a Satanist, Pike forbade the use of the word "Satan" under any circumstance. And, surprisingly, this brilliant Devil worshiper, Theurgist, Cabalist, and Illuminati leader was equally emphatic about not being a Satanist. "Satanism is a heresy," said Pike in his Paris speech.[35] Most people use Satan and Lucifer interchangeably to describe the anti-God entity known as the Devil. Pike's ilk of Devil worshipers never describe their god Lucifer as evil and believe that Satan is a Christian fabrication.

The crucial distinction between the two types of Devil worshipers is that Luciferians glorify Lucifer as the principle of good, "the equal to the Creator God of the Christians, whom they detest, as the principle of evil." Satanists, on the other hand, "recognize that their God Satan occupies a position in the supernatural sphere inferior to that of the Christian deity."[36] Therefore, the god Satan is referred to by his worshipers as "the Spirit of Evil" or "Father and Creator of Crime." Satanists "accuse the God of the Christians of having betrayed the cause of humanity."[37]

## THE PRODUCTS OF FREEMASONRY

"Why the name Freemasons?" Free from what? "Free from the fear of God," responded a defiant Eliphas Levi, a Masonic mentor of Albert Pike, to his own rhetorical question.[38] In spite of the evidence of an evil purpose at the heart of Freemasonry, I caution the reader not to rush to judge all Masons. Most of them have, in Albert Pike's own words, been deceived.[39]

The Masonic fraternity has succeeded in creating an ambiguous public perception. To many, Masons are charitable, fun-loving, Islam-worshiping Shriners who wear red fezes and march in festive parades and help crippled children and burn victims. To others, their secrecy is proof enough that the Masons are hiding something behind their bloodcurdling oaths. To a few, they are pagan Devil worshipers, working to destroy biblical religions and take over the world.

The truth is, Freemasons are like any other group. Most of them are average; they have a few geniuses and a liberal sprinkling of fools. Masonry, again like all other groups, energetically ignores its worst element—such as Freemason Aleister Crowley, who has allegedly taken the lives of 150 people, mostly young boys, in ritual sacrifices; Freemason Jesse James, murderer and thief; Freemason Karl Marx, murderer and thief; and Albert Pike, racist, Devil worshiper, and traitor against the United States. Instead, Freemasonry boasts of the great achievements among the sixteen American Presidents its fraternity has produced. Some Masons have indeed served this country well. However, two White House Freemasons, Thomas Jefferson and William Jefferson Clinton, provide conspicuous examples of the moral impairment of many ambitious Masons, especially when it comes to "race relations."

The squeaky-voiced Illuminist Freemason Thomas Jefferson was attacked in *The Johnny Cake Papers* by Thomas Robinson Hazard as being "a half-nigger," as part of a broader conspiracy to destroy him politically.[40]

Regardless of his own racial lineage, Jefferson had allegedly fathered many of his own Black slaves.

J. A. Rogers states in *The Five Negro Presidents* that there is adequate evidence to substantiate the charge that Jefferson and three other U.S. Presidents—Warren Harding, Andrew Jackson, and Abraham Lincoln—were Black. Rogers also said that there was insufficient evidence to name the fifth man, a modern-day president.

William Jefferson Clinton, it is alleged, has emulated the President for whom he is named. Whitewater Special Prosecutor

Kenneth Starr's probe of Freemason Clinton's alleged sordid activities includes questions about the possibility that "a certain woman . . . had given birth to Clinton's child" out of wedlock, according to a *New York Post* article entitled "Starr Probe of Bill's Sex Life."[41] Shortly before he was sworn in as President, the news tabloids, which have increasingly become the primary sources of investigative journalism since the Establishment media has gone AWOL on Bill and Hillary's personal lives, ran stories alleging that Clinton is the father of a young son, born to a Black woman. The stories, scrupulously avoided by the Clinton-friendly mainstream press, were accompanied by photographs of a sandy-haired, light-complexioned Black boy.

The February 18, 1992, issue of the *Globe* and the January 28, 1992, edition of the *Star* repeated the rumor about the then seven-year-old boy, who according to the *Globe* "looks just like Bill Clinton." He certainly does. Subsequent reports alleged that the boy, his grandmother, and mother have disappeared from Little Rock, Arkansas.

## CHRISTIANITY WITHOUT CHRIST?

No group is more critical of or threatened by Freemasonry than Christians, but ironically Christian churches are increasingly led by Masons and adopt the Masonic secular dogma of "the fatherhood of God and the brotherhood of man"—without Jesus Christ. Even the practice of "brotherhood" among Christians mimics the Masonic two-tier system of racial apartheid. The results of a survey of Christians suggests the message: Physician, heal thyself. Christians should remember that when you point a finger at someone else, four fingers are pointing back at you. At the least, it is a case of the pot calling the kettle black.

Between 70 percent of one and 90 percent of the other of the pastors of the two largest Protestant denominations in the United States are Masons, according to a disputed estimate by author Tom McKenney.[42] However, the Southern Baptist Convention reports that 14 percent of its pastors are Freemasons, believers in Christianity without Christ, as are 1.3 million of its 2.5 million members in the United States, a very conservative estimate because Masons generally do not disclose their Masonic affiliation.[43] In some parts of the South, the Masonic lodge doubles as a church. More and more those who are entrusted to preserve Christianity, as well as their followers, do not believe in its teachings.

A survey of ten thousand Protestant clergy, mostly White, I suspect, supports that alarming conclusion. It found that 51 percent of Methodists, 35 percent of United Presbyterians, 30 percent of Episcopalians, 33 percent of American Baptists, and 13 percent of American Lutherans do not accept Jesus' physical resurrection as a fact.[44] The virgin birth of Jesus is rejected by even larger percentages as is the belief in "evil demon power in the world today."[45] But the highest percentages—87 percent of Methodists, 95 percent of Episcopalians, 82 percent of Presbyterians, 67 percent of American Baptists, 27 percent of American Lutherans, and 24 percent of Missouri Synod Lutherans—rejected the belief that the Scriptures are "the inspired and inherent Word of God in faith, history and secular matters."[46]

Christianity is fast becoming the Masonic religion of secular humanism. It is essentially religion sans a personal savior and 69 percent of Americans identify with this New Age philosophy.[47] This is the religion now enforced by the schools and the courts. Neither the secular Masonic religion nor Christianity, nor any other religion, should be the basis for government policy or education. But the religion of Masonry is guiding public policy.

The Scriptures teach of the resurrection of Jesus Christ from the dead, which sets Christianity apart from all other world religions, and a faith that permits Christians to share the life of a Jesus who conquered death. And the Christian is taught that "if Christ has not been raised, your faith is worthless."[48] In a godless, antireligious (unless the religion is secular), materialistic America, one is coaxed to avoid that kind of testimony for fear of being labeled right-wing or a conservative fanatic. Since I am neither, this particular tactic to forestall the truth is ineffective against me. I love God and Jesus is the only way that I can be with Him. Whatever that makes me sound like is what I am.

Scripture predicts "a falling away,"[49] which has become a mass desertion from Christian dogma. Some Christians believe this defection is necessary before Christ will return. If so, Freemasonry and its secular influence in government and education is certainly doing everything it can to hasten that day.

## MASONIC IDENTITY POLITICS AND IMPEACHMENT INSURANCE

In this century, Republican and Democratic Presidents have appointed, and Masonic-dominated Congresses have approved, Masonic majorities on the United States Supreme Court.[50] During a thirty-year period, beginning in 1941, Masonic majorities on the Court "erected 'a wall' separating things religious from things secular. It was an epoch when prayer and Bible reading were deracinated from public education and when decision after decision succeeded in prohibiting any State financial assistance to religious schools."[51] The mainstream media never reports on this Masonic presence and its influence on the Court's rulings—as the same journalists almost certainly would if the Court were controlled by eight Jewish or Catholic justices—as was the case between 1949 and 1956 with an 8–1 Masonic majority.[52] Yet it can be depended on to defend Masonry.

In 1987, two conservative newspapers, *The Wall Street Journal*[53] and *The Washington Times*,[54] vilified Senator Patrick Leahy of Vermont for questioning Masonry's segregation policies against Blacks.[55] In fact, Masonry is highly discriminatory. The first Black on the Court, Freemason Thurgood Marshall, was forced into what the White Scottish Rite and York Rite consider the "clandestine" and forbidden Black branch, known as Prince Hall Masonry.[56] Nor did these editorial defenses mention the fact that the Ku Klux Klan was founded by Masons as an adjunct front group that inherited the White Masonic tradition of anti-Catholic, anti-Jewish, and anti-Black discrimination.

Hugo Black, a Ku Klux Klan member committed to the goal of a WASP state, and a Mason, was nominated to the Supreme Court in 1937 by a fellow Mason, President Franklin Roosevelt. As a U.S. senator, Black had shown a "frightening proclivity to trample [the] civil rights of the public at large."[57] The Senate confirmed the nomination of a member of the KKK by a huge 63–16 margin and liberal groups that normally would have opposed such a bigoted background ignored Black's Senate record and his militant intolerance and "supported Black vigorously," according to Paul A. Fisher in *Behind the Lodge Door*.[58]

It seems that liberal and conservative differences fade and the moral imperative for fighting White racism evaporates in the presence of achieving Masonic objectives. For example, men like Democratic Senator Robert Byrd and Republican Senator Arlen Specter, inventor of the "magic bullet" theory in the JFK assassination, have both taken the same secret Masonic oath of identity politics.

According to *The New York Times*, FBI Director Louis Freeh "is especially troubled by the scattered evidence of a Chinese plot to try to influence the 1996 elections."[59] However, Freemason Bill Clinton has a firewall against impeachment for his role in this or any of the other criminal acts of which he is suspected. The Masons in Congress in both parties who are obliged to honor his "distress signal" above the law will find a graceful exit for him—without criminal prosecution.

## MASONIC APARTHEID

Freemasonry is by definition elitist. Spiritual salvation, according to Masonic dogma, is beyond the reach of all Black men and all women, both of whom are considered "profane (unclean, unworthy)."[60] Masonry excludes women from membership because it is a phallic religion. A woman with her natural endowment, the female sex organ, some Masons joke, could never be called "Tubal Caine," which is pronounced "two balls and a cane." The absence of a penis is the basis of the blanket exclusion of women. Blacks are excluded from most White lodges of the Scottish Rite and the York Rite because they are Black—which is considered biologically and socially inferior. Not one Southern Jurisdiction Lodge has ever allowed a Black man to join, according to author John Daniel. That racist fact and the use of "Ja-Bul-On" ("The Word") as the so-called secret name of God were cited by the Southern Baptist Convention as outstanding problems, among others, it had with Freemasonry, although the SBC finally ruled that its members could join the Masonic order.

According to *World Book Encyclopedia,* one out of every twelve American males is a Mason, and twice as many Masons live in the United States as in the rest of the world.[61] And the majority of Freemasons are White Southerners in the Scottish Rite, among whom are former U.S. Senator Robert Dole, Senator Strom Thurmond, Senator Jesse Helms, and former Presidents George Bush, Gerald Ford, and Ronald Reagan, who, it is rumored, holds the distinction of being the first President to take the oath of office facing the Obelisk, the Masonic phallic-shaped Washington Monument.

Racism in White American Scottish Rite Masonry is, along with his love for Baphomet, a legacy of Albert Pike's strident bigotry. The number of Blacks in White Masonry is "just a fraction of a fraction of one percent of total membership,"[62] according to John J. Robinson's Mason-friendly *Born in Blood: The Lost Secrets of Freemasonry.* According to the coauthors of *The Deadly Deception,* being a White man is a necessary prerequisite to taking the oath for the first three Blue Lodge degrees.

White Freemasonry, the Scottish Rite and York systems, is entirely separate from the Black Prince Hall Grand Lodge, which is considered by the White wing to be "clandestine" Masonry. The White "brothers" consider Black Masonic activities to be a "spurious, illegitimate imitation."[63] Both Black and White branches of Freemasonry share the same pantheistic religious tenets, which are essentially non-Christian, and, to my knowledge, there are very few American Blacks, if any, involved in Illuminati Freemasonry, primarily due to their exclusion from the White elitist Masonic orders. However, there is no evidence that Blacks are not equally drawn to Luciferian or Satanic activities in Masonry or other occult groups.

Of the 250,000 Black American Masons, the Internet lists the Reverend Andrew Young, former Mayor of Atlanta and U.S. Ambassador to the United Nations; former Supreme Court Justice Thurgood Marshall; *Ebony* and *Jet* publisher John A. Johnson; W.E.B. DuBois, intellectual; Carl Stokes, first Black elected mayor of a U.S. city (Cleveland); Julian Bond, civil-rights-era activist; educator Booker T. Washington; Mayor Marion Barry of Washington, D.C.; Scottie Pippen, basketball star; and Jesse Jackson, a Christian preacher and two-time Democratic presidential candidate. Most of these distinguished Freemasons still living are members of the Prince Hall Grand Lodge, and none of them would be allowed to visit most White lodges without risking punishment.

A footnote to the "List of Famous Freemasons" on the Internet said:

The most perplexing and discouraging thing on the above list is to see all of the Black Americans who foolishly have

joined Freemasonry. Even if they let Jesse Jackson join a
lodge other than the discriminating Prince Hall Lodge,
how can Jesse imagine the old Anglo-Saxon bigotry of ancient Freemasonry has changed? The Masons are simply
using Jesse Jackson as window dressing. There has NEVER
been a more tragic case of Uncle Tom-ism than this one!

I would not use the appellation of Uncle Tom to describe
any of these Black Freemasons, but I would recommend Revelation 18:4: "Come out of her, my people, that ye be not partakers of her sins, and that ye receive not of her plagues." The
force of God does not abide with racial hatred, and there is only
one other force in the world. Masonic racism can only survive
in the church of the Devil. Come out of her, my Black brothers.

## MASONIC KKK

The true reason for barring Blacks from mainstream Freemasonry is White supremacy, which was evident in Masonry's essential role in creating the Mystic Knights of the Ku Klux Klan
as an adjunct group. The Internet writer raised the issue of
"Anglo-Saxon" bigotry, which hits the mark. Jews and Catholics were also originally barred from the Klan, which suggests
that racism alone does not explain its exclusionary policy. The
KKK's WASP bigotry was inherited from its Masonic origins.

Jesse James, the notorious outlaw, a Thirty-third-Degree
Mason, was also a member of the KKK's predecessor, the
Knights of the Golden Circle, founded by Southern Freemasons
for the purpose of reigniting the Civil War. The Knights assigned Jesse James the job of robbing Northern banks to finance
a second civil war. "It has been estimated that Jesse and the
other members of the Knights had buried over $7 billion in
gold all over the western states,"[64] Ralph Epperson asserts in

*The Unseen Hand*. The Knights, financed by British Illuminati Freemasonry, had allegedly also assigned another Thirty-third-Degree Freemason, John Wilkes Booth, to assassinate President Abraham Lincoln.[65]

After the Knights of the Golden Circle was publicly identified as the group that struck down Lincoln on behalf of the drug-pushing Freemason British Prime Minister Henry Palmerston, Pike changed the group's name to the Mystic Knights of the Ku Klux Klan in 1867. The Klan's name came from the Greek word *kuklos,* or "circle"; prior to its formation Pike had publicly called for a White "Order of Southern Brotherhood." For information on Pike's role as founder of the KKK, read *The Present Attempt to Dissolve the American Union: A British Aristocratic Plot* by Samuel Morse and *Ku Klux Klan: Its Origin, Growth and Disbandment* by J. C. Lestor.

The picture is very clear. Illuminati forces within Freemasonry and the British aristocracy have plotted against the United States since its birth. In fact, the Northern Jurisdiction of Freemasonry was founded by a British spy, John James Joseph Gourgas. Immediately following the Civil War (1866–1869), "most of the Klan's major leaders were Freemasons" and the "Black Codes" to re-enslave Blacks were written in the Masonic Grand Lodges and carried out by Masonic terrorists and their fellow bigots wearing sheets, the KKK.[66] Masonry was a one-stop shop for hate and violence. Now, perhaps, you know why they burn the Cross.

The most rabid segregationist governors in the South during the civil rights movement were Masons.[67] By 1924, future U.S. Supreme Court Justice Hugo Black, a Thirty-third-Degree Freemason, and approximately 1,125,000 other White men were Klansmen.

The power of the Mason-KKK nexus was most evident when an avowed enemy of the United States, Albert Pike, was charged with treason for atrocities committed against Union soldiers during the Civil War. He fled to British territory in Canada; but, bowing to Masonic pressure, Lincoln's successor, President Andrew Johnson, a Master Mason, pardoned the man who had helped start the Civil War and worked in collusion with the British to assassinate a President of the United States. And today, Pike is the only Confederate general who is commemorated by a statue in the nation's capital: "The Albert Pike, Ku Klux Klan Memorial Statue," as its critics refer to it. It was erected in 1901 because of pressure by the Masons in Congress and is maintained today by the U.S. Department of Labor because of the power of Masons in the United States, beginning with Freemason President Clinton.

"By 1987, decades after most American institutions had accepted racial integration, only four of the forty-nine Grand Lodges could count even one black member in their jurisdictions," writes William J. Whalen in *Christianity and American Freemasonry*.[68] He goes on to say that with "one curious exception, Alpha Lodge No. 116 in New Jersey and a handful of blacks reported to be initiated by lodges in New York and Massachusetts, regular Freemasonry remains ninety-nine and forty-four hundredths percent white."[69] The minuscule number of Blacks in White lodges belong to the Northern Jurisdiction of Scottish Rite Freemasonry, which started the Ku Klux Klan.

Albert Pike, the Supreme Commander of the Southern Jurisdiction of Freemasonry, slammed Black Masons, saying, "I took my obligations from white men, not from negroes. When I have to accept negroes as brothers or leave Masonry, I shall leave it."[70] This leader of worldwide Masonry, who acknowledged Nimrod as his spiritual ancestor and the world's first Mason, would rather have abandoned his beloved religion of Freemasonry than accept a Black Mason as his brother. Nothing proves that Pike, a Harvard man fluent in sixteen ancient languages, was a hypocrite more than the contradiction inherent in his scholarly knowledge of Babylonian mystery religions and his adherence to modern White Supremacy.

Pike knew that the founder of Freemasonry, Nimrod—the

original sun god—was a Black man. Masons cite as proof of Nimrod's sovereignty a 1560 *York Manuscript* and the *Cooke Manuscript,* circa 1450, also known as "The Legend of the Craft."[71] As earlier noted, Nimrod, the first king of the first city, is also known as Osiris, the Black Egyptian sun god; he is also called Ninus, another Black god.[72] The Black founder of Freemasonry is also called Zeus in Greece, Ra in Egypt, and Vishnu in India. But most of all, Nimrod is "Beel-saman," Lord of Heaven—the sun god of Illuminati Freemasonry and the pagan world.[73]

All Master Masons are introduced to Nimrod as Osiris, the sun god of Egypt, who is portrayed as a Black man with extremely thick lips. But none of these facts fits the political agenda of modern White-supremacist Freemasonry. Masonry's founding father, man-turned-into-god, would not be eligible for membership in today's White division of the Babylonian pagan worship that he created. An evil Black man is discriminated against because evil White men hate his race.

Pike and his successors hid the fact that the founder of Freemasonry was Black. And whenever a White Mason learns of his cult's Black origins, the hierarchy lies by explaining that in accordance with the principles of reincarnation, Nimrod reappeared as his own White son, who was conceived by Nimrod's virgin wife after his death. She was impregnated, the myth continues, "by Nimrod's spirit coming down on her from the sun . . . [and] entering her womb through a sunbeam."[74] Despite this revision of their own pagan history, all elite Masons know that all sun gods represent Nimrod—the Nimrod they symbolize as a period inside a circle, or a phallus inside a vagina.

## SOCIAL CRISES: RACISM AND PAGANISM

In spite of the opposition of Freemasonry and Christianity, White Christians are just as hypocritical as Freemasons in their dismissal and, sometimes, outright rejection of the fact that wisdom and Blackness were synonymous in the ancient world, according to Robert Graves's book *Mammon and the Black Goddess.*[75]

This prejudice was manifested in the alleged dynamiting of the nose of the Pyramid of Giza by the British because of the statue's broad African nostrils. This same racism is expressed today because of the presence of the statues of Black Virgins that dot the landscape of Europe and, to a much lesser extent, the United States. "We have traced her history from the great goddesses of the prepatriarchal period, especially Inanna and her handmaiden, Lilith," Ean Begg writes in *The Cult of the Black Virgin.*[76] But throughout the world, "Black Virgins are being whitened, stolen, removed to museums or withdrawn from circulation" to prevent a link to the ancient world.[77]

Although "a large portion of the ancient miraculous Madonnas of the world are black, why is such a surprising phenomenon so little known" and why are scholars so "uninquisitive"? Ean Begg inquires.[78] The ancient tradition of devotion to the statue of a Black Madonna is ignored by many White Christians for the same reason that many White Masons lie about their founder and spiritual father, the Black Nimrod. Apparently both groups find Blackness a greater sin than hypocrisy and deceit. But if a Christian cannot bow down and praise the Mother of Jesus because she is an African, he is also indirectly rejecting Jesus, and that is blasphemy in the eyes of the church. Thus, the only way out of this dilemma is for Mary to be White. The fear, of course, is that the truth may be that Jesus was also Black, and, if he were, their belief in God would dissolve because of their hatred of Black people. I have prayed to and worshiped a White Virgin, a White Jesus, and a White God all of my life—because God's goodness and truth tower over all physical features. If God, Jesus, and Mary are Black, I could love them no more than if they are White. Nor can I love a Christian more than a Muslim, Jew, or Hindu.

Everything that is pagan to a Christian because it is not explicitly Christian is not necessarily evil—Satanic, Luciferian, or otherwise. Besides, Christianity is paganized, and a cursory look at history reminds us once again of the cultural cross-fertilization of all civilizations and customs. In fact, the Roman Catholic Church in Europe failed to convince the people to halt the observance of various pagan holidays, so eager to recruit them, it put a religious exterior on the various pagan rites and celebrated them as Christian holidays.

The celebration of Easter, for example, predates Christianity. It was a pagan celebration of fertility and the beginning of spring, the vernal equinox.[79] These were sexually licentious events, accompanied by animal and human sacrifices to placate various gods. "Easter" derives from the name for the Anglo-Saxon goddess of spring.[80] The word Easter, the Christian celebration of the resurrection of Jesus, derives from one of the names of Semiramis,[81] the mother of the gods and the wife of Nimrod, also called Ninus, Bel, Belus, and Baal because of the confusion of the tongues following the Tower of Baal debacle. Babylon received its sordid reputation from her obsessive behavior. She was served by prostitute priestesses and bisexuality was her trademark. Semiramis was also known as Isis, her Egyptian name, and as Ishtar, the fertility goddess. The Ishtar egg, a symbol of impregnation or fertility, was decorated to celebrate the spring each year.[82] The English word "Easter" comes from Ishtar.

"Lent," the forty-day period that precedes Easter, calls for fasting and abstinence. Centuries earlier, the ancient Egyptians observed "a forty-day Lenten fast in commemoration of Osiris."[83] Secret societies throughout the ages and among the British ruling class, including an Illuminati branch, Cecil Rhodes's Circle of Initiates, are modeled after the Cult of Isis.

As Easter worships the vernal equinox, Christmas, the celebration of the birth of Christ, is a pagan celebration of the sun's rebirth at the winter solstice, and its roots are also planted in ancient pagan idolatry. *The Shocking Truth About Christmas* by Russell K. Tardo summarizes the evidence and points to the probability that Christ was not born on December 25. December 25 was the date of the most celebrated holiday of ancient times, the birthday of the sun god Mithra, another name for Nimrod/Osiris, the central symbol for the Masonic emphasis on erotic sex. Mistletoe is one of the appurtenances of this sensual holiday; the custom of kissing under mistletoe originated with men kissing one another to affirm their homosexuality and to highlight temple prostitution during the Roman festival called Saturnalia. (Saturn is another name for the sun god of fertility.)

Halloween and Mardi Gras leave little to the imagination with regard to their origins or customs. Halloween is an unadulterated anti-Christian celebration of Satanism, replete with devils, witches, skeletons, ghosts, etc. It originated as the "Festival of Samhain," the Devil, held by the pagan Druids, who were so evil the Romans ran them out. Mardi Gras is the French way of celebrating eroticism. Its fertility god is Pan, half man, half goat—all sex—as Luciferian as it gets. "Santa" uses the same letters as "Satan." Christmas, originally the Christ mass, is now X-mas, and "X" is a symbol of the Devil. It is now the Devil's Mass.

Again, we find that Luciferian Occultism is an integral component in the development of our youth. The figure of Count Dracula, a demonic force, has become a role model in the popular culture for young Americans, and the character's acts of murder, ritual sacrifice, drinking of blood, and necromancy are sold to our children as "normal" behavior.

You and I may not belong to secret societies, but as you can see, they have the potential of playing a sinister and divisive role in our society. To fight the Illuminati Ruling Class Conspiracy, we have to make certain that our leaders are people who derive their sense of self-esteem and empowerment from God, not from esoteric symbols and elitist cults.

# 5

# KARL MARX'S TROJAN HORSE: THE FED

*And when men cease to believe in God, they will not believe in nothing, they will believe in anything.*
—THEODORE J. FORSTMANN

The evil goal of the Illuminati Ruling Class Conspiracy, as we have seen, is to enslave the world. But how do you enslave a democratic Republic, such as the United States? The answer is with *money*. Whoever controls a nation's wealth controls that nation.

Democracy can exist only if the people, through their elected representatives, control the money supply by controlling the banking system. In the United States, the government has delegated its authority over money and credit to a private central bank, the misleadingly named Federal Reserve System. The name is a hoax since there is nothing federal about this bank of issue that is largely owned by a consortium of European (Anglophile) elitist financiers.

In our Republic, the democratic process was subverted when

the Illuminati Ruling Class Conspiracy seized control of the nation's money supply. Thus, in today's United States, democracy is only a theoretical possibility. De jure slavery for Blacks ended in 1865, but de facto slavery for everyone began in 1913 with the passage into law of the central bank and the income tax. The Illuminati Ruling Class Conspiracy now controls the United States government and oppresses the American people by confiscating more and more of their property (income) through printing-press inflation and taxes.

## MY FEAR

My biggest fear in writing this book is that most people, intimidated by the mystique of economics that has been manufactured by the secret society of Illuminati bankers, will not even try to grasp the key to the Conspiracy's control over their lives. Most of us have been brainwashed into silence and submission by the notion that concepts such as *money supply, inflation, gold standard,* and *capital* are the exclusive province of the educated elite. The truth is there is nothing mystical about money.

Do you know why the poor are getting poorer and why income inequality is steadily getting worse? Do you know, for example, why the U.S. government intentionally keeps a substantial percentage of working-age Americans unemployed? Or how the government is systematically depriving American families of more and more of their incomes?

If you bear with me, I will answer these questions and reveal the economic underpinnings of the Illuminati Ruling Class Conspiracy. In the absence of such understanding, information about the Conspiracy amounts to little more than unrelated and idle, often counterproductive gossip.

I want to stress that it is not my intention to slander bankers and financial experts (except for the comparatively few who are

Illuminists, Illuminati agenturs, or drug money launderers). These men and women perform a vital service in society, and my quarrel is not with them or the stockholders of banks. However, many of these people of good character have probably never considered the devastating impact of the central banking system on the average American and the nation. I am, however, compelled to indict the current system on the basis of its immorality.

## THE CURRENCY OF FREEDOM

Freedom, economic and political, was the driving force of the American Revolution. The founding fathers understood the relationship between money and liberty. They were adamant, therefore, that the supply and value of money in the United States be controlled by the federal legislature—the duly elected popular representatives, who are directly accountable to the people.

Thomas Jefferson, for example, knew the power conferred by control of the money supply, having witnessed how the Illuminati oligarchy used the Bank of England, the British central bank, to rob the British people, the American colonies, and the subjects in its empire.

> If the American people ever allow private banks to control the issue of their currency, first by inflation and then by deflation, the banks and the corporations that will grow up around them will deprive the people of all property until their children wake up homeless on the continent their Fathers conquered.[1]

Jefferson may have been a Jacobin; an apologist for the evil founder of the Illuminati, Adam Weishaupt; an Illuminist subversive, as John Quincy Adams claimed; a racist hypocrite who preached the inferiority of Blacks by day and impregnated his Black slave by night; and perhaps a traitor as President. But his occasional utterances on the economics of freedom cannot be faulted. The economic principles implicit in Jefferson's statement are of crucial importance.

These basics are as true today as they were in Jefferson's time. In a monetary system based on paper currency, the value of money is determined by the real assets backing the currency, such as gold, real estate, etc. If the supply of currency is inflated—if more money is printed—without a corresponding increase in assets, the value of the currency decreases. Prices become inflated in proportion to the inflation of the money supply. When money is worth less, it takes more of it to buy goods and services, and therefore prices rise. Inflation defined as rising prices that result from higher labor, raw material, or production costs is a ploy used by the Illuminati Ruling Class Conspiracy to blame the oppressed for the causes of their oppression. (We will return to this issue in the next chapter.) If money is issued and controlled by private banks that are not accountable to the public, these institutions can arbitrarily determine the value of money by inflating and deflating its supply. These private banks, then, are empowered to control the economic and, by extension, political life of the nation.

That is precisely why Article I, Section 8, Paragraph 5 of the Constitution of the United States is explicit about the powers and duties of Congress "To coin money, regulate the value thereof, and of foreign coin, and fix the standard of weights and measures." It makes no provision for the abdication or delegation of these duties by the Congress.

## AMERICA'S PRIVATE BANK

At this point, I would like to ask you to take out a dollar bill, or any other denomination of American currency. What you are holding, as you can read at the very top on the front of the bill, is a "Federal Reserve Note." It is money issued by a private bank in the name of the United States government. Andrew Gause, author of *The Secret World of Money,* names the benefactors of the Fed's indirect operations.

Its stockholders. The May, 1914 organization chart of the Fed shows that they issued 203,000 shares. National Citibank took 30,000 shares, First National Bank took 15,000 shares, and then those two banks merged in 1955 to create Citibank. With that merger, they held one-quarter of the shares of the New York Fed. The National Bank of Commerce was Paul Warburg's bank. He was the primary architect of the Federal Reserve system, and he took 21,000 shares. Manufacturers Hanover, Rothschild's bank, took 10,200 shares. Chase took 6,000 shares and Chemical took 6,000. These six banks owned 40 percent of the stock of the Fed. As of 1983 they owned 54 percent, and here's how it breaks down: Citibank owns 15 percent, Chase Manhattan owns 15 percent, Morgan Guaranty owns 9 percent, Manny Hanny owns 7 percent, and Chemical Bank owns 8 percent. Citicorp, of course, is the number one bank of the United States now, and Chemical and Chase just merged, making them the number two. Manny Hanny is gone, making J. P. Morgan number three, then First Chicago Trust.

By 1982, these same six banks (Manny Hanny in particular) had loaned two-and-one-half times their net worth to Latin American countries. The proper thing for the Fed to have done would have been to say, "Hey, you loaned two-and-one-half times your net worth to Brazil, and they didn't pay you. Better luck next time!" But that's not the way it happened. The Federal Reserve

Banks, again "in the national interest," purchased that entire bad debt, with the credit of the American people, as loans, and they called them assets. The obligation to pay the loans went from the Brazilians to the Federal Reserve Bank's Open Market Committee, thereby passing the burden of that debt onto the American taxpayers. Chemical, Citibank, and all the others are riding high today because the Fed assumed all of their debts in the name of the American people.[2]

## AMERICA'S OWNERS

The overwhelming problems in the United States stem from the fact that our money—and therefore the nation—is enslaved by the Illuminati Ruling Class Conspiracy. We have already seen how the Illuminati and the ruling class oligarchy have conspired in various ways to gain dominance over America. The establishment of America's private central bank was the watershed at which all of these other conspiracies met. In *The Secrets of the Federal Reserve: The London Connection*, Eustace Mullins explains the opposition to this unconstitutional action that made a bank of issue the country's central bank and nullified Article I, Section 8, Paragraph 5 of the Constitution.

In this country there was a long tradition of struggle against inflicting a central bank on the American people. It had begun with Thomas Jefferson's fight against Alexander Hamilton's scheme for the First Bank of the United States, backed by James Rothschild. It has continued with President Andrew Jackson's successful war against Alexander Hamilton's scheme for the Second Bank of the United States, in which Nicholas Biddle was acting as the agent for James Rothschild of Paris. The result of that struggle was the creation of the Independent Sub-Treasury System, which supposedly had served to keep the funds of the United States out of the hands of the financiers.[3]

Mullins also points out an apparent connection between London merchant bankers and the economic panics in America of 1873, 1893, and 1907. Mullins's charge fits in with the British Crown's plans (discussed in Chapter 2) to repossess the United States as a servant of British Illuminati imperialism.

British Prime Minister Winston Churchill, who once sent Mussolini a letter praising Fascism, liked the idea of British hegemony anywhere in the world, but especially in the United States. The "British Empire and the United States," he stated, "will have to be somewhat mixed up together in some of their affairs for mutual and general advantage."[4] Many writers believe the advantage was all Britain's.

The Federal Reserve Act, according to Andrew Gause, was actually conceived as a way to funnel America's wealth to Great Britain. Gause also believes that the British Rothschilds indirectly controlled the United States monetary system.

My contention is that the Federal Reserve Act was put into place in order for the wealth of the United States to be stripped and transferred to Britain so that she would be able to win World War I. . . . behind the scenes, the banking powers in the U.S. wanted to help the British all they could, so they created this wonderful Federal Reserve System with its private notes, calling it the money of the United States, then loaning it to Great Britain, while at the same time circulating it here at home. Then on through the Twenties, when the war was over all of that money created by the Fed came home to roost.

If you question whether the real purpose of the Federal Reserve was, initially, to provide England with funds to fight World War One, ask this question: Hadn't the English banking interests been trying to institute the Federal Reserve System for the previous 100 years? Clearly they had control of U.S. monetary policy. The Rothschilds had control of the United States' monetary system through the House of Morgan.[5]

Gause contends that J. P. Morgan—of the Rockefeller-Morgan-Aldrich combine that dominated American business and politics in 1913—was a deep-cover American agent of the European banking empire of the House of Rothschild. The financial firm of Kuhn Loeb, on the other hand, was Rothschild's official North American agent. A secret meeting of bankers and politicians at Jekyll Island, in Georgia, was convened to plan the Federal Reserve System; the meeting was organized and led by Senator Nelson Aldrich, an associate of J. P. Morgan and a member of the Rockefeller extended family, and by Paul Warburg, a partner in Kuhn Loeb. "Between Kuhn Loeb and J. P. Morgan and Co., the Rothschilds' interests dominated the planning for the Federal Reserve."[6]

Lord Rothschild, you will remember, along with Cecil Rhodes and other Oxford elitists, was a cofounder of the modern Illuminati vision of world conquest by the British. It is Cecil Rhodes's $150 million bequest that funds the Rhodes Scholars training program, but it was the Rothschilds who in all likelihood gave Rhodes control over the diamond fields of South Africa, where he made his fortune.[7]

Rothschild's and Rhodes's vision became reality when the British recaptured America through the creation of the Federal Reserve Bank. "The foreign influences behind this bank [Hamilton's First Bank of the United States], more than a century later, were able to get the Federal Reserve Act through Congress, giving them at last the central bank of issue for our economy."[8] The Fed has been the instrument of the transfer of America's enormous wealth to Britain. "On almost any measure you care to take, London is the world's leading financial centre."[9] In other words, despite the loss of her territorial empire in the non-White world, Britain has expanded its economic empire. *Capital City,* a book by Hamish McRae and Francis Cairncross, says that the central bank of the United States government is the reason that England is a financial powerhouse.

> Daniel Davison, head of London's Morgan Grenfell, said, "The American banks have brought the necessary money, customers, capital and skills which have established London in its present preeminence . . . only the American banks have a lender of last resort. The Federal Reserve Board of the United States can, and does, create dollars when necessary. Without the Americans, the big dollar deals cannot be put together. Without them, London would not be credible as an international financial centre."[10]

Mullins writes: "London is the world's financial center, because it can command enormous amounts of capital, created at its command by the Federal Reserve Board of the United States."[11] The Federal Reserve Bank of New York, the eight-hundred-pound gorilla of the Federal Reserve System, had its majority stock purchased in 1914 by three New York banks that had and have a London connection.[12] The entire Federal Reserve System of the United States, many believe, is manipulated by "The City," a sovereign nation inside the city of London where only seventeen firms are allowed to operate as merchant bankers.[13] Of those seventeen banks, five control the Federal

Reserve Bank of New York. Those five are listed below in numerical order of their capitalization, the pecking order of "The City":

> Number 2 is the Schroder Bank. Number 6 is Morgan Grenfell, the London Branch of the House of Morgan . . . Lazard Brothers is Number 8. N. M. Rothschild is Number 9. Brown Shipley Company, the London Branch of Brown Brothers Harriman, is Number 14. These five merchant banking firms of London actually control the New York banks which own the controlling interest in the Federal Reserve Bank of New York.[14]

## THE BONES CONNECTION

"The City," it is important to remember, is where the "Pilgrims," Cecil Rhodes's philosophical descendants, originated. Many of the major players at Brown Brothers Harriman, one of the Fed's owners, for instance, are allegedly alumni of Yale's ultrasecret Skull and Bones, an Anglophile senior fraternity, also known as The Order. The common link between the American WASP Establishment and the British Masonic international money lords is the United States Federal Reserve System.

The core of the Harriman influence in The Order today survives through intermarriages with the Paynes and the Vanderbilts, and there are now twenty to thirty Anglophile families that have intermarried. Fifteen Skull and Bones men graduate each year from being Yale "Knights" to "Patriarchs" at a plethora of unbelievably powerful positions in education, religion, law, government, the military; on the boards of foundations; and Brown Brothers Harriman and Company, where they manage the enormous fortunes of fellow Pilgrims and Brahmins.

A few Blacks and Jews recently became Bones men (and as

of 1991, women were admitted), probably as window dressing. Ironically or deviously, I don't know which, The Order refers to itself as Jewish and to the outside world as Gentile, although Bones men have been exclusively White Anglo-Saxon Protestants. Perhaps "Gentile" is a cryptic term for those who lack an occult kinship with the Jewish Cabala, the study of which was a tradition among the Knights Templar in England where the New England WASPs originated. The Templars used the symbol of the skull and crossbones, the sign of the Master Mason and now of the Skull and Bones fraternity at Yale. The Anglophile fraternity also has suspicious similarities with Cecil Rhodes's Circle of Initiates, especially the Circle's cult of Isis model at Oxford, and with Adam Weishaupt's old Order of the Illuminati in Bavaria. All three secret societies—The Order, The Circle of Initiates, and the Illuminati—were founded at universities by intellectuals and aristocratic elitists. And all three are occult orders that are suspected of being related because of similarities in their methods and objectives.

The old-line American families, the descendants of the original settlers in Massachusetts, The Order's inner circle, "arrived on the east coast in the 1600s from various parts of Great Britain when Templar Kings ruled England during the time Sir Francis Bacon was promoting America as the 'New Atlantis.' Many of the American families, no doubt, can trace their origins to the old Templar families." According to Antony Sutton in *America's Secret Establishment:* "They are Whitney, Lord, Phelps, Wadsworth, Allen, Bundy, Adams, etc. The second group are families who acquired wealth in the last 100 years, sent their sons to Yale and in time became almost old line families, e.g., Harriman, Rockefeller, Payne, Davidson."[15]

Insiders call this ultrasecret senior society The Order, as in the Order of Skull and Bones. It was also once known as the Brotherhood of Death. Still others have known it for over 150 years as Chapter 322, a German secret society that was founded at Yale, which has the only known chapter in the United States. Chapter 322 of what? The Illuminati from Germany? That suspicion is raised because William Huntington and Russell Alphonso Taft, The Order's founders, imported the society from Germany in 1832. Taft's stay in Germany must have included exposure to the extraordinary popularity of Hegelian principles among Illuminists in intellectual circles. Since everything about the chapter is ultrasecret, few facts are known.

## THE POLITICS OF MONEY

The conspiracy to inflict a central bank on the United States stretches back to the very birth of the nation, as we have seen. It did not succeed, however, until the beginning of the twentieth century. The "booms and busts" of the late 1890s and the Panic of 1907—manufactured by the bankers—led to the loss of jobs, homes, and confidence. This economic uncertainty, together with a sustained propaganda campaign by the bankers, was enough to convince the public that the government lacked the financial expertise necessary to manage the nation's money. The mystique of money had been created and used to flim-flam the people into accepting the separation of money and state. The politicians in Congress either bought the lie or were bought off.

The vote on the Federal Reserve Act was conveniently taken on December 23, 1913, two days before Christmas, when only "three members of the Senate" were present, according to "The Money Masters: How International Bankers Gained Control of America," a video transcript published in *Monetary Reform* magazine. It was "a unanimous consent voice vote" of only three senators, two of whom knew very little about banking or the legislation they were enacting.[16] The American public knew even less.

Illuminati Thirty-third-Degree Freemason, anti-American Socialist, "Colonel" Edward Mandel House's puppet, President Woodrow Wilson, hurriedly signed the unconstitutional "federal" bank into law within hours. House, the Conspiracy's designated insider in the Wilson White House, openly boasted of this triumph in implementing Illuminati control over the monetary system of the United States. And as Senator Charles Lindbergh, Sr., commented in 1923:

> The financial system has been turned over to the Federal Reserve Board; that board administers the finance system by authority of a purely profiteering group. The system is private, conducted for the sole purpose of obtaining the greatest possible profits from the use of other people's money.[17]

Most members of Congress did not—and still do not—understand the Illuminati system of American central banking. The handful who did were intimidated into silence and inaction. Those who were critical of the Fed were branded as pariahs, losing political patronage within their own party and the ability to raise campaign funds. In short, the Illuminati Ruling Class Conspiracy quickly demonstrated that standing up to it leads to political death, and the Fed was hard-wired into America's political system and given its autonomy.

Congressman Louis T. McFadden of Pennsylvania, who in the 1930s served on the House Banking and Currency Committee, was one politician who could not be silenced or purchased. He forcefully made the point that the Fed was not part of the government and was actually cheating the government and the people.

> Mr. Chairman, we have in this country one of the most corrupt institutions the world has ever known. I refer to

the Federal Reserve Banks hereinafter called the Fed. The Fed has cheated the Government of these United States, and the people of the United States out of enough money to pay the Nation's debt.

This evil institution has impoverished and ruined the people of these United States, has bankrupted itself, and has practically bankrupted our government. It has done this through the defects of the law under which it operates, through the maladministration of that law by the Fed, and through the corrupt practices of the money vultures who control it. Some people think that the Federal Reserve Banks are United States Government institutions. They are not Government institutions, they are private monopolies which prey upon the people of these United States for the benefit of themselves and their foreign customers, foreign and domestic speculators and swindlers, and rich and predatory money lenders.[18]

Today, the American system of government is hopelessly compromised by our politicians' dependence on the central bankers. A hard look at the Fed by a Congressional committee is almost unthinkable. Both major political parties have become statist Fed sycophants. The Republican Party platform speaks of it in glowing terms, neglecting to mention, of course, the inflation that results from such Fed practices as secret "currency swaps" that produce phony assets. In 1980, Congress passed the Depository Institutions Deregulation and Monetary Control Act, which conferred even more authority on the Fed. And the President, always hoping for an election year inflation of the money supply in order to fool the people with a contrived image of prosperity—and in order not to be outdone by the legislative branch—adds his fawning pledge to "respect the independence" of this derelict system.

The immoral connection between the United States government and the Illuminati money machine is clearly illustrated by taxpayer-financed bailouts of the private banks that own the Fed. In *The Secret World of Money,* Andrew Gause explains how the Federal Reserve makes money for its owners.

The interest the Fed collects on its bond holdings are minuscule compared to the money it can generate from its many unreportable activities. Their biggest profits are all indirect and "off the books." They make it from their perfect information, and from being able to monetize anything they want. As the Federal Reserve, you can monetize a billion-dollar note written by a six-year-old. You can do whatever you want. Here's a perfect example. The Mexicans were getting ready to default on fifty billion dollars' worth of bonds. The primary loser would have been J. P. Morgan and Co. The Secretary of Treasury, Robert Rubin (the former vice-chairman of Salomon Brothers), went before the Congress of the United States and told them that it was of vital national interest that the Mexicans should not default on their loan, and that Congress should give the Mexicans fifty billion dollars. The Congressman replied that they didn't object to that, but they wanted to learn a little more about what the money would be used for. And with that, the President promptly announced that he didn't actually need Congressional approval for a bailout, as he could just take money out of his Currency Stabilization Fund and give it to the Mexicans. The money was given to the Mexicans, and the Mexicans promptly gave that money to Citibank, Salomon Brothers, and every other private Fed-connected bank that bought their worthless bonds. Obviously, it was the cartel who owned the New York banks and who runs the Fed from behind the scenes who profited from this Fed operation. That was a classic example of how the Fed made billions for its owners.[19]

Former Republican Senator Barry Goldwater adds: "Most Americans have no real understanding of the operation of the international moneylenders. The accounts of the Federal Reserve System have never been audited. It operates outside the control of Congress, and manipulates the credit of the United States."[20] There you have it: the Illuminati Ruling Class Conspiracy at work.

## ECONOMIC TYRANNY

It is critical that we do not get diverted by the fact that rich bankers are getting richer through the Federal Reserve System. That is, in part, only a by-product of the Fed's much more sinister purpose—to give the Illuminati Ruling Class Conspiracy tyrannical control over the people of the United States. "The creation and perpetuation of the Federal Reserve System is the most gripping, insidious economic tyranny yet accepted," states Ernie Ross in *Bankers and Regulations*. "There is no place for it in the future of a free America."[21]

A tyranny can be imposed and expanded without force by confiscating the private property of the people (including income), thus making them dependent on the tyrant for the means of survival. This principle was laid out with devilish clarity by Karl Marx and Friedrich Engels in 1848 in the *Communist Manifesto*. In effect, the *Manifesto* is the Illuminati's Ten Commandments. The Illuminati, operating covertly, it is speculated, paid Marx and Engels to write an anti-God, antifamily position statement favoring a totalitarian system of government so the Illuminists could also enter the political arena on the radical left. Today's Communists prefer to be called Marxists; however, whatever name it goes by, it is still the anti-God religion of statism. The *Manifesto* introduces the scheme of transferring wealth, not from the rich to the poor, but from the workers to the Illuminati elitist class. The fifth plank of the *Manifesto* embodies the Illuminati's political doctrine (Illuminati Luciferian Occultism is its religious dogma); it explains economic tyranny under the heading: "Centralization of credit in the hands of the State by means of a national bank with State capital and an exclusive monopoly."[22] That is a near-perfect description of what Rothschild's agents accomplished in the United States in 1913, now known as the Federal Reserve Bank.

The second plank of the *Manifesto* calls for "a heavy or graduated income tax."[23] Prior to passage of the Sixteenth Amendment to the Constitution in 1913, taxes on income were illegal in the United States. Since the introduction of the personal income tax, the average American works almost seven months of each year just to pay taxes.

Marx knew that his plan for economic tyranny would not be accepted easily in a democracy. He therefore included in the *Manifesto* the insightful provision that the Illuminati Ten Commandments should be applied differently in different countries. In the United States, the *Communist Manifesto*'s Plank 2— promoting a graduated income tax—and Plank 5—a central bank—were sold to the people as democratic institutions aimed at preventing economic chaos and financial panics, such as the one in 1907 that had been manufactured by Illuminati agenturs, two German immigrants, Joseph Schiff and Paul Warburg.

Schiff was allegedly sent to the United States by the Illuminati's European economic royalty specifically to acquire control of America's money supply, which he did with the establishment of the Federal Reserve System. Both confessed conspirator Carroll Quigley and Rabbi Marvin Antleman, author of *To Eliminate the Opiate,* agree that Masonic money created a Warburg financial presence within the U.S. banking system, along with

"J. P. Morgan and John D. Rockefeller as front men"[24] to support Schiff's assignment.

The devastating effectiveness of Marx's plan for totalitarian control by the Illuminati was demonstrated by the Bolsheviks in Russia. After seizing political power by means of a violent revolution, Communist leader Vladimir Lenin "used the printing press to destroy the people's savings and redistribute the wealth by sharing the poverty."[25] Lenin had followed Marx's instructions in Plank 5. He created a central bank and intentionally issued so much currency that the money already in circulation became worthless. "The resulting inflation raised the general index of prices to 16,000 times what it was in 1913. It had its desired effect. The middle class was eliminated as a class in Russia."[26]

Lenin proved that, as the famous Marxist economist John Maynard Keynes put it, "the best way to destroy the Capitalist system was to debauch the currency."[27] "Debauching" the currency is, in effect, plain old counterfeiting—increasing the money supply for personal gain. Of course, when the government does it, counterfeiting becomes legal. The inflation of the money supply devalues the currency, undermining the value of private property.

Freemason Keynes explains in *The Economic Consequences of the Peace* how "debauching the currency"—creating inflation by printing new unbacked notes of debt—gradually reduces the standard of living by secretly confiscating the income of the citizens and transferring it to the owners of the central bank that does the confiscating. As you read Keynes's analysis, bear in mind that he is a Marxist who is honestly explaining how rising prices result from government-printing inflation of "dollars," thus permitting the government to confiscate savings and income without leaving a clue.

By a continuing of inflation, governments can confiscate, secretly and unobserved, an important part of the wealth of their citizens. By this method they not only confiscate, but they confiscate arbitrarily, and while the process impoverishes many, it actually enriches some.

There is no subtler, no surer means of overturning the existing basis of society than to debauch the currency.

The process engages all the hidden forces of economic law on the side of destruction, and does it in a manner not one man in a million is able to diagnose.[28]

As Keynes says, it is such a clever process that, if reading it here for the first time, you probably find this definition of inflation and a confiscatory scheme hard to believe or even unacceptable. And even if you tentatively agree with Keynes's characterization, you probably believe that this is something that happens in other countries, that it could never happen in the United States, because this is a democratic Republic. That is exactly what the Illuminati Ruling Class Conspiracy would have you believe. Nevertheless, inflation created by the Illuminati Federal Reserve System is robbing Americans of their wealth and forcing them to worship at the altar of statism for government handouts.

# 6

# STATISM: THE RELIGION OF OPPRESSION AND THE SCIENCE OF CONTROL

*Deficit spending is simply a scheme for the "hidden" confiscation of
wealth. Gold stands in the way of this insidious process. It stands
as a protector of property rights. If one grasps this, one has no difficulty
in understanding the statists' antagonism toward the gold
standard.*
—Alan Greenspan, Chairman,
Federal Reserve Board

Unlike the United States, the political ideology of Germany, both prior to and following World War II, never embraced the rights of the individual. Instead, the Hegelian dialectical process guided Germany by a system of "rational tyranny."[1] Individual freedom was not tolerated. According to Hegel, the state is God and the duty of the citizen is to serve God by serving the state—the state being Absolute Reason. It is apparent why these ideas must be kept in secrecy in the United States.

The Illuminati, those intellectuals who believe they have overcome the superstition of "false" religion, use this "absolute reason" to manipulate a society from both the left and the right simultaneously. The Illuminists are both the Capitalists and the Communists. "Both Marx and Hitler have their philosophical roots in Hegel," explains Antony Sutton, author of *The Secret*

*Cult of the Order.*[2] The Order produced both Patriarch W. Averell Harriman, friend and financier of Communism, and Patriarch George Bush, Capitalist conservative, whose father, Patriarch Prescott Bush, was a partner at The Order's favorite financial house, Brown Brothers Harriman. This is a classic example of Hegelian dialectics in action. Another example can be found in the behavior of Bill Clinton since becoming President of the United States.

Yalie Bill Clinton participates in Hegelian dialectical process from somewhere near the middle of the political spectrum (a Republicrat) as he stakes out the leftist position on affirmative action, while his "adversary," undisputed Bonesman, CIA-affiliated William F. Buckley, publisher of the *National Review,* practices the art of decrying "reverse discrimination" from the right. On the issue of drugs, they switch. Buckley is leftist in his campaign to openly narcotize the masses, while Clinton plays the stern, antidrug fighter as Commander in Chief. Major policy issues are always directed by members of The Group in England, The Order in the United States, and the Illuminati everywhere.

In mental-spook parlance, the Hegelian process of dividing and manipulating a population is referred to as "managed conflict." Of course, the conflict first has to be created; then it is manipulated as a wedge in order to stimulate the forming of opposing groups, and finally is resolved to the satisfaction of a handful of elitist puppeteers, e.g., the Trilateral Commission and the Council on Foreign Relations. G.W.F. Hegel, the German philosopher, taught that this Machiavellian scam also had a bonus: It allows the people to feel that their opinions matter. The presence of a Parliament or a Congress helps to confirm the existence of a participatory democracy.

Most of the candidates for the federal legislature in the United States are also selected according to the same rationale of opposition, their candidacies actualized by The Order's and the Illuminati's money, and the people are given the illusion of being permitted to confirm one or another of the opponents at the polls. If things go as planned, however, in the near future, the confirmation aspect will not even be necessary. The Illuminati will simply announce the leaders.

The Hegelian principle of bringing about change by means of a conflict between opposing forces is achieved by means of a three-stage process, involving thesis, antithesis, and synthesis. The idea to be implemented into policy, the desired change, must, in the thesis stage, become a predicament (commonly called a problem). The emergence of this proposal through the media, in the form of a legislative proposal, a "White paper," etc., will trigger the emergence of an opposing force, or antithesis. This second stage is designed to guarantee that both sides in a polarized public will fear the loss of statist privilege or an entitlement.

Panic and hysteria will break out, and perhaps violence, as has been the case with abortion foes, homosexual rights advocates, and the Christian right—and of course there's that old staple, conflict between Blacks and Whites. There's no end to the available supply of suckers, and the spook agenturs on both sides know how to stir them up by instilling fear, panic, and hysteria.

In the end, the Illuminati in The Order and The Group will win. "The final outcome will be neither thesis nor antithesis, but a synthesis of two forces in conflict,"[3] Antony Sutton observes. This synthesis, the third stage of the Hegelian dialectical process, sees the Illuminati-sponsored power elite offer the solution to the predicament (problem) it created in stage one, thesis. After the psychological conditioning of the population in the antithesis stage (stage two), the predetermined outcome can now be implemented as the choice of the people. The synthesis (stage three) automatically becomes a new thesis and starts the Hegelian cycle all over again.

Under this system of Hegelian politics only a power elite can enforce a decision. In this Hegelian scheme, the imposed synthesis reaffirms and preserves the state as God and the individual's religious duty to serve the state.

Economic tyranny, as we saw in the previous chapter, is a surefire way to enslave people and make them dependent on the government for survival. In that process, confiscation in the form of taxation has been the despot's weapon of choice. But even in a pseudo democratic Republic, such as America has become, it is politically inconvenient to rely too heavily on this tried-and-true method; more subtle means are necessary. Never at a loss for a way to exploit the people, the devilishly clever Illuminati bankers have come up with government-debt creation and monetary inflation.

Thomas Jefferson had a firm, insider's understanding of the conspiratorial politics of this world and the people in it who prefer money and power to God's Divine plan. He warned future generations of Americans that the Illuminati concept of a free lunch paid for by debt leads to war and more taxes, both profiting the money cabal: "To preserve our independence," Jefferson said, "we must not let our leaders load us with perpetual debt. We must make our election between economy and liberty, or profusion and servitude. It is incumbent on every generation to pay its own debts as it goes—a principle which, if acted on, would save one half of the wars of the world."[4]

Americans did not listen. After we opened the gates of the nation to Karl Marx's Trojan Horse—the Fed—the government began to accumulate debt at an appalling rate, all in the name of the people and for the "good" of the people. In 1930, the national debt was $16 million. By 1946, it had ballooned to $269 million. Today, it is almost $7 trillion. That works out to about $70,000 in IOUs in the name of each American family, with 1 percent of everything Americans earn going to pay the interest. Of course, with compound interest payable to the "central" bankers, it is impossible to ever retire this "national" debt. It feeds on itself and fuels inflation of the monetary supply.

The government, in this covert way, is now confiscating over half the income of the citizens of the United States and is on its way to taking the rest. That is why today American families need two incomes to merely survive, while thirty years ago one job would have sufficed.

The noted economist John Kenneth Galbraith has explained how inflation acts as a "method of income redistribution," by transferring income from "the poor to the rich."

> Inflation takes from the old, the unorganized, and the poor and gives to those who are strongly in control of their own incomes. . . . Income is reallocated from the old to the people of middle years and from the poor to the rich.[5]

That goes a long way toward explaining how the Federal Reserve central bank has become "staggeringly wealthy," according to *The Wall Street Journal*, "with $451 billion in assets" in 1996.[6] It also explains how, through its stock in the Federal Reserve, the Illuminati Ruling Class Conspiracy has forced Americans to bend their knees at the altar of statism.

## THE CHAIRMAN'S GOLDEN RULE

In writing this book, I have come to appreciate the brilliance of the current Chairman of the Federal Reserve Board, Alan Greenspan. His leadership could be of inestimable value in confronting the devastating economic predicament this nation will face after the stock market's inevitable crash in the near future. I lament the fact, however, that as Chairman of the Federal Reserve Board, Greenspan refrains from telling the truth, the way he did in his 1966 article, "Gold and Economic Freedom," in which he explained how the welfare statists cemented their hold on America when they removed our currency from the gold standard.

The article was originally published in a newsletter called *The Objectivist* and reprinted in Ayn Rand's *Capitalism: The Unknown Ideal* the following year. In it, Greenspan explains that all "statists" are united in "an almost hysterical antagonism toward the gold standard" and asserted that "gold and economic freedom are inseparable."[7] Statists, he continues, know almost instinctively that "the gold standard is an instrument of laissez-faire and that each implies and requires the other."[8]

To know the source of the statists' preference for worthless paper notes of debt over a paper currency backed by gold, Greenspan argues, you must know "the specific role of gold in a free society." Money, he says, is "that commodity which serves as a medium of exchange, is universally acceptable . . . as payment . . . and can, therefore, be used as a standard of market value and as a store of value, i.e., as a means of saving." It is "the common denominator of all economic transactions." Such a commodity, historically a metal, creates the opportunity to move beyond a primitive barter economy and is necessary for "a division of labor economy."

Gold has been that commodity and "the sole international standard of exchange" since World War I.

> If all goods and services were to be paid for in gold, large payments would be difficult to execute, and this would tend to limit the extent of a society's division of labor and specialization. Thus a logical extension of the creation of a medium of exchange is the development of a banking system and credit instruments (bank notes and deposits) which act as a substitute for, but are convertible into, gold.[9]

Greenspan then gives a candid and insightful insider analysis of why it was necessary for the economic royalists to do away with the gold standard in order to confiscate the American people's wealth through "welfare schemes" (entitlements) that drive the national debt. A gold standard to back our currency would prevent this theft by the spendthrift statists in both parties, Greenspan believes.

> Stripped of its academic jargon, the welfare state is nothing more than a mechanism by which governments confiscate the wealth of the productive members of a society to support a wide variety of welfare schemes. A substantial part of the confiscation is effected by taxation. But the welfare statists were quick to recognize that if they wished to retain political power, the amount of taxation had to be limited and they had to resort to programs of massive deficit spending, i.e., they had to borrow money, by issuing government bonds, to finance welfare expenditures on a large scale.

Chairman Greenspan said that welfare statists have used the elimination of the gold standard to covertly steal our wealth and savings through deficit spending and inflation. Since taxation must be capped, he said, the scheme to confiscate citizens' wealth takes the form of huge deficit spending by issuing government bonds. Banks erroneously treat these bonds as the equivalent of tangible gold deposits. These fiat paper reserves (government bonds) cannot support the supply of monetary claims, thus creating higher prices and a reduction in the value of goods. The gold standard ensured that the amount of credit the economy carried did not exceed available tangible assets. "Gold stands in the way of this insidious process. It stands as a protector of property rights," said the Federal Reserve chairman.[10]

That is the Alan Greenspan you will never hear from again, a brilliant man, speaking with integrity and clarity. "On April 19, 1993, after his speech to the Economic Club of New York,

I asked Chairman Greenspan whether he still agreed with his reasoning and conclusions [in "Gold and Economic Freedom"]," reports Larry Parks, Executive Director of FAME, (Foundation for the Advancement of Monetary Education).[11] "He said 'Absolutely,' and added that he had recently reread the article." In response to why he no longer speaks out, Greenspan said that these are not popular ideas among some of "my colleagues" at the Fed, Parks asserts. " 'But you know where all of this is leading to.' He gave me a pained look and walked on."[12]

Greenspan, I want to believe, is essentially an honest man. I am sorry to see him [nearing the end of his life] with so much power and so little integrity. In the end, he is at best a puppet of the very system of welfare statism that he condemned as evil.

## WHERE IS AMERICA'S GOLD?

In "Gold and Economic Freedom," Alan Greenspan also explains how the Illuminati Ruling Class Conspiracy went about destroying the gold standard in 1931 when Great Britain abandoned it completely, thereby triggering a "world-wide series of bank failures."

The Federal Reserve created more paper money when the United States economy floundered slightly in 1927. At the same time, the Federal Reserve successfully helped Great Britain survive its gold losses when the country refused to increase interest rates. The extra credit that was generated in the economy was infused into the stock market. In an effort to balance the excesses of the resulting stock market boom, the Federal Reserve inadvertently started a backlash that reverberated throughout the world. Great Britain had completely abandoned the gold standard by 1931. This reinforced the erosion of confidence in the economy, precipitating global bank failures and the Great Depression of the 1930s.[13]

It is very significant that Britain again played a pivotal role in precipitating a worldwide disaster: the Great Depression. I doubt that it was innocent incompetence, as Greenspan suggests, that caused the fatal chain reaction. The players, the methods, and the outcomes all bear the fingerprints of the British Illuminati money lords.

In the United States, the gold standard was tacitly abandoned when the central bank was created in 1913 and welfare statism was sold to a frightened, insecure people as a saving grace. In the first three years of the Great Depression, more than five thousand banks had failed, taking with them nine million savings accounts; the national income was reduced by half; and fifteen million people were unemployed. Industry and agriculture were a shambles. Freemason President Franklin Delano Roosevelt interjected the government for the first time into the management of the economy with a New Deal financed by newly unbacked government IOUs, and we were on our way to the *Novus Ordo Seclorum*—"New Secular Order"—the statistics promised on the dollar bill and to $7 trillion in national debt.

Anglophile conspirators were not satisfied with simply forcing the United States to abandon the gold standard for its currency; it wanted America's gold as well. In 1941, when we entered World War II, the United States owned nearly two thirds of the world's "good gold stock," .995 fine delivery gold. In 1945, $24 billion of good gold stock was at Fort Knox. By late 1959, twice the amount of U.S. gold reserves was found in Europe. By 1964, if you can believe the James Bond movie *Goldfinger*, Fort Knox housed only $15 billion in gold.

In 1944, Freemason Henry Morgenthau, Roosevelt's Treasury Secretary, met in Bretton Woods, New Hampshire, with British and European bankers; British Masons, including Freemason Marxists John Maynard Keynes, Anthony Eden, and Bertrand Russell; and other American Illuminati agenturs. At the now famous Bretton Woods conference, this Anglophile group—which has "the same Anglophile central bank stockholders who controlled the majority of stock . . . in the Federal Reserve Bank" and the International Monetary Fund (IMF)[14]—agreed to launder the gold looted by the Nazis through the Bank for International Settlements (BIS) in Switzerland, according to author John Daniel.

The Bretton Woods conference was also responsible for creating the International Monetary Fund (IMF), whose alleged purpose was to finance industrial development in underdeveloped countries. The IMF and the World Bank were later established under the authority of the United Nations. "The same Anglophile central banks' stockholders, who controlled the majority of stock in BIS and the Federal Reserve Bank, were also the major stockholders in the IMF."[15]

The IMF and the World Bank were organized as the United Nations' instruments for confiscating the world's gold. American gold was transferred to the European central banks as America's annual "contributions" to the IMF. It took only fourteen years, from 1945 to 1959, "to liquidate American gold reserves."[16] According to Daniel's eyewitness sources, the gold was shipped out from Fort Knox in milk trucks and driven to the World Bank in Washington, D.C. "From there it was shipped to Europe and Japan to rebuild those devastated nations."[17]

What Americans have left today of their gold stock is "gold alloy" of .85 fineness or less, "mostly coin melt" that came from Roosevelt's 1933–1935 seizure of gold coins from American citizens, around the time he put the Illuminati seal on the dollar bill.[18]

The gold bars at Fort Knox have not been inventoried (not audited by checking the seals on vault doors) since 1933.[19] The value of America's gold alloy stock is today estimated at about

$2 billion.[20] We are indeed, thanks to the Illuminati Ruling Class Conspiracy, the world's number one pauper nation.

## THE DIALECTIC OF BLAME

You can fool some of the people some of the time, as the saying goes. But you can screw all of the people all of the time, if you fool them into believing that it is someone else who is screwing them. The Illuminati statists knew that to enslave the people of the United States by covertly confiscating their income through monetary-supply inflation they would have to blame something or someone else for the steady erosion of our standard of living.

But in order to steal Americans' money with government inflation of the money supply, the financial camarilla in "The City" (inside London) must remain hidden and unknown to the American people and inflation must be blamed on everything but bloating the money supply. A. Ralph Epperson explains:

> Inflation, to be successful, must be concealed from those who stand to lose the most: the money holders. Concealment becomes the goal of those who do the counterfeiting. Never must the true cause of inflation be properly identified. Inflation must be blamed on everything: the market place, the housewife, the greedy merchant, the wage earner, the unions, oil shortages, the balance of payments, the common housefly! Anything but inflation's true cause: the increase in the money supply.[21]

The Illuminated statists came up with an ingenious solution: Define *inflation* as rising prices and then blame working people for driving up the prices by buying food, clothing, and shelter, and asking for a decent wage. In terms of the Hegelian dialectic: Price inflation was presented as the predicament (thesis); workers' demands for higher wages and full employment as the cause (antithesis); and the Fed's Nairu scheme, as the solution (synthesis). The state law became the central force—the deity—in our lives, promising security and prosperity.

This strategy of disinformation and Hegelian brainwashing has worked very well. "Too Many Jobs?" a recent story in *Time* magazine, reported exuberantly that "the alarm bells in the inflation firehouse known as the Federal Reserve Bank must be going off."[22] The national economic consensus, the article explained, is that "inflation is inevitable when the unemployment rate drops below 6 percent, because wages rise as the labor market tightens."[23] That is the Illuminati Ruling Class Conspiracy's party line in a nutshell.

The Fed's big lie about inflation has had a profound effect on the economy. Whenever unemployment goes down (more people find jobs), the stock market heads south also. It even crashes. Conversely, stocks climb when unemployment (misery) climbs, because the Fed rewards investors for behaving like trained inflation-seals with higher interest-rate returns.

Intentionally misleading news reports tell us that "the Fed uses high interest rates to head off inflation" or that "the economy's steady growth triggers higher inflation." The Fed, for its part, has responded to the threat of "inflation" by devising the evil Nairu (nonaccelerating rate of unemployment) scheme, which keeps 6 percent of Americans permanently unemployed. Six percent translates into 8 million people out of work. When you count those groups that are no longer included in the data gathering, the figure is closer to 20 to 30 million unemployed souls.

"Why would any well-intentioned person want to reduce investment in the future and put people out of work?" asked Robert Eisner, professor of economics at Northwestern University, in a 1996 *New York Times* editorial. Eisner, of course, knows the answer to that question. The Federal Reserve aims for a sluggish 2 percent annual growth on "the dismal dogma . . . the belief that there is a natural rate of unemployment beyond which the economy cannot grow without bringing accelerating inflation."[24] The bedrock of the government's economic theory is the belief that a specified amount of jobless misery is necessary and "natural."

In actuality, Nairu is an unemployment plan; it is high-tech slavery, reminiscent of *Secrets of Iron Mountain,* a 1967 best-selling book that includes a fictional proposal for the reinstatement of slavery in a technological form: enslavement of people who are unemployed because they have no computer skills.[25] The 6 percent Nairu figure is equivalent to about 25 percent of the Black and Hispanic population—the impact among low-income Whites is also higher than 6 percent. The actual number of unemployed Blacks and Hispanics—marked for planned obsolescence and government control in the form of some sort of welfare statist handout—is about 50 percent, or over thirty million people. In my opinion, the Fed Chairman, in fact, routinely instills fear in workers with his policy to depress wage demands.

The real cause of inflation, of course, is the Fed's printing press, which continually "debauches" the dollar. But facts such as this do not make it into headlines such as "Economy Surging." Media propagandists like *Newsweek*'s Robert Samuelson arrogantly debunk other media organizations and individuals who do not spout the government's dogma. Samuelson calls people who report the fact that the government is reducing living standards and job security for most Americans economic "dunces." Statistics implying lower living standards lie, according to Samuelson.[26]

The propaganda is effective: A recent survey showed that 70 percent of all Americans are confident they will achieve the American Dream. The way things are going, though, the American Dream will be nothing more than the Illuminati statists' Nairu Unemployment Plan. Sadly, most Americans seem to have been conned by the dialectic of blame the Illuminati Ruling Class Conspiracy has used as part of its strategy to have itself worshiped as the source of human rights. Karl Marx had turned Hegel's thesis-antithesis-synthesis model into the basis for Communist "dialectical materialism," and the crony Capitalist Fed relied on that same Hegelian dialectic to blame America's working people for being robbed.

## A NATION OF "NIGGERS"

The new world in which the only color of freedom is green demands a new "nigger." New conditions dictate that the new class of niggers cannot be race based. You are now a nigger when you don't know that you are being robbed of your money and your freedom. Niggers get no respect, die in wars so other people can profit (the Vietnam War produced an $80 billion profit for the companies that sold products to the military),[27] and have their human rights confiscated on a daily basis and their property taken from them by the statists every April 15.

With statism as "the spiritual center of society," says Theodore J. Forstmann, "the statist has no use for the Golden Rule. [Do unto others as you would have them do unto you.] The statist does not speak of government as a collection of bureaucrats, agencies, and limited constitutional powers but as the embodiment of the collective good—as community itself."[28] The "spiritual authority of the Golden Rule" is derived from the assumption "that there is a Creator and that we are all equal in His eyes."[29] In the absence of the Golden Rule, our society has splintered into an "interest-group democracy," in the words of David Boaz, author of *Libertarianism*.[30]

The Illuminati Ruling Class Conspiracy uses the Hegelian

dialectic to disempower the people by pitting one group against another. It has refined the method of dividing and conquering along lines of race, sex, religion, and political beliefs to a diabolical degree, in the process offering the ruling class a convenient cover. The Conspiracy's mass communications bureaucracies, especially within the mainstream media, create one crisis of division after another, and then the Conspiracy's statist bureaucracy steps in and manages the crisis. The state's solution is more state, in other words, more power and control for the elitists.

I wonder if Forstmann is aware that he is benignly describing the Illuminati Ruling Class Conspiracy. Whether you call the phenomenon "statism," "Communism," or "Illuminism" is irrelevant. You are describing humans, in the absence of God's love, in bondage to an evil oligarchy.

# 7

# THE ILLUMINATI-SPONSORED AMERICAN RACE WAR

*The government rightly believes that as long as there is discord along racial lines, there will never be unity among all Americans. Without unity the American people will never be able to rid America of an oppressive federal government intent on destroying the freedoms of all Americans.*

—MICHAEL WILLIAMS HAGA,
*Taking Back America*

The tactics of blame and division are the covert weapons of the Illuminati Ruling Class Conspiracy. As already noted, the Hegelian dialectical process practiced by the Conspiracy uses wedge issues as a means of social and psychological control of society. In his *Pawns in the Game*, William Guy Carr explains how "the Princes of Masonry"—a cabal of some of the most powerful "international-minded bankers, industrialists, scientists, military and political leaders, educationalists, economists, etc."—gain dominance by setting people against each other.

> They are men who have accepted the Luciferian plan for the rule of Creation as being preferable to that of Almighty God. They worship Lucifer as required by [Albert] Pike

in his book *Morals and Dogmas*. They acknowledge the authority of no mortal except their leader. They give loyalty to no nation. They direct the CONTINUING LUCIFERIAN CONSPIRACY to prevent God's plan, for the rule of Creation, being put into practice; they plot to obtain absolute control of this world and everything in it. They use all subversive movements to divide masses of the people into opposing camps on political, social, racial, economic and religious issues, then arm them, and make them fight and destroy each other. They hope to make humanity follow this process of self-destruction until all existing political and religious institutions have been eliminated. They plan to crown their leader King-despot of the entire world and enforce the Luciferian dictatorship with Satanic despotism.[1]

Of course, the "secrets" the initiates are felt unworthy to receive are useless, philosophical mumbo-jumbo, not knowledge of good and evil. Those secrets amount to unadulterated superstition, which is used to achieve the political and economic ends of the Illuminati Ruling Class Conspiracy.

## THE DIALECTICS OF RACE

Adolf Hitler's Third Reich is an enduringly infamous instance of the Illuminati's use of race as a weapon of control. The Aryan messiah and his disciples of the "master race" were explicit in their objective of remaking the world in their own image. According to Gerald Suster, author of *Hitler: Black Magician,* "Those who see in National Socialism nothing more than a political movement know scarcely anything of it. . . . It is even more than a religion: it is the will to create mankind anew."[2]

Hitler's jackbooted Nazi butchers created a religion of racial hatred—with the insignia of "the moving cross" (the swastika) and occult torchlight ("illumination") rituals at Nuremberg—that cast the world into the pit of destruction and chaos. Joseph Goebbels, the Nazi propagandist, in the prescribed Illuminati fashion, incited the German people to violence with the Illuminati's favorite dogma, that the end justifies the means—including mass murder:

> A time of brutality approaches. . . . We shall only reach our goal if we have enough courage to destroy, laughingly to shatter what we once held holy, such as tradition, upbringing, friendship and human love.[3]

The Nazis chose the Jews and other racial minorities as their antithesis—the cause of all of Germany's and the world's problems. They appealed to the fears, insecurities, and loathing of a nation that was suffering economic and political crises after its defeat in World War I, and in this way spread panic and hysteria. Armed with the faked *Protocols of the Learned Elders of Zion,* the Nazis blamed the Jews for everything from selling out the country during the war to feeding off the misery of the German people; ethnic hatred became an emotional outlet and a rallying cry for a separate, susceptible German people. Most important, of course, it was a convenient device to propel the Nazi Illuminati into power.

## THE RACIAL STATES OF AMERICA

In August 1997, a White police mob in New York City took a thirty-year-old Black male suspect, a security guard named Abner Louima, into the bathroom of Precinct 70 in Brooklyn and angrily rammed the long, rough wooden handle of a plunger into his rectum. Following the historical ritual pattern of White male homosexual rape, the White policemen shoved the phallic instrument, covered with the victim's blood and feces, into his mouth. "One of the cops accused in the infamous 70th precinct torture returned to the scene of the alleged crime . . . to a hero's welcome," the *New York Post* reported in an article entitled, "Hugs for Louima Cop at Scandal Precinct."[4]

This act of sexualized violence is chillingly reminiscent of the ritual lynchings of the early part of the twentieth century, with their fixation on the penis (Sigmund Freud posited penis envy) and their homosexual overtones. The lynching ritual was a sporting event for White men, in which they expressed their neurotic fear of Black men's manhood. LYNCHING TERMED A TYPE OF DIXIE SEX PERVERSION the March 16, 1935, headline of the *Baltimore Afro-American* opined.[5] In *One Hundred Years of Slavery,* the ceremonies in these racist sexual rituals is chronicled. Among the sordid events is the story of a mob of two thousand Whites in Newnan, Georgia, on April 23, 1899, that cut off the ears, fingers, and penis of a Black man accused of murder. These body parts were then sold as "souvenirs," for which extravagant sums were paid. The Black man was then burned alive.[6] The victim's penis was usually cut off and stuffed in his mouth, and often sold as a trophy to the highest bidder.

The fact that some White men in positions of power still feel threatened enough by a Black man to sodomize him with a plunger points to the fact that the Illuminati dialectic of racial division is doing its job in America. While the overwhelming majority of Whites find racial acts that took place in New York and in the past unconscionable, there is a growing hard core that is in various stages of preparedness for a final resolution of "the Black problem." Blacks typically respond with hatred and/ or self-hatred and more dependence on Whites. And inexorably, the races are speeding toward mutually assured destruction, while the Illuminati Ruling Class Conspiracy profits from the mutual misery.

## THE CONSPIRACY OF DIVISION

The racial hatred that exists in this country is a result of social conditioning, planned and administered by the Illuminati Ruling Class Conspiracy.

The Illuminati chose Blacks as the antithesis—the cause of the predicament (problem)—in the American version of their Hegelian racial dialectics. There is irrefutable historical evidence that Blacks have been the preferred victims of conspiracies by the United States government. See details in this chapter and *Black Lies, White Lies* for the historical background and examples. From slavery to the Ku Klux Klan, to the Woodrow Wilson administration Military Intelligence Division's war on Black Americans, to the Nazi-like Tuskegee syphilis experiment, to the FBI's infiltration of civil rights groups, to the widely suspected government role in the assassinations of Martin Luther King, Jr., and Malcolm X, the government has used a variety of tactics to undermine the Black community in this country.

In my first book, *Black Lies, White Lies: The Truth According to Tony Brown,* I reported on government-sponsored gas-chamber experiments; the use of LSD experimentation on unsuspecting citizens; clandestine "body snatching" of thousands of poor urban Blacks in the 1950s to study the effects of radioactive fallout; the "ethnic weapons" in the United States' biological and chemical arsenal—genetically programmed to read racial differences, especially African and Semitic blood types, and including the exposure of unsuspecting civilian Blacks in Savannah, Georgia, and Avon Park, Florida, to yellow-fever-bearing mosquitoes. Put it all together, and you get a scary insight into the government's ongoing campaign to destabilize and marginalize the Black population of the United States.

It is very significant that it was President Woodrow Wilson's administration that "effectively declared war on all Blacks as suspected traitors" very shortly after having turned over the country to the Illuminati central bankers.[7]

The government's campaign against Black America beginning in 1917, which I have briefly surveyed earlier, was the supreme act of citizenship nullification. In recent years, there have been even more insidious drug and propaganda attacks upon Black communities. External forces have overwhelmed Black neighborhoods with heroin and cocaine and White society has been encouraged to blame victims of these incursions for their "moral weakness" and "criminal tendencies." At the same time, the fears of a shrinking White majority of their loss of government entitlements have been stirred up by statist affirmative action programs. It is such fears and manipulated perceptions, and their mirror images among Blacks, that may be driving us into a race war. And if the Illuminati plot succeeds and we do fight each other, at the end there will only be Black and White American losers and Illuminati Ruling Class rulers.

## TUSKEGEE CONSPIRACY

The best-documented example of a government conspiracy against Blacks is the infamous Tuskegee syphilis experiment, on which I began reporting in 1972 on my PBS television series, *Tony Brown's Journal.* Begun in 1932, this was a forty-year syphilis study carried out in Tuskegee, Alabama, in which the United States Public Health Service and the Centers for Disease Control and Prevention used Black men as nonconsenting guinea pigs. The mostly White doctors watched as 400 poor Black men, who thought they were receiving treatment, wasted away over four decades, while unwittingly putting their families at risk. All but 1 of these men—399—died between the years 1932 to 1972.

The Tuskegee experiment illustrates beyond the shadow of a doubt that the United States government is prepared to go to genocidal lengths to undermine and control the Black community. Elitist hatred of Black men as members of a "notoriously syphilis-soaked race" allowed the doctors to view them strictly as subjects, rather than human beings.[8]

Another disturbing history lesson of the Tuskegee conspiracy is that social conditioning can teach us to dehumanize not only members of other races but our own as well. This lesson comes to us in the person of Eunice Rivers. Rivers, an ambitious young Black nurse who had graduated from the Tuskegee Institute Nursing School in 1922, was the daughter of Albert Rivers, a poor and uneducated farm worker from Jakin, Georgia. In spite of her background, she served as Special Scientific Assistant in the government's Nazi-like "experiment."

Nurse Rivers's job, in addition to her nursing duties, was to transport the men to and from the clinic and to make sure that they never received treatment for the disease anywhere else. She performed the duties prescribed to her under this genocidal plan with unyielding precision. For example, when Charles Pollard, one of the men under observation, attempted to take a bus bound for a treatment center in Birmingham, Rivers literally chased him down. As Pollard recalls, Nurse Rivers pulled him out of the bus line, yelling, "You can't go down there; you can't take them shots!"[9]

Eunice Rivers was "not troubled by the duties she performed" and was "comfortable not treating the men,"[10] according to James H. Jones, author of *Bad Blood*. She "seized upon her doubts about the drugs [used to treat syphilis at that time] as an excuse to justify not treating the men."[11] In a rare on-camera appearance in a documentary film that I produced for television, Nurse Rivers seemed to confirm Jones's assessment of her as she tried to defend what she and her coconspirators had done: "I don't know, I haven't any thoughts about it . . . I don't know. I think that this was something that they were sincere in themselves."[12] To me, her response indicated a deep ambivalence and an insincere innocence. I felt she was lying.

The terrible truth seems to be that having full knowledge of the racist intent of the Tuskegee experiment—the intentional destruction of a group of defenseless, poor Black men whose backgrounds were very much like that of her father—did not create a crisis of conscience in Eunice Rivers. Her elitist education—read brainwashing—taught her to follow orders and subordinate her humanity for the good of the state, her God.

## THE COVERT WAR AGAINST BLACK AMERICA

The attempt to destabilize Black communities by the introduction of drugs is the very same strategy used by the Illuminists in Britain who narcotized and disabled the Chinese people with opium before their armed invasion in the mid-nineteenth century. In the next chapter, I will present evidence that strongly suggests that the crack-cocaine epidemics that wrecked entire Black communities in the 1980s and 1990s were planned. If these allegations are true, a covert war against Blacks that was begun in 1917 by Illuminati puppet President Woodrow Wilson is continuing.

In my first book, *Black Lies, White Lies,* I expanded on the facts presented by Stephen Thompkins in a 1993 series of articles in the *Memphis Commercial Appeal* on the U.S. Army's espionage campaign, conducted by the Military Intelligence Division (MID), in the Black community. For my book, Thompkins provided me with documents, some of which were not included in his articles.

When America entered World War I in April 1917, one in ten of its citizens was Black—about twelve million people. As

America drew closer to war, Army leaders suddenly realized how dangerous Blacks could be to national security if they organized against their government. Blacks were well positioned to thwart the war effort if they were so disposed.

"Negro unrest," as it was termed by the MID, was a major fear of President Woodrow Wilson's administration and the War Department. After declaring war on Germany in 1917, the United States government effectively declared war on all Blacks in America as suspected traitors. The MID created an internal security network to spy on every outspoken and prominent member of the Black community and to recruit Blacks to spy on each other. This domestic spy network was the largest ever assembled in a free country.

This intelligence operation was the forerunner of the FBI-led COINTELPRO counterinsurgency program of the 1960s. During the Kennedy and Johnson years, 400 Blacks were added to the FBI's "security index" of 10,000 "racial agitators" listed by their "degree of dangerousness."[13] The listing was begun in 1939, undoubtedly by MID, since the index was formally called the "Bureau War Plans." All Black Americans were viewed as potential enemies of their own country. In 1918 and during World War II, Blacks were suspected of being potential agents of Germany. In the 1960s, Blacks, especially the leaders of Martin Luther King's Southern Christian Leadership Conference, were regarded by the FBI as Communist subversives.

In 1963, President Kennedy and his brother Robert, the Attorney General, believed that King's anti-Vietnam War posture and his civil rights marches alienated Whites and threatened Kennedy's reelection chances. In *Racial Matters,* Kenneth O'Reilly writes: "The Kennedys were active on another civil rights front, spying on the movement through the FBI."[14] It was no secret that Kennedy's successor, Lyndon Johnson, hated King for his suspected Communist ties and opposition to the Vietnam War. Johnson, according to O'Reilly, had titillating gossip about Black people and "Black-scare stories" supplied to him by the FBI.[15]

By the 1960s, MID had developed into a greatly expanded and sophisticated American intelligence community targeted at civilians, and especially Blacks. According to one of Thompkins's *Commercial Appeal* articles, Army spying on civilians "expanded in the 60s because the FBI and local police forces proved unreliable."[16] In May 1963, military intelligence started using U-2 spy planes to watch Black protests in Birmingham, Alabama. More U-2 sorties on Blacks followed, as did even more expensive surveillance by the more advanced SR-71.[17]

But it was the fear of Martin Luther King, Jr.'s influence on Blacks that moved the U.S. military to prepare for an outbreak of war with Black America in April 1968, the month that King was assassinated.

## KILL M.L.K.

When riots erupted in Detroit in the summer of 1967, 363 of the 496 Black men arrested for firing rifles and shotguns told undercover Army intelligence agents that King was their "favorite Negro leader."[18] That alarmed the military establishment, which had insufficient war power within the country to halt an armed rebellion led by the charismatic Black leader, who it felt was taking advantage of them because of the civil unrest over the Vietnam War.

Their intelligence gathering convinced them of "King's plans to ignite violence and mayhem"[19] nationwide in April 1968 with his Poor People's campaign in Washington. These "West Point geniuses" had no "clue" how to stop King, wrote Thompkins. If an April uprising occurred, as expected by the military, there were not "enough combat-type troops to react,"

Ralph M. Stein, an analyst in the Pentagon's Counterintelligence Bureau in 1968, told Thompkins.[20]

The response was to mobilize the U.S. military into a state of preparedness against the Black community. Military planners "covertly dispatched Green Beret teams to make street maps, identify landing zones for riot troops and scout sniper sites in 39 racially explosive cities."[21] Some 124 cities were scouted as war zones, and, naturally, troublemakers were identified.

On April 4, 1968, Martin Luther King, Jr., stepped out onto the balcony of the Lorraine Motel in Memphis, Tennessee, and at 6:01 P.M. was killed by one bullet from an assassin's rifle that went through his jaw and neck. James Earl Ray was identified and convicted as the lone gunman. However, there is widespread belief that it was a government conspiracy that killed King and that Ray—a crook and a liar, whose testimony in part conflicts with that of witnesses and who is widely suspected of knowing more than he is telling—was only a patsy.

A syndicated columnist in the *Miami Herald*, citing my book *Black Lies, White Lies* as the source, reported that Army intelligence was conducting surveillance on King on April 4, the day he was murdered.[22] The author dismissed that fact as irrelevant and said that watching and killing King were worlds apart. He would be absolutely correct if King were being shadowed by the Boy Scouts, but as I explained in my book, the surveillance team was composed of twelve Green Berets of the 20th Special Forces Group, a unit that was notorious for being the dumping ground for "crazy guys" who had worked in Vietnam in murky clandestine operations with the CIA and similar groups.[23]

I also reported in my book that, according to Thompkins, the day before King was killed, he was monitored by Army agents from the 111th Military Intelligence Group from a sedan filled with electronic equipment.[24]

In December 1997, retired Army intelligence agents who monitored King in Memphis in the days before he was murdered there spoke publicly for the first time. They denied any "foreknowledge of the assassination."[25] As many as ten undercover agents of the 111th Military Intelligence Group were in Memphis and some of their arrivals and departures coincided with King's arrivals and departures, newly declassified documents show.[26]

In *Orders to Kill*, William Pepper identifies the masterminds of the conspiracy against King as a "cabal of government leaders and organized crime figures."[27] Pepper also resurrects Ray's mysterious handler Raul, who could be forced to come forward if a new trial were ordered. Raul now allegedly lives in Westchester County, New York. The accused man denies that he is the mysterious Raul. He also claims to be a retiree with a modest home but is represented by one of New York's most expensive law firms.[28]

King's family has publicly stated their belief that Ray was an innocent front-man for a conspiratorial cabal and that Lyndon Baines Johnson, the thirty-sixth President of the United States, bears direct responsibility for the assassination.[29]

The existence of a conspiracy and of Raul are debunked as imaginary by the mainstream press that believes conspiracy theorists only succeed in persuading those who are already convinced. Among the most outspoken is author David Garrow, who is certain that Ray pulled the trigger and who accused the King family of being "irresponsible and misinformed."[30] But Garrow obviously dismisses the evidence that moved the House Select Committee on Assassinations to conclude in 1978 that indeed a conspiracy had been behind King's death.[31]

Following the Select Committee's findings, a number of questions still remain unanswered. Was James Earl Ray working for a group of White supremacists from the St. Louis area who paid him $50,000 to assassinate Martin Luther King, Jr.? Was there a shadowy gunrunner, Raul, who was James Earl Ray's control in an alleged conspiracy to murder King? Was there close to King a Black informant known as Copperhead, who today is a popular Democratic legislator? Chances are that we will never know the answers to those questions. The Illuminati Ruling Class Conspiracy's hold on the truth is too great. One thing is clear, though: Blacks who raise their voices to demand justice and human rights are routinely killed.

## THE ASSASSINATION OF MALCOLM X

At 3:00 P.M. on February 21, 1965, Malcolm X was assassinated in front of four hundred witnesses on the stage of New York City's Audubon Ballroom in Harlem. Shortly afterward, three men were brought to trial and found guilty of the murder. But circumstances surrounding the trial, the assassination itself, accounts in the press, and subsequent actions were so peculiar that to this day the question of who killed Malcolm is unanswered.

For over twenty years, beginning at a time when interest in the subject was at its nadir and mention of any of Malcolm's teachings was enough to get you kicked out of the television business, I have conducted an investigation on national television of the circumstances surrounding the death of Malcolm X. After examining Malcolm's life and death, I have concluded that the facts do not point to the clear-cut conclusion that Elijah Muhammad's Nation of Islam gave "the call" to kill Malcolm.

Beyond a doubt, members of the Nation of Islam pulled the triggers of the guns that blasted Malcolm into martyrdom, but a great many among the members of the Nation of Islam were undercover police and FBI agenturs. It is estimated that four of the five top posts in the Nation were held by police and government informants. So even if the Nation of Islam gave the order to assassinate Malcolm X, we must ask who exactly gave the order, a racist government faction or a manipulated, Malcolm-hating Nation of Islam agitated by Minister Louis X, now known as Minister Louis Farrakhan? Or was it the Illuminati, which was manipulating both of these entities to keep control of its most lucrative drug market and to maintain a passive Black population, an oppressed underclass whom oppressed Whites could blame for all of the ills of society that were in fact being engendered by the Illuminati Ruling Class Conspiracy.

Despite revisionist history, Malcolm was not widely admired among Blacks, especially the middle class, because he preached separatism at a time when most Blacks pursued assimilation. Even Blacks branded him a "radical militant" because of his outspoken attitude toward Whites. By any objective standard, however, Malcolm X was a great man, primarily because he would always accept change as an inevitable part of intellectual and spiritual growth. He, in fact, rejected the dialectic of Black-White enmity after his trip to Mecca.

After his break with the Nation, Malcolm broadened his scope to include the international scene. Malcolm wanted to galvanize international public opinion against the United States for its oppression of Black Americans; to do so, he felt, he especially needed the support of independent African states, which would enable him to bring the racial question before the United Nations. So in the summer of 1964, Malcolm returned to Africa for a four-month tour of fourteen countries. In his autobiography, Malcolm notes that he was followed throughout Africa by unidentified persons, one of whom he described as "a thin-lipped, olive-skinned man."[32]

On July 23, 1964, Malcolm was in Cairo, Egypt, to deliver a scathing attack on America's domestic and foreign policies before an African summit conference. Shortly after that address, he collapsed in his hotel room with severe abdominal pain. According to Eric Norden, in an article in *The Murder of Malcolm X*, Malcolm was rushed to a Cairo hospital, suffering from toxic poisoning, and had to have his stomach pumped.[33] Malcolm later said he had been deliberately poisoned. Throughout the fall of 1964, Malcolm worked primarily on his plan to indict America in the United Nations. According to Norden, Malcolm had been under surveillance since he broke with the Nation of Islam, but now there were as many as "three different agents shadowing him at one time."[34]

In early February 1965, Malcolm flew to London to address the Council of African Organizations. From there he was scheduled to fly to Paris to deliver another speech. However, on February 9, when his plane landed in France, he was not allowed to step off the plane and was ordered by agents of the French government to leave the country immediately. Later, Malcolm said that his being barred from France led him to believe that the plotters of his death were much bigger than the Nation of Islam. Malcolm confided to Alex Haley on February 20, 1965, the day before he was murdered, "The more I keep thinking about this thing, the things that have been happening lately, I'm not at all sure it's the members of the Nation of Islam. I know what they can do, and what they can't, and they can't do some of the stuff recently going on."[35]

On February 20, Malcolm X called a meeting of his new group, the Organization of Afro-American Unity. That night, he stayed alone at the New York Hilton Hotel. A Hilton house detective later reported that three Black men asked about the location of Malcolm's room that evening. On February 21, Malcolm left the hotel in his blue Oldsmobile and drove to the Audubon Ballroom, where his organization's meeting was to take place. He entered the main ballroom about 2:30 P.M. Shortly after 3:00 P.M., approximately four hundred people had crowded into the ballroom, sitting on folding wooden chairs.[36]

The February 22, 1965, edition of *The New York Times* reconstructed what happened from eyewitness accounts. One of Malcolm's aides introduced him. The applause stopped, and the people sat down. Malcolm lifted his goateed face and said, *"Al Salaam Alikim."* The crowd murmured its response of "Peace be with you also." And then the assassin's decoys made their move. They were in a middle row, and they stood up and started pushing each other. One was saying, "Get your hands out of my pocket; stop messing with my pocket."[37]

Malcolm's bodyguards started to move toward them to break it up. And up on the stage, Malcolm stepped out from behind the lectern, saying, "Now, brothers, break it up; let's cool it." Alone on the stage, with one hand up in the air, he made a perfect target. A man—police say it was Thomas Hagen—ran down the aisle with a shotgun. When the shotgun was right in front of Malcolm X, both barrels raked him.

Several questions arise from press accounts of what happened that day. In all three New York morning newspapers, descriptions were given of the capture of two suspects at the Audubon immediately after the murder. In later editions of the same papers and from then on, only one suspect was said to have been captured at the scene by police, and the press never questioned this discrepancy.

The February 22, 1965, *New York Times* stated: "The police indicated two suspects were being questioned." One of those suspects was identified as Thomas Hagen. In a later paragraph, the capture of the second suspect was described. The *Times* reported that Patrolman Thomas Hoy, twenty-two, who had been stationed outside the 166th Street entrance of the Audubon, said that when he "heard the shooting," he rushed in. He saw Malcolm lying on the stage and "grabbed a suspect," who, he explained, was being chased by Malcolm's followers. "As I brought him to the front of the ballroom, the crowd began beating me and the suspect," Patrolman Hoy recounted. He said he put this man, not otherwise identified later, into a police car to be taken to the Wadsworth Avenue station.[38]

A late city edition of the same paper indicated that only one person, Thomas Hagen, was captured at the scene. There is no further mention of a second suspect from then on. In the February 22 early edition of the *New York Daily News,* the same discrepancy occurred: "Two men and the reputed assassin were taken by police from the hands of a howling mob of Malcolm's followers. Both men were spirited away by the police."[39] Again, later editions made no further mention of a second man.

Because of the mystery surrounding the second suspect, several independent writers in lesser-known publications wondered if he could have been a police agent. Other questions followed. What had the man arrested by Patrolman Hoy done to make the crowd think him a suspect? Why did the police not release this suspect's name, as they had Thomas Hagen's? Was there any connection between the government's surveillance of Malcolm and his assassination? The mysterious second man was described by eyewitnesses at the Audubon Ballroom as a "tight-lipped, olive-skinned man with slanted eyes,"[40] an echo of Malcolm's description of a man he said followed him throughout Africa and Europe.

Malcolm X warned Blacks that outside forces had targeted Black communities for drugs long before the drug threat became a popular issue, and certainly long before drugs devastated White communities. Novelist Jay Kennedy believes that it was because of his opposition to drugs in the inner cities, the Chinese drug cartels' first American stronghold, that the People's Republic of China had him killed.[41] As you will see in Chapter 8, this explanation fits the facts of the drug war waged against America by the Illuminati Ruling Class Conspiracy.

## DIVIDED WE FALL

In recent years, there have been even more insidious drug and propaganda attacks upon Black communities. External forces have overwhelmed Black neighborhoods with heroin and co-caine and White society has been tacitly encouraged to blame the victims for their "moral weakness" and "criminal tenden-cies." The fears of a shrinking White majority of its loss of gov-ernment entitlements have been stirred up by statist affirmative action programs. It is such fears and manipulated perceptions among Blacks and Whites that may be driving us toward a race war. And if the plot succeeds and we do fight each other, at the end there will only be Black and White American losers and Illuminati Ruling Class rulers.

I have come to believe that the perennially strained "race relations" between Blacks and Whites are the result of manipu-lation by the ruling oligarchy for the purpose of preventing a unified population that could focus on the conquest of America by a cabal of elitists. Affirmative action is a case in point. Touted as a program designed to foster equality, it almost exclusively builds mistrust and division.

In the affirmative action world, Blacks have 100 percent of nothing. Only a handful of them get any help, and the ethnic beneficiaries cluster among the most affluent and the best edu-cated in each group. Middle-class White women, of course, get the lion's share (estimated at 80 percent) of the jobs and busi-ness opportunities that result from these class preferences. For instance, after Clinton's announced initiative, "Mend it, don't end it" (thesis), to reform affirmative action for Blacks, I sus-pected that the fix was already in. Therefore, it came as no sur-prise when shortly afterward Clinton announced that all White women could be declared as "socially disadvantaged," therefore eligible for the bulk of business set-aside preferences by the gov-ernment. The Hegelian conspirators wanted affluent White women to have a greater stake in affirmative action so they would become a policing force to restrain Blacks' near monop-oly and, at the same time, preserve the program as a means of government control over White women and Blacks and as a wedge issue between all Blacks and Whites. As a result, both groups remain divided and conquered.

Even within the Black community, it pits the middle class against the underclass. Affirmative action, as it has been traditionally practiced, is a program in which those who are professionally qualified, but need protection from discrimination, crowd out those who need remedial help, effectively preventing the latter from having the opportunity to aquire needed job skills, especially computer training, that might enable them to get out of poverty and/or into the middle class. Under the current Hegelian system of government-imposed synthesis, any affluent group or individual can be arbitrarily declared disadvantaged and feast at the statist deity's trough of plenty.

The result of this elitist fig leaf is that White women and the mostly middle-class qualified achievers from non-White ethnic groups who no longer need help, and certainly not preference, are preferred while poor Blacks and Hispanics who reap no benefits from affirmative action are made the scapegoats and blamed for not having improved their lot, despite, the logic goes, the sacrifice that the White population has made to help them. That failure demonstrates that Blacks and Hispanics are irresponsible and even perhaps a genetically inferior group, some argue.

## AFFIRMATIVE ACTION: THE WEDGE ISSUE FOR A RACE WAR

The policy called affirmative action was never based on a true concern for Black people, as both friend and foe of the plan tend to believe, and certainly not on a concern for the poor and unqualified because it is exclusively for a qualified middle economic class. In this Hegelian scheme, the imposed synthesis reaffirms and preserves the state as God and the individual's statist duty to serve God, while preserving the perennial schism between Blacks and Whites. Americans aren't stupid, just unsuspecting and naive about conspiracies.

The typical American has never heard of Georg W. F. Hegel and has never studied the science of economics. And for good reason. The average American college graduate has had only one course in economics, and it used a textbook based on the Marxism of John Maynard Keynes. Furthermore, there is no textbook that deals with the historical or political theory of the Hegelian dialectic, thanks to Hegelians themselves, such as John Dewey, a member of The Order who helped plan America's modern educational system.

In such a world, where the public is systematically and institutionally deprived of the information necessary to make informed economic and political decisions, the Illuminati Ruling Class Conspiracy flourishes. Its so-called crisis managers use and plan conflict to achieve their objective of German Hegelian rule by an economic royalty, via the respective governments of the world.

## The Hegelian Conspiracy: Thought Control

The German root philosophy of G.W.F. Hegel—the state as God, freedom resulting only from worship of the government, rejection of individualism, the state (actually the power elite that controls the state) as absolute reason—must be kept secret from Americans whose Constitutional tradition is one of individual rights, a subservient government, and a supernatural deity as a personal God. That is why in America, the Illuminati is forced to go through the motions of democracy; in banana republics, it rules outright through bare-knuckled dictatorships. However, America is becoming more openly ruled as a totalitarian state.

This is a reminder of how the Hegelian process works: First (thesis), the government announces a new policy or plan that implies a loss for both sides. Second (antithesis), both sides engage each other in a conflict because they are psychologically conditioned to project onto the opposing group their anxieties about losing ground. Third (synthesis), after the government-induced threats of the loss of benefits, the state demonstrates its so-called conflict management skills and imposes a compromise (synthesis), which is bound to generate a new (thesis) plan, which in turn is inevitably followed by a fresh round of conflict (antithesis) and compromise (synthesis) with the government exercising power over the two hostile groups. The vicious cycle of manipulation never ends.

American democracy has now succumbed to the Hegelian dialectical process and its use as a system of thought control. In that respect, there is no wedge issue that has been more successful in the public arena than affirmative action preference programs.

Do you believe that the current excuse to establish parity between historically disadvantaged groups and the White population, euphemistically called affirmative action preferences, is the best effort that a country as powerful as the United States can make? I don't. Therefore, I conclude that an affirmative action concept that diminishes opportunities for most Whites, demeans the small percentage of the upwardly mobile non-Whites who personally benefit, focuses on well-educated White women, and ignores all poor people is designed to achieve the maximum amount of group conflict and the minimum benefit to those who need it the most.

## AFFIRMATIVE OPPORTUNITY BASED ON ECONOMIC CLASS

Affirmative action preference programs to help Blacks get jobs in the corporate sector or entrance into college are not of much use to the average Black twelfth grader who reads four years behind the average White student, and affirmative action programs do absolutely nothing to close "the appalling, unacceptable racial gap in educational performances in the K-12 years."[42] Besides, the average Black student who is most likely to read at the same level as the average White student probably shares a similar socioeconomic status, which is arguably a better predictor of performance than race.

Thus, with little benefit to anyone but a group of hand-picked Blacks and other non-White ethnics, affirmative action's true purpose seems to be to allow the President to use race as a foil for his political objectives. For example, he used his ethnic agents to raise an army of intellectuals and fair-minded people who will politically bond with him to save affirmative action and subsequently help advance his hidden political agenda. The President began this recruitment campaign with the appointment of a philosophically one-sided race commission and a Clinton acolyte as its leader.

John Hope Franklin, the chairman, promptly narrowed a so-called national dialogue on race to a discussion of affirmative action and welcomed only those who agreed with *his* view and conclusion that endemic White racism is the problem and affirmative action is the solution. Clinton's panel never focused on racial healing; it defined itself right from the beginning as a pro-middle class advocacy group.

Dissenters in this nondemocratic debate were treated with contempt. The Blacks who disagreed with Franklin's liberal Clinton politics were labeled Uncle Toms, and the Whites who were not politically correct were, naturally, labeled racists. Both noncooperating groups were disinvited from the so-called healing process, which was a very odd way to bring about a two-way dialogue on racial matters and mend the fences. The idea of Blacks and Whites and other groups getting along was so thoroughly discredited by Franklin's narrow-mindedness and unscholarly broadsides against the most egregious anti-Black Blacks that even the friends of affirmative action were compelled to attack the unfairness and intransigence of this alleged racial healing process, just, I suspect, as its Hegelian planners wanted. The Clinton administration was pulling the strings behind the scenes. With friends like Bill Clinton, affirmative action and poor Blacks and Hispanics don't need Republican enemies.

The Republicans and conservatives played the anticipated role as the destroyer of the very idea that people who are not White have a legitimate right to ask for help from the nation as a whole. This niggardly attitude sheds no light on solving the problems that affirmative action acknowledges but ignores. The conservative role in this antithesis (conflict) phase is to raise the specter of "reverse discrimination" (an oxymoron) and scare the pants off the White population.

As both sides demonstrate quite eloquently, neither the Republicans or the Democrats, nor the liberals or conservatives, all of whom work for the power elite, are interested in helping the American people get along better or improve their lot. These agenturs are like their puppet masters, orchestrating the decline of the nation, notwithstanding their ethnic or cultural background or their political affiliation. They are Hegelians, first and foremost.

For both the Democrats and the Republicans, affirmative action is a political football. Posing a thesis and creating an antithesis of conflict around the implementation of affirmative action as an anti-White program has only led to an end to affirmative action, and to a loss of any empathy that most Whites may have felt toward Blacks and Hispanics.

Clinton's affirmative action advocacy and the Republican opposition to the idea are both designed to further marginalize Blacks and Hispanics. The conflict management of the preference policy selects a William Buckley, intellectual elitist type to attack preferences from a mythical "right," and Faustian Oxonian Rhodes Scholar spooks such as President Clinton to defend it from a make-believe "left" in order to politicize an entrenched conflict. For example, Clinton's strategy of faint praise for Colin Powell successfully obfuscated the fact that millions of people who need an opportunity are not getting it because preference programs for well-qualified people are disguised as programs for the ordinary citizen.

In defending affirmative action, Clinton is clever enough to imply that Colin Powell's success is entirely the result of a preference program, a broad brush stroke that paints over all of the toil, sweat, brains, and tears of the Blacks in the military who have achieved their rank by virtue of performance. However, Clinton conveniently leaves out the crucial fact that General Powell had graduated second in his class from the prestigious Command and General Staff School before he was placed on the all-White list for consideration for promotion to brigadier general.

The issue is that a man of Powell's achievements was omitted from the eligibility list because of his race. Affirmative action only did for Powell what it should have done; it protected his Constitutional right not to be discriminated against because of his race. Clinton twisted this fact to suggest that Powell became a general because he was Black. But Colin Powell is neither typical of the Black population nor of the American population; he is above average in most respects. What should be the number one priority of the nation is a program that provides opportunity for the typical American who needs a hand up. Programs designed to help the country at large should not be confused with efforts to protect the rights of those who are qualified but overlooked because of race or gender.

Clinton, the alleged policy "wonk," pretends that he cannot find the solution to reform affirmative action, as he so effortlessly proposes a plethora of new ideas for health care, foreign policy, or the budget. He could end discrimination in the workplace for college-trained non-White ethnics and women by simply doing his job—getting the Equal Employment Opportunity

Commission to fine violators and giving the agency the clout and the resources to do so. Instead, Clinton avoids the obvious solutions and focuses on preferences that offend Whites and demean Blacks, amid a backdrop of appointments of a handful of privileged non-Whites, his political emissaries to control opinion in their respective ethnic subpopulations.

In the business world, preference hires in the workplace are a necessary component to reach targeted markets domestically and globally. To the business minded, diversity for its own sake is a waste of time. But many have learned that work force diversity has a bottom line. Middle-class Blacks, for example, make more money selling insurance to middle-class Blacks for All-State Insurance than Whites did, All-State learned. Affirmative action in the corporate sector is perceived very favorably because affirmative action in the business sector was always a natural bridge to cultural diversity, a bottom-line program that increases profits. On the average, companies are more efficient and make more money with more diverse work forces; the government Hegelians can't stop that economic reality. See my book *Black Lies, White Lies* for a more thorough discussion of this issue.

And notwithstanding its merits, agitating for benefits for Blacks at the expense of Whites on the basis of the slavery of Blacks in America is fraught with problems: For example, slavery was an upper-class WASP institution, most of the non-WASP ancestors of today's White population arrived in America after slavery, and most of the Anglo-Saxons during slavery lived one cut above the Black slaves. The average White was not a slave owner and not very well off. Racist, perhaps.

The Hegelian process will also reaffirm many Whites' faith in statism and the government's defense of their hegemony as a majority power. According to its architect, Hegel, the debate (antithesis) gives both sides "the satisfaction of feeling themselves to count for something."[43] Both sides are losers, but both sides will believe the system of statism works for them. In a nutshell, that's Hegelian control of political thought.

I know what you're thinking: The present government-imposed synthesis is good because it produces compromise decisions. My answer is that if the compromises are intended exclusively to create conflict between groups, rather than a compromise (synthesis) that solves the predicament and improves life for all concerned, it is counterproductive.

Contrary to commonsense logic, today's class-based affirmative action is a Hegelian prototype whose government-imposed synthesis denies those in the lower socioeconomic class the opportunity to obtain the skills needed for employment. Even an elitist Black named Julian Bond boasted that affirmative action is not a program to help those in the lowest socioeconomic class. Affirmative action was obviously introduced by the government neither to create economic or educational parity between Blacks and Whites nor to alleviate poverty or the lack of education among the poor of all groups. Only an affirmative opportunity program providing for preferential treatment based on socioeconomic factors and proportionate to a targeted subpopulation's aggregate numbers on welfare can meet the stated goals of affirmative action.

## SOLUTION: OPPORTUNITY, NOT PRIVILEGE

The key to helping the entire Black community, the philosophical starting point for affirmative action, is to give preference to poor Blacks and low-income members of other culturally ethnic groups and to develop the majority of Americans who are poor, most of whom are White, as the backbone of America's twenty-first-century, information-technology work force. The result of affirmative opportunity: The nation prospers and the talk of a race war moves away from center stage and once again becomes a fringe issue.

Let me propose an affirmative "opportunity" model to replace the current affirmative action predicament. Fairness and an evenhanded treatment of everyone, without a reserved status for any community of interest, is the only way to help the entire country and the only way to do that is to help (prefer, really) those who are the most economically disadvantaged. Socioeconomic status in America is largely disguised as a race issue. The twenty-first century will not focus on race and gender. It will be a millennium of the haves and the have-nots. The haves will have a computer and the have-nots will not.

If affirmative action were defined by need, which is determined by economic class, it would help the poor of all races, as well as the middle class. Affirmative opportunities, such as computer training programs that lead to good-paying jobs in six to twelve months and move the unskilled into the middle class, would break the poverty cycle. It is apparent that if you wanted to help Blacks and bring the maximum number of all poor and disadvantaged Americans into the mainstream, that is what you would do. Moreover, there would be little, if any, political opposition to such a universal and practical program.

Only the highly skilled can succeed in our new high-technology-based economy. Since most people in the United States are White, Whites in the lowest income categories must also get a preference in any viable program that will ultimately help the country. Blacks, as a result of centuries of systemic oppression, are found in lower socioeconomic classes in disproportionately large numbers. Therefore, those Blacks who are stuck on the lowest rung of the socioeconomic ladder would receive, based on need determined by economic class, a disproportionately larger portion of affirmative action resources for training for technical-information jobs and entrepreneurship, for college preparation, and so on.

As this plan proceeds and succeeds in producing much-needed information-technology workers (346,000 high-tech jobs are now vacant) and college graduates, fewer people would live in poverty. The K-12 educational gap and poverty overall among the non-White ethnics and the White poor would be sharply reduced. And the disproportionate percentage of Blacks eligible for this affirmative opportunity would be reduced permanently.

## POLARIZED ASSIMILATION

Unachievable assimilation programs that polarize and racial preferences that are designed to assist the middle class and stigmatize Blacks are part of a conspiracy against all Americans.

Blacks do not take Whites' jobs on a large scale with affirmative action preferences; government policies such as those behind trade agreements export them by the millions to countries offering low-wage labor. A majority of Whites favor giving Blacks a hand up, but not a preference for jobs or college. White indifference to Blacks' aspirations is not the major contributing factor in Black failure. Government-induced dependence has sapped the competitiveness of many Blacks and has institutionalized transgenerational poverty, which, in turn, has guaranteed more dependence on welfare statism. This control of the population ensures the Conspiracy's hegemony.

It is a scheme that was perfected by the Cecil Rhodes Oxford Illuminati. The purpose of the Illuminati welfare system is not to elevate the poor—who are believed to come from inferior genetic stock—but to warehouse them for the benefit of the Illuminati Ruling Class Conspiracy. Why has the British-influenced American Establishment over the past several decades taken trillions of dollars from taxpayers and given it to poor Blacks and Whites so that they could remain idle, without teaching them the few work skills that would enable them to become employed? It is a deliberate campaign of triage against them.

Triage is genocide in slow motion; the government kills off those it no longer needs with unemployment, drugs, disease, or whatever is handy—or a deliberate policy of "benign neglect."

Today, more and more technically illiterate Whites are also being put into this triage system. The new information-driven economy has a zero tolerance for excess labor; it can no longer afford to subsidize a preference program that is based on White supremacy, and America's new niggers are the technologically displaced of all races. In the past several decades, White men have lost more economically than any other group. With the increasing loss of their unjustified preference, White males are for the first time being forced to take a realistic look at statist America, and the psychological adaptation to this triage process is extremely traumatic for many of them, who have reacted with denial and paranoia. White women are receiving a much larger share of the available jobs, mainly because they are increasingly the most highly skilled group. However, some White men find it easier and more ego gratifying to blame Blacks, an "inferior race" that allegedly plays unfairly by demanding preferential treatment, for their loss of opportunity and standing. This psychological compensation may help White men justify their image of themselves as noble victims, but it denies reality.

The problem is, there is nothing noble about being a victim, and projection is a neurotic, low-level defense mechanism. Moreover, when Blacks perceive White men as the enemy merely because those White men want to keep their jobs, then Blacks are demonstrating a comparable neurosis; that is an inappropriate way of dealing with a conspiracy against all Americans—Black, White, Red, Yellow, and Brown—of a similar economic status. There can be no winner when those caught up in the affirmative action controversy begin to play the blame game. The situation has been designed solely to create racial antagonism. Even the handful of those whom affirmative action programs actually benefit are stigmatized as losers, and are tracked in their professional careers as incompetents.

Blacks have historically understood the fundamentally oppressive nature of this system, but have mistakenly placed the blame for all of its faults on the presumed separatist attitudes of all Whites. The Conspiracy's Hegelian divide-and-conquer system feeds Black and White fears and gives people like Thomas W. Chittum something to worry and write about. The difference is that Chittum and millions of other Whites are mentally enlisting in what I euphemistically call the Ozzie-and-Harriet militia, America's "Manchurian candidates." Though they may not have been hypnotically programmed, they are nevertheless being psychologically prepared to kill Blacks, Browns, Yellows, Reds, Jews, and non-WASP White immigrants when the appropriate cue is given. Blacks, however, are the primary targets of the "Manchurian candidates," who are becoming psychologically predisposed to ignite over a predetermined stimulus, which can take any one of many forms—a jury nullification decision, renewed affirmative action for Blacks, an independent act of violence of a Black against a White, urban riots, even incendiary rhetoric directed toward Whites.

## A MANUFACTURED RACE WAR

Carl Rowan's *The Coming Race War in America: A Wake-up Call* gives a textbook example of divisive racial dialectics. Tom Wicker, a contemporary White political pundit and former *New York Times* columnist, opined that Rowan's book is an "overwrought" treatment of the subject.[44] Rowan, a Black former Trilateralist and progagandist for Lyndon Johnson, offers an apocalyptic message in divide-and-conquer rhetoric. In my opinion, Rowan fuels the fears of Whites with his threat of impending war, while reinforcing the stereotype of violent Blacks. His race-war scenario is followed by a pleading for more welfare statism, and an Establishment solution to the predicament it created in the first place.

*Civil War II: The Coming Breakup of America* is Thomas Chittum's tome predicting a racial Armageddon in the United States. The author is a former soldier of fortune and Vietnam veteran who now spends his time speaking out on behalf of White people, although he was never called upon to do so, and spreading the message of a "deadly war—already in its infancy"—between Whites and a non-WASP population that has, he says, turned America into a living hell for White Anglo-Saxon Protestants.

> Social, political and economic forces are pulling America apart and driving her toward a bloody war that may fracture the nation into several different countries, divided along ethnic lines.
>     Riots . . . gangs . . . militias . . . exploding crime rates . . . mass immigration . . . rising unemployment . . . falling wages . . . these are all factors that will fuel the fires of war.[45]

Compounding an already dangerous situation is the inciteful behavior of a few Blacks. One Black zealot boasted, "I want to be one of the flamethrowers of God, break White folks' backs. I want to give you hell all the way to your [Whites'] graves. I ain't scared to die, and I'm ready to kill."[46] Having already started the fire of race-baiting, Conspiracy agenturs continue to use such inflammatory rhetoric as fuel in the hopes of igniting an outbreak of warfare.

The war-eager White supremacists want to persuade normal White people that all Blacks are armed and dangerous, and ready to attack White neighborhoods. In his book, in a section called "Civil War II Checklist," Chittum cites an article in *Harper's* magazine by Paul Butler, a Black lawyer, that urges Black jurors to consider not convicting Black defendants. Jury nullification such as this, Chittum stresses, is a significant omen of an impending violent confrontation between Blacks and Whites. Besides being unconstitutional, the idea of freeing a criminal solely because he is Black sends an unmistakably anti-White message. It is also an unreasonable, unnecessary provocation that can only heighten the readiness of the entire White population to seek a "final solution" to its "Black problem." This is the kind of racial confrontation the Illuminists need in order to continue to rule.

## THE WHITE WAR PLAN

"America was born in blood," Chittum writes. "America suckled on blood. America gorged on blood and grew into a giant, and America will drown in blood. This is the spectre that is haunting America, the spectre of Civil War II, a second civil war that will shatter America into several new ethnically based nations."[47]

If you conclude that he's a racist or that his book is "a call to violence," Chittum insists, you are missing the point. Rather, his war plan is the result of an "objective examination of the historic, demographic, political, economic, and military developments" that force him to conclude that "reverse discrimination" is a greater threat to national security than international terrorism. You can sum up his "objective examination" in two words: affirmative action.[48]

The objective facts that affirmative action has preferred more middle-class White women than Blacks, and that it has done more for a handful of middle-class Blacks than the multitude of disadvantaged ones, were obviously omitted from this former computer programmer's calculations, as was the strong possibility that affirmative action is a divide-and-rule wedge issue whose main purpose is to elicit from the White population as many irrational Timothy McVeighs and "objective" Thomas Chittums as possible. Chittum's graphic vision of the racial Armageddon includes White-manned artillery "blasting our cities to flaming wastelands infested with psychotic snipers . . . packs of feral dogs . . . doomed refugees. . . . Bands of guerillas . . . raping, looting, murdering. . . . The hungry will fight to the death over scraps of garbage. . . . Behold the vision of Civil War II."[49]

In "thinking the unthinkable," Chittum becomes the self-appointed war strategist for a "dominant group" that is threatened by the loss of its hegemony. Any movement toward social and economic equality when considered in the light of the projected reduction of the White majority, from nearly 80 percent of the population to just over 50 percent by the year 2050, upsets America's delicate balance of power and is totally unacceptable, Chittum writes. Chittum is not alone with this fear. Another White man has said: "We don't want to be a minority in our own country."[50] Some Whites believe that the cultural cohesion and stability of the nation depends on a WASP-assimilated White majority and its democratic majority tyranny. Chittum may not be a racist, as he maintains he is not, but he has almost total disregard for the Constitution or the Declaration of Independence. However, Constitutional integrity is the least of Chittum's concerns. How to kill and contain Hispanics, his main worry, and Blacks, unfortunately, is the focus of his obsession.

Chittum offers key signs that can serve as barometers for "our inevitable slide into all-out ethnic warfare" and aid us in determining when "the multiethnic American Empire will shatter."[51] Those signs include the use of attack aircraft and armored vehicles by the local police, which came to pass in 1992 in Los

Angeles with the flushing out of snipers in a Black housing project. The Los Angeles Police Department's handling of that conflagration moved beyond riot control and took on the trappings
of war, according to Chittum. Armed ethnic militias are another
sign, of which the armed militia of Korean merchants defending
their property against an armed militia of Blacks during the Los
Angeles riot are but one example. Barricades erected to keep
"foreigners" out are another sign; such barricades represent,
says Chittum, psychological boundaries in the hearts and minds
of the ethnic groups that deploy them. Such ethnocentric attitudes, he predicts, will eventually lead to attacks on police and
military installations. Intuitively, the rioters are psychologically
forming a new nation.

As a would-be historian basing his predictions on an analysis
of past events, Chittum is completely inept; all of his criteria for
a race war are historically spent, contradicted by actual events.
Blacks faced off against tanks and helicopters in the streets in
Detroit in 1967. Irate Jews laid siege to a police precinct in
New York in 1991. Armed Black gang members and Korean
merchants do not constitute militias. And psychological and
ethnic separatism and nationalism have been among the core
values of White America since it was founded. Many Blacks have
now arrived at the same conclusion. But these are not the criteria for a race war. Instead, they are only the flimsy excuses that
Chittum uses to rationalize his warlike impulses; the same can
be said for the threat he perceives from an alleged explosion of
the Black population, which in reality will increase only mod-
estly (by about 2 percent) by the year 2050.

No, Chittum and the real armed-and-dangerous militias of
disgruntled White supremacists are looking to find a pretext,
and in its absence are willing to fabricate one, for starting a civil
war—but for reasons that are totally removed from the defense
of an embattled White America. Indeed, they are driven by the
pathological need to commit genocide against Blacks, Hispan-

ics, other non-Whites, immigrants, non-Anglo Saxons, and Jews.

In sum, the presumed threat of Blacks to the nation, and of Mexicans to California, is merely a red herring, a pretext for eliminating all non-WASPs. Chittum's racial attitudes are evidence that he is another "Manchurian candidate," diabolically programmed to kill his enemy's enemy and then die in his own excrement.

From a false premise and a faulty historical analysis, Chittum, the Manchurian candidate and victim of the Illuminati Ruling Class Conspiracy, proceeds to the examination of the conditions necessary to fire the first shot or slit the first Black or Latino throat: active support from at least 10 percent of the marginal Anglo-Saxon subpopulation; "secure sanctuaries" from which to launch attacks on non-White population centers; and "ongoing aid from a foreign government"—money, arms, diplomacy.[52] In my opinion, 10 percent of the White population has already been psychologically conditioned by the Hegelian spooks of the Illuminati to murder Blacks.

To make matters worse, this doomsday scenario is being exacerbated by, I estimate, about 10 percent of the Black population that believe that Blacks can win a violent confrontation—and by an Illuminati-spook-dominated Black ruling class cabal that has ever more stridently accelerated its demands for statist preferences, which can only succeed in driving more and more moderate Whites into the arms of the White supremacist militias. There are also signs now emerging of cooperation between Syria and other Illuminati-financed, terrorist-sponsoring nations and American White militias. These White supremacist "patriots" and America's enemies confer openly on the Internet about destroying America.

Chittum finds theoretical support for an approaching war in Gore Vidal's *The Decline and Fall of the American Empire*, a 1992 polemic in which Vidal states that America is "now in a prerevolutionary time," ripe for an ethnic rebellion similar to that which occurred in the old USSR in the late 1980s, and in a 1995 work by Peter Brimelow entitled *Alien Nation,* the thesis of which is that America's borders are vanishing under a "vast whirling mass of illegal immigrants."[53] An *Atlantic Monthly* article concluded that Brimelow's proposal to deport all illegal aliens could only be accomplished "at gunpoint."[54]

Chittum also draws inspiration from the perennial Republican presidential wannabe and CNN resident Nativist, Patrick Buchanan, whose ideas have influenced Chittum's theory of Bantustans for Blacks, modeled after the South African Black enclaves bearing this same name. Chittum has adopted his champion's conclusion that the "racial resentments and ethnic hatreds" surrounding the debate over affirmative action during the 1996 California elections made it "clear that America is headed towards Balkanization."[55]

Chittum has concluded that the only viable solution to affirmative action preferences is a White-initiated bloody race war that totally isolates Blacks and Hispanics in segregated geographical regions of the country. Once again, Chittum offers Blacks two poor choices: perpetual White racism to protect the majority's privilege, or banishment for those who survive a race war to the southern tip of Florida and a Black Belt in the South, with Atlanta as the first capital of Black America.

Under the second scenario, a war's outcome would depend on strategic locations of various "enclaves," as Chittum calls his war zones. Despite a commitment from the military to recast itself in the 1990s into an internal security force "to provide domestic national assistance," Whites in enclaves to the north of Atlanta, for example, are "gone with the wind" because they can easily be surrounded by Blacks and the "federal cavalry" will be preoccupied up north with urban gangs. Not to worry, however; the military's "heavy firepower can be counted on in the inevitable showdown,"[56] the militarist consoles.

The "Nueva España" armies will run the Anglos out of Texas, New Mexico, Arizona, and southern California. Japan will invade the Northwest. Parts of Canada will join the Anglophile states of New England and return to their British roots in a confederation. If Whites can exit the South fast enough to outrun the sudden invasion of Blacks, Whites can form a "second Confederacy." The new "independent black nation" will replace today's Black Belt on the postwar map.

In addition to this scenario, Chittum provides war maps of selected states. Blacks of the Chattanooga, Tennessee, enclave and Whites in Dare County, North Carolina, "a snow White mini-Rhodesia," are surrounded by the opposite-race enemy. "They're history," Chittum predicts."[57]

Chittum believes that with the exception of a handful of Establishment writers like Buchanan and Charles Krauthammer, who in *Time* magazine predicted that "diversity and ethnic separatism" means that "America's destination is the Balkans,"[58] the majority of journalists are afraid to spit out the facts of a possible race war.

Chittum is not all wrong, despite his outlandish solution to the affirmative action issue and his population projections for 2050. He's right when he says there is enough Black racism to make Whites worry and that he is entitled to object to affirmative action without being labeled by a manipulative media as a racist. A racist he may be, but opposing affirmative action does not necessarily make him one. In the media, discussions of race relations are highly ritualized, and the only participants who are allowed are Illuminated spook types like Bill Clinton and Hegelian Negro acolytes like Harvard's Randall Kennedy who only create more tension between Blacks and Whites with their soliloquies.

Chittum says that the so-called war on drugs is a red herring designed to distract attention from the military's new domestic role of controlling the population as an army of occupation. If he's right, the government could make it easy for traffickers to bring drugs into targeted areas—as it did when it allowed Lucky Luciano to distribute heroin in the Black community in the 1940s—and create crime and chaos, then use the resulting turmoil as an excuse for a larger military role in those communities. Local police forces are being militarized with weapons and hardware donated by the military at a time when crime is going down. AK-47s, SWAT teams, and combat helicopters on local police forces are the result of a crime hysteria, whipped up by a fear of Black men. But their intended use could be against the emerging threat from an aroused White population.

Before we all rush into a deadly race-based war, perhaps we should pause and consider what Blacks and Whites have in common. The same conspiracy killed Martin Luther King, Jr., and Malcolm X, John F. Kennedy, and Robert Kennedy. The same people who poison White children's minds and sell them drugs poison Black children and murder them with drugs. The same someone or something has steered the richest nation in the world into bankruptcy. The same people who made an $80 billion profit from the Vietnam War got draft deferments for their elitist sons. The same Conspiracy that unconstitutionally confiscates Black property, confiscates White property. In short, the same Illuminati Ruling Class Conspiracy that oppresses Blacks oppresses Whites, Browns, Yellows, and Reds as well.

The steady stream of revelations of "government medical experiments and nuclear testing without informed consent and with dangerous consequences" for Americans of all stripes has convinced Ed Koch, a former mayor of New York, that "we were betrayed by our own government."[59] Koch calls for "an official ombudsman in government . . . to protect the people from the government."[60] America also needs, instead of armies of Blacks and Whites at one another's throats, an army of deprogrammers for the psychological victims of the racial hatred that has replaced patriotism.

## AN OFFER TO MY ENEMIES

The following is an open letter to Chittum, White supremacists, *Turner Diaries* freaks, and America's Ozzie-and-Harriet militia members:

Do you really believe that the psychotic idea of burning America down or blowing it up and killing its people in order to be able to rebuild it is patriotic? It is treasonous, and if you think that way, you are not fit to be called an American. You are trying to accomplish from the inside what even Karl Marx and the Illuminati knew was impossible with a gun from the outside. If you want to destroy America—no matter what her faults are—you are worse than the freedom-hating Illuminist-Communists who are stealing both of us blind.

If you are so American, why are you not man or woman enough—brave enough—to reach out to those who do not look like you but share your love for this land and fight for the human rights granted us by the Creator and taken from us by the Illuminati? Can you admit that your misplaced hate is wrong and destructive to even those you love? Obviously, you are aware that you and your White friends are also victims. Therefore, would it not be logical and productive if you and I jointly declared war on the real enemy.

If you do not already recognize how threatening the quest for human rights and Americanism can be to the Illuminati Ruling Class Conspiracy's grip on the United States, just consider the enormously positive impact on the nation's economic and educational advancement that would occur if Blacks and Whites realized that the racial strife between them is largely manufactured by evil people who consider both groups suckers. And both groups *are* suckers for playing the game of mutually assured destruction.

Rapprochement between Blacks and Whites is garlic to the

Illuminati Ruling Class Conspiracy vampire. Can you imagine the fear that would run through the heart of the evilarchy if Blacks and Whites, along with all other Americans, united in a common cause to reinstate democracy, reclaim their property, and seek God's guidance as we restore our human rights? Among these rights is the right not to be bussed as a token for liberal racism and to live with whoever we choose, as long as we do not violate the human rights of any other American.

Or are you more comfortable with your neurotic racism and second-class citizenship? Perhaps you enjoy your current status as an Oswald-style patsy, scheduled to die in your Illuminati masters' next war to protect the British oligarchy's financial empire and drug cartel. And why have you learned to hate me more than you love your children? It is their future you are helping the cabal destroy. What about a principled defense of human rights rather than assisting an ignominious slaughter of our freedom by the Illuminati Ruling Class Conspiracy?

No one with any self-respect from the other race is asking you to marry them, go to school with them, or live next door. Most people just want to live in peace with whoever wants peace and the love of God in their lives. Black people and White people are basically the same. Most of us are average; we have a few geniuses and a liberal sprinkling of fools. Put down your gun, my friend, and pick up the truth.

You heard right; I said "friend." You may not like me, and I may not particularly care for you, but you and I had better get one thing straight: We are all we have got. I am not interested in spending Sundays over at your house; I am obsessed with freedom. If you are a real American, you will work with me to eliminate the income tax and relegate the IRS to processing a national sales tax. We need to remove the Illuminati Seal of the Devil from our money and get the mark of the Beast out of our hands.

The most essential struggle is between good and evil. The

strife between White and Black is the representation of a society distorted by the Illuminati. Racism is the result of human beings' failure to improve themselves spiritually as well as materially. In the inner struggle between good and evil, we must all develop the courage to become spiritually empowered or all is lost for all of us.

# 8

# THE DRUG WAR
# AGAINST U. S.

*The only secret in the world is the history you don't know.*
—HARRY S. TRUMAN

Novelist George Orwell was an insider in British Illuminati Freemasory who had been recruited, according to author John Daniel, by Aleister Crowley, icon to many rock and roll stars and "the Beast 666," into the Masonic sex and drug lodge, the Order of the Golden Dawn.[1] In *1984*, George Orwell created a frighteningly realistic portrait of "Big Brother," a ubiquitous, oppressive government.

Some writers believe it was Orwell's covert warning of the Illuminati's plans to take control of the United States of America during the latter half of the twentieth century. *1984*, the secular humanist "peace" promised by the Illuminati Conspiracy, is now, and here's Orwell's insider portrayal of it:

Are you prepared to give your life? To commit murder?
To commit acts of sabotage which may cause the death

of hundreds of innocent people? To betray your country to foreign powers? To cheat, to forge, to blackmail, to corrupt the minds of children, to distribute habit-forming drugs, to encourage prostitution, to dissemi-nate venereal diseases; to do anything which is likely to cause demoralization and weaken the power of the peo-ple? Are you prepared to commit suicide, if and when we order you to do so?[2]

The Illuminati Ruling Class Conspiracy is controlling the United States through its hold on the money supply and is be-lieved by many to be destabilizing the country with drugs.

We have already seen how the British Illuminati oligarchy, with Cecil Rhodes leading the way, planned to gain control of America's money supply and politics through the creation of a central bank. The United States then "would fight Great Brit-ain's wars and pay her bills."[3] Once the Conspiracy succeeded in forcing the Fed on the American people, the United States did in fact save Britain in World War I and World War II, and guaranteed hegemony for British-controlled oil companies with the Persian Gulf War.

Beginning with China in the eighteenth century, according to Daniel, "destabilization of nations through drug addiction became Great Britain's foreign policy. This foreign policy con-tinues to this day."[4] Since 1978, "statistical data and analysis confirms that the United States is now the prime target of desta-bilization by the international drug trade—which we have shown can be identified with English Freemasonry."[5]

The data overwhelmingly confirm the thesis that the United States is being destabilized by the international drug trade. Sixty percent of all drugs sold worldwide—a trillion-dollar-a-year market—are purchased by Americans, who represent only 4 per-cent of the world's population. The illegal sales of drugs ac-count for "capital flight" that transfers half a trillion dollars a year out of the U.S. economy. "Stripped of our assets" through a debased currency and national debt, bleeding capital to the drug pushers, and paying the high social cost of drug addiction, the nation is dangerously unstable and headed for chaos and violence. It's not an accident, Daniel says.

> Destabilization begins by weakening an economy— through the loss of dollars sucked out of the economy through the illegal drug trade. In 1978, the worldwide revenue from illicit drug sales was estimated at $200 billion annually, with sixty percent of that gross coming from drugs sold in the United States alone. This means that $120 billion annually is lost from our economy. By 1986, universal illegal drug sales more than doubled, topping $500 billion, with over $300 billion annually drained from the United States economy. These figures were confirmed by many sources throughout the 1980s. *U.S. News & World Report,* on March 18, 1985, released a new study by Congress, which confirmed that the illegal drug trade had grown dramatically in the United States "at a rate of 10 billion dollars a year since 1978 to an estimated annual gross today of 110 billion dollars. Social costs, which include crime, treatment and drug enforcement, total 100 billion more. . . . The House Narcotics Committee reports that illicit drug use in the U.S. exceeds that of any other industrial nation and is emerging as one of this country's major health problems." What do all these figures mean? Simply that when cash is paid in illegal transactions for drugs and arms, our government gets no taxes for these transactions, and "capital flight" takes that money out of circulation in our nation.[6]

Destabilization can already be seen in the frequency and acceptance of violent outbreaks in the form of group rioting. A stock market crash would create the chaos and social disorder that the race-war fanatics need to provoke the average citizen to take up arms. As the Los Angeles–style food, class, and race riots escalate, the White race patriots are poised to create widespread anarchy. Law and order will cease. "Big Brother" will emerge to lead a permanently fractured, Balkanized, permanently Third World America. Of course, those groups thought to be non-American or non-Anglo-Saxon, which will be considered one and the same, will be disposed of by the crudest of methods. Welcome to *1984 America*.

## DRUGS: AN INSTRUMENT OF CONTROL

The Dutch established the historical precedent for the use of drugs by a national government for profit and Hegelian control over an entire population in the middle of the seventeenth century with their opium trade aimed at the Indonesians. The Dutch employed opium "as a useful means for breaking the moral resistance of Indonesians who opposed the introduction of their semi-servile but increasingly profitable plantation system. They deliberately spread the drug habits from the ports, where Arab traders used opium, to the countryside."[7]

By 1838, when the British ruling class's trading companies in league with the government had become the largest international drug cartel by creating a drug addiction crisis that was destroying China, opium had become the leading product in world trade. At this point, Britain invaded and defeated a narcotized, dysfunctional China with only ten thousand troops and took the island that is now called Hong Kong and $28 million in silver as booty.

Hegelian control of China was absolute because of the Opium War, which started after Britain began selling opium to the Chinese to cut its trade deficit. In a desperate attempt to stop the British and halt this genocide, the Chinese government banned the sale of opium. The British prevailed and decimated the country's economy and population with its drug trafficking. Britain victoriously waged war against the narcotized and hapless Chinese in 1840 and 1860[8] and uniquely positioned the British empire to distribute the "black dirt," as the Chinese call opium, throughout the world.

The British "Company" networks owned opium refineries in Shanghai and Hong Kong and banks in Canada and the Caribbean that financed the opium trade and laundered opium profits.[9] "During the last century British finances protected by British guns controlled the world narcotics traffic."[10] The Opium Wars against China are textbook examples of how the Illuminati combines Hegelian dialectics (imperialism) and Luciferian Occultism.

The Chinese in the nineteenth century and Americans—with Blacks as primary targets—in the twentieth century have been conquered by opium and heroin and crack cocaine provided by the Illuminati Ruling Class Conspiracy. The objective in both cases was to use drugs to suppress the targeted populations by sapping their energies and undermining their morality.

Today's priesthood of the Illuminati money lords are using the following strategies to subdue America: (1) promoting an ideology of secular humanism, which is merely a cover for the old Devil worship of the Illuminati Conspiracy (one of the fruits of this egotistic philosophy is the attitude in most Americans today that *they* are not responsible for their actions, but are victims; (2) flooding the country with drugs, just as Freemason Henry Palmerston, Great Britain's Prime Minister, poisoned China with opium in the nineteenth century, and as the Anglophile network does in America today; (3) pursuing a policy of triage whenever there is an opportunity, as there was to engender and pursue the Vietnam War in the 1960s and '70s, a war that was tantamount to human sacrifice because it was fought neither to defend the United States nor with the aim of winning (some 58,000 Americans died in Vietnam; their average age was eighteen; another 500,000 returned home as drug addicts).

Another example of this policy of triage is the therapy for so-called AIDS, a drug disease, which uses toxic drugs that cause the DAIDS—drug-acquired immune deficiency syndrome—that kills the victim. (See my book *Black Lies, White Lies* for the details.)

## THE OPIUM WARS

China was invaded by England in 1839 in what came to be known as the First Opium War, whose objective was to force the Chinese to buy opium from the English, and later on from other Europeans and Americans. By 1931 and the Manchurian Conquest, England had prosecuted "ten Opium Wars against China."[11] The First Opium War was initiated by Lord Palmerston, the British Prime Minister and Freemason occultist. During the Second Opium War, Edward Bulwer-Lytton, spokesperson extraordinaire for the Cult of Isis and Cecil Rhodes's Illuminati mentor, was the Colonial Secretary. These wars were compatible with Palmerston's and Bulwer-Lytton's Luciferian values undergirding British imperialism.

The English Illuminists modeled themselves as a modern Priesthood of the Temple of Isis, an imperialistic, racist cult that "formalizes the elements of a capability for social control, exploitation, and destruction of creative will in a subject population."[12] That's an excellent description of the political doctrine known as "British imperialism," and in a nutshell states the mission of the Illuminati political religion. And social control, exploitation, and destruction of the will of the people all over the world has been achieved, in large part, by trafficking in opium and its psychoactive derivatives. During Britain's First Opium

War against China, one fifth of the Chinese population was enslaved by addiction to opium; this included the wealthy as well
as the poor, and it created an epidemic larger than that of the
Great Plagues.

## THE AMERICAN TARGET

Today, the drug cartels run by the Illuminati Ruling Class Conspiracy reach into every government in the world. In fact, entire
governments, including China's and Britain's—in alliance with
America's Establishment—are structured to politically organize
and militarily protect drug interests.

The official party line is that this analysis is Taiwanese propaganda and that the People's Republic of China (PRC) has no
role in the drug trade. However, the evidence to the contrary
is quite impressive. On June 23, 1965, then Chinese Prime
Minister Chou En-lai, in conversation with Egyptian President
Nasser, outlined China's "twenty-year plan to finance political
activities and spread addiction"[13] in the United States. Chou
En-lai is quoted directly by editor Mohammed Heikal in *The
Cairo Documents:*

> Some of them [U.S. troops in Vietnam] are trying
> opium. And we are helping them. . . . Do you remember
> when the West imposed opium on us? They fought us
> with the opium. And we are going to fight them with
> their own weapons . . . The effect this demoralization is
> going to have on the United States will be far greater
> than anyone realizes.[14]

As a down payment on their twenty-year plan, the Chinese
sent 500,000 American veterans of the Vietnam War back home
as drug addicts. As early as 1960, diacetylmorphine (heroin)

that had originated in Hong Kong was seized in the United States. By the 1980s, "the resurgence of the Golden Triangle drug flow to the West, surpassing the heyday of the Vietnam War, shows that Beijing [China] is on a new drug offensive."[15] The Hong Kong–based *Liberation* monthly reported in December of 1989 that "the People's Republic of China provides 80 percent of the high-quality heroin selling on the international market."[16]

On May 16, 1975, the *San Jose Mercury News* broke a story alleging a Chinese connection.

> A secret federal report, the *Mercury* has learned, pin-points the People's Republic of China as the producer of quantities of heroin that have been detected in the Bay area. The report, completed six months ago, supposedly is being kept under wraps by the federal government for fear its release could affect detente between the U.S. and China.[17]

Jack Anderson had made the same claim in a syndicated column, "Protecting Beijing," on May 26, 1972, that was based on a leaked White House memo.

I cannot prove that the U.S. government participates in distributing drugs to its own people, but it is common knowledge that it does not protect them from those who do. Drug-infested areas, regardless of who provides the drugs, are oppressed territories, usually wastelands of urban blight, most of whose inhabitants are without a voice or moral conviction, and often even hope. These areas also seem mysteriously impregnable to police intervention, and suffer the benign neglect of both government and private enterprise.

All of America is now under attack, not just the urban ghettos but the affluent suburbs, the universities, the rural areas. The inner cities served as the early beachheads for the launching of the drug war against the American people. The population targeted for the massive expansion of prisons now under way is the majority White population, which is being destabilized by drugs and morally devolved by its offspring. To shield this agenda, Blacks were once again used as the scapegoat population (the specter of fear was again raised among Whites that Black men would attack them), in order to win the crucial public support for more jails. In fact, violent crime among Blacks is overwhelmingly directed toward other Blacks.

Whether it was the government or someone else doing the government's dirty work for it, the bottom line is that, under attack by drugs, America has reached the final stage of Illuminati synthesis—control through wholesale drug-induced immobilization and disease, and moral corruption. This is totalitarian statism.

Blacks in America are not the primary target, just the first and best target of opportunity. British and American intelligence recognized that reality when they rewarded Lucky Luciano and the Mafia with the exclusive drug franchise in Black neighborhoods. For more information, read Jonathan Vankin's book, *Conspiracies, Cover-ups and Crimes*.[18]

## BLACKS FIRST:
## THE GOVERNMENT-MAFIA CARTEL

Every Black person who saw the movie *The Godfather* was especially stung by the scene in which the Mafia chieftains, in reaching a moral compromise to overcome the taboo against distributing heroin, agree to confine sales to Black neighborhoods. "They're animals anyway. Let them lose their souls." The American narco killing fields began in its Black neighborhoods, on screen and off.

Charles "Lucky" Luciano and his "107th Street Gang" had

distributed heroin in New York City as early as 1915. However, this founding father of street drug trafficking in the United States did not hit it big in the heroin trade until after World War II. By then, Luciano had accomplished two Herculean tasks. He had "organized Sicilian gangs into a nationwide structure and aligned them with their Jewish counterparts controlled by the likes of Meyer Lansky and Bugsy Siegel."[19] With this merger, Luciano "created the national organized crime syndicate—the Mafia, La Cosa Nostra, the Outfit, the Mob," the organization that as late as the 1980s the Governor of New York, Mario Cuomo, would deny existed.

Luciano's other coup was that he now had the United States government, as well as British intelligence, behind him. What more could a convicted drug runner, panderer, and suspected murderer want? "The military first bonded with organized crime in 1942," according to author Jonathan Vankin.[20] The Office of Strategic Services (OSS), the forerunner of the Central Intelligence Agency, had just been organized by the U.S. government with cooperation and "technical assistance" from British intelligence's Special Operations Executives (SOE). Sir William Stevenson, SOE's representative in America, recruited Luciano as an SOE-OSS operative.[21]

Luciano negotiated with OSS-SOE from his jail cell where he was serving a fifty-year sentence. He was moved by his new associates in the spying trade to a cushy jail, where he served only about ten years. During his incarceration, he met frequently with Lansky and other Mafia leaders, as well as with England's and America's top intelligence officers. They wanted help from the gangsters in controlling sabotage on the New York docks. Rumor has it that Luciano's people burned a ship, the *Normandy,* in order to force U.S. officials to seek his help in controlling the sabotage that the cunning Luciano probably initiated.

The intelligence community also wanted Luciano's help in

Italy where he served as an OSS-SOE case officer in the overseas phase of "the military-Mafiosi joint venture," as Jonathan Vankin calls it in *Conspiracies, Cover-ups and Crimes.* When General George S. Patton needed help clearing a path for the Seventh Army through the countless booby traps in Sicily, he got it from Luciano's Cosa Nostra brother, Sicily's mob boss Calogero Vizzini. During the occupation period, the American military picked the Mafia bosses to become the mayors, instead of the leftist resistance leaders, the partisans, who had fought the Germans.[22]

U.S. law enforcement never had a "better opportunity to wipe out the problem of heroin"[23] than at the end of World War II and in the years immediately following. Demand was down because junkies had been forced to go cold turkey during the war. American customs officers, on the lookout for spies during the war, were very effective. The Chinese Communists, before they took over the Golden Triangle region of Southeast Asia and the opium trade from the British, killed off the Asian opium operatives.

According to Jonathan Vankin:

> After World War II, there were a scant twenty thousand addicts in the whole U.S.A., down from ten times that twenty years earlier. A mild tightening of the thumbscrews and heroin could have been, for all practical purposes, banished from the country. Instead, the exact opposite happened.[24]

The partnership of the government, the military, the international intelligence community, and organized crime had the means and the motive to open up Black communities as the first importation centers for opium derivatives in the United States. And at the command center of this cabal today, with the necessary addition of international banks to launder narco dollars and with the People's Republic of China as the main supplier, is the Illuminati Ruling Class Conspiracy.

## LOS ANGELES DOPE

In August 1996, the *San Jose Mercury News* (the same paper that courageously reported on China's drug trafficking activities in 1975) published a three-part series by Gary Webb charging that the CIA was flooding South Central Los Angeles and inner-city areas nationwide with crack cocaine.[25] It was alleged that the CIA, through Nicaraguan middlemen, had sold drugs to the indigenous gangs in Los Angeles, the Crips and the Bloods, and used the profits to fund the war being fought by the Reagan-supported "Contras" against the Communists in Nicaragua.

The *Mercury's* site on the World Wide Web was getting 100,000 inquiries a day. Black radio talk shows discussed little else, and Black newspapers gave the story headline status. Because of all this attention, the pro-CIA and -government Establishment media could not ignore the charge outright, as is the custom, nor could they trivialize the charges as another example of Black paranoia.

*The New Republic,* a liberal magazine, stated in a pop psychology profile of thirty-three million Blacks by Cinqué Henderson that illustrates this attitude that "the gross material disparities" resulting from separation from the White population has resulted in "equally vast psychological ones" for Black America.[26] I interpret that to mean that separation from Whites created the Black socioeconomic predicament and the estrangement from the master race, being "the unloved," as *The New Republic* headline put it, has driven Blacks to a schizophrenic inability to test reality. Paranoia, therefore, equals rejection by Whites. Oh, if life were only about White people, it would be so simple. Unfortunately, it is also about conspiracies to feed your children crack cocaine.

Fortunately, the *Mercury* management does not suffer from this delusional thought. Neither is it in the inner circle of the media elite. On the other hand, it is too credible and prestigious to dismiss.

The media lid on the story was sealed, however, when within weeks, *The Washington Post, The New York Times,* and the *Los Angeles Times,* the big three of American newspaper journalism, assured the public that they had thoroughly investigated the matter and that what had seemed to many intelligent people a convincing body of information, confirming the federal government's role as a drug trafficker in Black communities, was all nonsense and the result of poor journalism at the *San Jose Mercury News,* which subsequently transferred Webb to a smaller office in Cupertino, California. He resigned in December 1997.

*The Washington Post,* on October 4, 1996, explained that its investigation found that the "available information did not support the conclusion that the CIA-backed Contras played a major role in drug trafficking in the United States." The *Post* even quoted Webb as saying that his series never claimed that the CIA knew about drug trafficking: "This doesn't prove the CIA targeted the Black communities. It doesn't say this was ordered by the CIA. Essentially, our trail stopped at the door of the CIA." The *Mercury* editors maintained, however, that the evidence pointed in the direction of a government-sponsored plot—despite the absence of a smoking gun tying the CIA to the inner-city drug sales or the fact that the *Mercury* was being held to a higher standard of journalism by its critics at the *Times, Post,* or *Los Angeles Times.*

In a later series, the *Los Angeles Times* flat out said that the crack epidemic in Los Angeles was not the result of a master plan and was not orchestrated by the Contras or the CIA. Both the CIA and the Justice Department launched probes into the

*Mercury*'s allegations. Then Webb began to contradict his own report in personal interviews, and the *Mercury*'s otherwise rather gallant editor, John Ceppos, said in an editorial addressed to the "American people and inner-city residents in particular," that the series on L.A. dope "fell short of standards."[27] Closure.

The Establishment had spoken, and, with the exception of an unprecedented visit to Los Angeles by the CIA's director in a C-SPAN-televised, predictably raucous town-hall meeting with local Black activists, it was on to more important matters of state. The media and the nation could now focus on the urgency of Ebonics and a California ballot proposition that would kill affirmative action and protect our democracy from what is widely perceived to be a poorly educated, irresponsible, paranoid Black population.

Along the way, however, a two-year investigation done in the late 1980s by the Subcommittee on Terrorism, Narcotics, and International Operations was unearthed.

> In the end, the committee found that the CIA and the *contras* had, indeed, used a number of traffickers, criminals and brigands to smuggle arms or stand at airports. But the committee could not prove that these individuals' freelance criminal activities had been sanctioned, organized or furthered by the intelligence agency, much less that they were all part of an organized scheme to underwrite the contra war.[28]

The CIA strongly denied any role in conspiring with the Contras to sell and distribute narcotics. But what was proved by this official body is that the CIA used "traffickers, criminals and brigands" in illegal activities. One of the traffickers, Danilo Blandon, a Nicaraguan drug wholesaler and Drug Enforcement Administration informant, told the Senate Intelligence Committee at an underreported closed-door meeting on November

25, 1996, that he was no longer associated with the Contras when he sold cocaine to Rickey Ross, a Los Angeles gang member.[29]

The CIA's record of covert activities contributes to the suspicions that it does function as a secret society that wages genocide against Blacks by inducing Black youths to become addicted to powder and crack cocaine. In addition to the CIA being conspicuously AWOL in the war to keep drugs out of the country, the most recent evidence of its involvement in the drug trade is the arrest of General Ramon Guillen Davita, the commander of the Venezuelan National Guard and "the CIA's most trusted man in Venezuela," who was indicted on drug trafficking charges by a federal grand jury in Miami just three months after the *Mercury* story broke.[30]

Guillen, who also worked with the U.S. Drug Enforcement Agency, was charged with smuggling twenty-two tons of cocaine into the United States while he was head of "the National Guard anti-drug bureau."[31] Three years earlier, *60 Minutes* reported that Guillen smuggled more than a ton of cocaine into the United States.[32]

Whatever the CIA's role was in the flooding of inner cities with crack, it could not have done it alone. Several agencies of government and many institutions in the private sector that are also AWOL in the so-called war on drugs would have been needed as coconspirators: the Drug Enforcement Administration, the FBI, the Customs Service, the Pentagon, the State Department, the IRS, Congressional oversight committees, as well as local law enforcement agencies, the courts, and, definitely, the White House as well as the banks and financial institutions that launder billions of narco dollars would have been essential to the operation. Whatever else you name it, this again describes the Illuminati Ruling Class Conspiracy.

In December 1997, the CIA and the Justice Department (which oversees the FBI) announced the conclusion of year-long investigations. Both reports found no evidence linking the CIA, "directly or indirectly," to Nicaraguan or other drug traffickers in California.[33] The CIA also promised another inquiry on two Congressional investigations that "found allegations of CIA association with drug smugglers in Central America during the 1980s."[34]

January 1998 marked the first time a U.S. attorney general had ever invoked an order that "allowed a report to be withheld from the public if its release would reveal sensitive information."[35] The secret report dealt with the principals in the August 1996 *San Jose Mercury News* story on the CIA, Nicaraguan rebels, and crack cocaine dealers.


## BLAME VERSUS RESPONSIBILITY

At the height of the South Central Los Angeles–CIA scandal, some media pundits began to blame the public for taking the drugs that are being made available. It reminded me once again of the British and Americans blaming the Chinese for consuming the opium they forced on them at gunpoint in the nineteenth century.

Some of these pundits made the accusation that many Blacks were predisposed to pathological behavior, especially drug addiction. Claude Lewis, a Black journalist for the *Philadelphia Inquirer*, challenged blacks to use their will to fight the drug scourge. In a column entitled "Even If the CIA Flooded Inner Cities with Crack, Blacks Didn't 'Say No,' " Lewis argued: "The reason I doubt theories of genocide against blacks is that I don't think a determined government would need to strain much to pull it off. Especially since so many blacks, given their history, would unwittingly help such a plot succeed."[36]

In a chapter in *Conspiracies, Cover-ups and Crimes*, Jonathan Vankin remarks: "I think individual drug problems may be the fault of individuals, but despite current enthusiasm for persecuting 'the casual user,' America's drug problem appears to have been inflicted upon it."[37] In other words, blaming Blacks for taking drugs does not constitute a policy to eradicate drugs. Nor does it absolve the Conspiracy and its government agenturs of distributing those drugs.

Republican and Democratic administrations have demonstrated that the responsibility for the reign of death among Americans resulting from drugs is bipartisan. Drug czars in the administrations of both parties occupy themselves mainly with putting on public relations stunts and making excuses. They do not do anything substantial, and they are not expected to do anything. The depth of the conspiracy to do nothing is revealed by the fact that Nancy Reagan's "Just Say No" campaign was the most effective antidrug program any administration has offered. It was a genuinely felt effort, but conveniently unfunded and ad hoc, so as to limit even its very modest public relations success. And thanks to the Illuminati Ruling Class Conspiracy, Americans keep saying yes.

## THE AMERICAN NARCO LIFESTYLE

Just as the Conspiracy has targeted the Black community for drug distribution, it has apparently targeted America with a death-wish message. With so much Conspiracy attention focused on the unsuspecting drug markets of America's inner cities, the Establishment adds its own firepower, as it were, offering the public movies that are tailored to sell more drugs and that reinforce a "gangsta" way of life. The essence of the new American lifestyle is summed up by the advice of real-life gangster Pretty Boy Floyd: "Live fast, die young, and make a good-looking corpse." The best brainwashing money can buy are the current crop of prime-time sitcoms that glorify dysfunctional,

Ebonic-speaking role models. Specialized TV channels are designed to promote narco hip, the media-manufactured style epitomized by the ugly and angry "gangsta" looks of the urban Black youth and the "heroin chic" looks of the suburban White youth. The symbols of this media-driven cultural message translate into hedonistic pleasure seeking, in other words, secular humanism.

Do you think I am exaggerating? Are you willing to bet your child's life on that? You probably already have if you believe that you live in a world of accidental events. The spate of British rock "stars" beginning with the Beatles, who with their drug message emerged onto the American cultural landscape in the early 1960s, were no accident. Just think about the titles of some of the Beatles' hits: "Day Tripper"—could that be referring to a morning pick-up hit of heroin? "Yellow Submarine"—a yellow quaalude or downer? "Strawberry Fields Forever" is drug-culture talk for poppy fields and poppy, the strawberry-red poison. "Hey Jude" is code for marijuana. According to pop-culture historian William Brian Key: "The Beatles popularized and culturally legitimized hallucinatory drug usage among teenagers throughout the world. The Beatles became the super drug-culture prophets and pushers of all time."[38]

The cover of the Beatles' *Sergeant Pepper* album pictured the Grand Master of three degenerate British Masonic orders, Aleister Crowley, alleged to have taken 150 lives, mostly young boys, in human sacrifices in the homicidal, drug-dealing Ordo Temple Orientis (OTO) Masonic Group, once a breeding ground for the Hitler movement.[39] Also included on the cover were Illuminati Freemason Satanist Karl Marx; Rosicrucian (Satanist) Freemason Carl Jung; and Marxist Freemason H. G. Wells. Why those three men on the album cover? Ringo Starr reportedly explained that they were "people we like and admire."[40]

The evil propaganda messages found in some Beatles'

songs also reveal what the group liked and admired. The subliminal technique of "backward masking" exposes hidden
messages when the record is played backward. The Beatles'
song "Revolution 9" in reverse says, "Turn me on, dead
man," instead of "Number nine, number nine." The "backward" message from Led Zeppelin's "Stairway to Heaven"
is "My sweet Satan . . ."[41]

The Beatles were the outriders of the Illuminati "British Invasion" of the 1960s and 1970s with its exhortation to drugs,
Devil worship, sex, and death. Ozzy Osbourne, former lead
singer for Black Sabbath, worships Luciferian Aleister Crowley
as a demigod, as does Led Zeppelin's Freemason Jimmy Page
and Rolling Stones' Freemasons Mick Jagger and Keith Rich-
ards. All of the British rockers were allegedly initiated into
Crowley's Hermetic Order of the Golden Dawn, which allegedly promotes "the consumption of hashish, combined with
sexual perversion."[42]

There are special Masonic lodges in England that exist exclusively for the purpose of teaching musicians secret techniques. Musical tones can be used to move energy in the body
and manipulate muscles, arteries, and nerves to produce emotional reactions. Freemason Wolfgang Amadeus Mozart pion-
eered such techniques in his work *The Magic Flute* in order to
incite revolutionary fervor and anti-Christian sentiment. Rock
and roll, according to Mark Spaulding, author of *The Heartbeat
of the Dragon,* "was specifically designed to instigate REBEL-
LION in the listener . . . as well as undermining their inborn
God-ordained moral code."[43]

## MUSIC TO KILL BY

You may suspect that I am overstating the case for the devastating influence of moral rot on American life, especially on the
lives of the young. Let me share with you the spiritual belief of

Christians that in his presinful days, Lucifer, according to Ezekiel 28: 12–15, may have been equipped by God with musical
instruments. "Some Bible scholars believe he may have had
charge of the musical worship of God before the throne—sort
of a heavenly choir director,"[44] William and Sharon Schnoebelen wrote in *Lucifer Dethroned.* They suspect that this is why
the Devil today has dominated certain musical forms, especially rock.

The Thirty-third-Degree English Freemason, drug addict,
self-avowed Satanist, and alleged murderer of 150 babies as sacrifices at Ordo Temple Orientis (OTO) rituals Aleister Crowley,
is the patron saint of many rock and roll artists today.[45] Some
of these stars are members of the sexually licentious and homicidal OTO Masonic lodge. As I said, Crowley adorned the cover
of the Beatles' *Sergeant Pepper's Lonely Hearts Club Band*
album, according to Beatle Ringo Starr, as someone the Beatles
"like and admire."[46] The Beatles were the first rock band to use
the "Il Cornuto" Devil sign (the index and small fingers of the
hand forming the Devil's horns, the other three fingers tucked
in) on the front of the Beatles' *Yellow Submarine* album cover.[47]
Those were the days when Devil worship was subtle. It's now
as bad (as in rotten) as the music. In fact, you can find out
for yourself.

You can test the influence of Devil hate via music on your
or your child's mind by putting a plant in front of a music
speaker of Marilyn Manson, Motley Crue, or the latest Satanic
band. Place a second plant in front of another music speaker
playing religious music or, say, a Whitney Houston love ballad.
Based on anecdotal evidence, the plant nearest the Devil's music
will grow away from it and the plant near the love (God) sounds
will grow toward it.

Which spiritual direction was the fifteen-year-old boy growing in who showed his father a Marilyn Manson (a male Satanist) CD just before killing himself with a hand grenade?[48] Did a

fourteen-year-old open fire on a student prayer circle in a West Paducah, Kentucky, high school, killing two students and wounding four others because praying to God bothered him, as he warned earlier? Almost robotically, as if being turned on and off by mind control, shaking and crying, he emptied his gun into the unsuspecting group of young people. "I'm sorry," he said, as he dropped his gun into a pool of blood. I suspect that he is one of millions of young Manchurian candidates now being manufactured with Satanic messages in modern music and in the movies where the Il Cornuto salute to Satan is ubiquitous.

Hidden mostly, the secret Masonic handshakes (pressing the thumb of the right hand over the knuckle joints or between the knuckle joints on the other hand) proliferate throughout the movies. Dean Grace compiled a list of over 183 films (*Guide to Masonic "Handshakes" in the Movies)* in which the handgrips of the first three degrees of Freemasonry can be observed between the actors. *White Men Can't Jump,* a 1992 movie with Wesley Snipes ("Sidney") and Woody Harrelson ("Billy"), not only flashes Masonic pass grips throughout, but it offers an occult bonus. Dean Grace explains:

Because Woody Harrelson's father Charles Harrelson has in some circles been implicated in the assassination of JFK, I find it interesting that early in the film Billy tells his girlfriend Gloria a funny Jeopardy TV game show question. (What were) "The last words of Lee Harvey Oswald?—It wasn't me, it was the C.I. AAaagh!" Billy then grimaces the way Oswald did after being shot by Jack Ruby. Halfway through the film at the Brotherhood Tournament Billy taunts his future basketball opponents by saying, "What? Are you still throwing those bricks (basketballs)? What is this, a Mason's convention?"[49]

Following our British master's lead, America is now producing homegrown Illuminati Pied Pipers for the impressionable youth to idolize and mimic. And just as the radicals of the 1960s who dropped LSD and preached free love have conditioned their children for today's narco lifestyle, so, too, are the British-bred Illuminati troubadours transmitting the new music-borne drug-and-death ethos to their offspring and a new generation of Americans.

A world of subliminal death imagery, according to conspiracy theorists, is being beamed into the minds of the public through the rhythms and lyrics in drug-loving rap and rock. The overt message of decadent chic and the hidden message of sex and death are airbrushed into our psyches with powerful and enduring subliminal effects.

Sex and death are equated in these subliminal messages. Death, in this way, becomes a kind of eternal eroticism, an embedded death wish that can best be achieved through suicide, and, of course, drug usage is gradual suicide. The suicide rate among White teens, the chief consumers of so-called rock music, is, in fact, their leading cause of death. The only debatable issue here is whether this insidious message is being systematically communicated. Despite the protestations of Madison Avenue to the contrary, techniques of subliminal mind-control have been developed and, in some cases, already outlawed.

Was William Brian Key, author of *Subliminal Seduction,* the raving madman that the American Association of Advertising Agencies made him out to be when he accused the trade of eroding the moral fiber of our society by "embedding" obscene and taboo words and pictures that manipulate behavior? Can the letters S-E-X be found in the ice cubes of a Gilbey's gin print advertisement? In an ad for Tanqueray gin, did Key really see an upright penis that "promises subliminally to improve your erection" or was he just selling his books?[50] Do embedded symbolic penises and vaginas in ad illustrations and the labia that Key said he saw in the frosting on a Betty Crocker cake mix box "moisten the housewife's vagina," as Key claims?[51]

In one of his books, *The Age of Manipulation,* Key targeted the now outlawed "Joe Camel" cartoon character, which sold billions of dollars' worth of Camel cigarettes to young people by creating a subliminal hold on them. Joe, the ultracool cartoon figure, was so effective in selling cigarettes that it took governmental intervention to retire him. Key's explanation for this phenomenon is that the male and female genitals are sketched on the face of the sexy cartoon smoothie. The consumer is compelled to buy the product because of the unconscious pleasure derived from the concealed sexual imagery. Advertising executives, of course, reject these allegations.

However, warfare experts say that it is possible to develop a weapon—"deliverable by computer, television or film"—that would produce effects similar to "epileptic-like spasms" that were experienced in December 1997. Over seven hundred Japanese children who were watching television were sent to the hospital.[52] A five-second scene in a cartoon showed flashing red lights emanating from a character's eyes in *Pokeman,* the cartoon that is scheduled for syndication in the United States.[53]

I do not know if Madison Avenue uses hidden persuaders, and if it does, if the creative people have as much fun seducing our unconscious minds with hidden sexual and death symbolism as the Masons have with our pagan-symbol-cluttered national seal on the dollar bill. But I do think it quite likely that in the lingo of the American narco lifestyle, "Cool, dude," in the suburbs, and "Chill," in the urban centers mean it's time to relax with some psychoactive substance or with some sex, in other words, to symbolically die.

## GESTALT ROT

Is it just accidental that each year more and more drugs are sold to younger and younger children? Drug pushers on street corners and in schools do not advertise. Neither do the Wall Street pushers. How is the population stimulated to purchase such large quantities of drugs? If drugs are sold because of their euphoric effect, why does the number of first-time users keep increasing? Why are people who have never tried drugs buying death in increasingly large numbers?

It is the result of the lure of the American narco culture, which is the gestalt of a nation in an advanced stage of moral rot. The American narco lifestyle sells the drugs, but that American lifestyle is being manipulated by forces much more powerful than advertising agencies, I believe. That is why the United States has no peer anywhere in the world in terms of the deterioration of its population, especially the young.

"Why Are Young People Killing?" is the title of a recent article in *People* magazine. The article went on to say: "Coincidence—or scary trend? A spate of murders allegedly committed by teens leaves experts, family and police seeking answers." The cover of the issue of *People* in which that story appeared was even more explicit: "Kids Without Conscience? Rape, murder, a baby dead at a prom." *People* magazine may have said it all. Anyone without a conscience, guilt associated with an immoral or illegal act, is clinically diagnosed as a "sociopath." We are beginning to produce them by the generations.

The standard politically correct excuses given for the causes of such widespread antisocial behavior—parental absence or neglect; poverty; physical, psychological, and sexual abuse—do not explain the depth and breadth of this sociopathic and pathological behavior. Most of the new societal brutes described in *People*'s survey were privileged middle- and upper-class Whites. "They need no more reason for hurting another human being than they have for peeling an orange," a psychiatrist told *People*.[54]

*People* described a generation that has broken the standing record for murders committed by teenagers; within a year, the number jumped from 1,000 to 4,000. Teens are "committing crimes of incomprehensible callousness": A teenage couple from Texas is charged with the frivolous murder of a girl; a New Jersey high-school senior delivered her own baby in a bathroom stall, left the baby in the trash bin, and returned to the prom; and two New York teens were charged with killing and gutting a man in Central Park. All of this has the feel of a mass psychological adaptation to shared stimuli.

Why are youths killing? We recognize that every cause has an effect and every effect has a cause; therefore, I think it is reasonable to assume that something has happened that is provoking some already fragile personalities to kill and commit other antisocial acts. Some of them may be unable to distinguish between fantasy and reality—between toys and real guns, for example. When this phenomenon first appeared among Black youth in what the "illuminated" scholars and journalists opportunistically labeled "Black-on-Black murder," the Establishment agenturs concluded that it was the result of poverty, a pathological culture, and bad genes.

With what is now obviously an epidemic of vicious murders, baby killing, and overall amorality among White teens, "White-on-White murder" can be understood in neither sociological nor racial terms. In today's society, Whites cannot be considered racially or culturally inferior, although until the mid-twentieth century, the Irish, Jews, Slavs, and Italians were generally not considered White, which meant Anglo-Saxon. And since many of these White perpetrators are privileged, poverty and cultural pathology must be ruled out as precipitating factors.

Without racism in the equation, however, it becomes clear that all young people have been targeted for some form of mind control: psychological warfare. Pick your own villain, but there has to be one. My choice is the Illuminati because this picture of "social control, exploitation, and destruction of creative will" fits its stated objectives and "Big Brother" techniques, and the campaign is too massive and well coordinated for anyone else to pull it off. The "elements" of hedonistic pleasure-seeking and psychoactive drugs are used to create a new societal aesthetic—or value system. That sounds like British Masonic occult tactics to me.

## THE ALI SHUFFLE

Muhammad Ali resisted the U.S. government's attempts to first entice and then bully him into killing in the Vietnam War, saying, "Them Vietnamese never called me a nigger." Because he successfully resisted the government's campaign of psychological conditioning—brainwashing—being waged against the youth of America, both Black and White, he was of no use to the Illuminati. Ali's being a Black man was not the issue; he was in the way of profits and drug supplies. So he was publicly ostracized, financially penalized, and targeted by the ever-cooperative media for notoriety and demonization. But the psychologically strong and positive psychological Ali Shuffle helped him resist Big Brother's manufactured death trap.

As many have said before, if you give me your child and let me select his or her music, clothes, art, movies, television, and friends, I can produce the kind of person I choose—a personality for good or evil. *Occult Theocrasy*, written by Edith Miller in 1933, explains that music can be used for "the purposes of occult dominion. In order to control a person's otherwise positive mind, it must be conditioned to become passive and negative."[55]

"A mind that is positive cannot be controlled. . . . Minds

consciously working to a definite end are a power, and power can oppose power for good or evil."[56] If you direct your mind to love God, family, and moral virtue, Big Brother's subliminal mind control stands no chance. Teach your children "the Ali Shuffle" to ward off the Illuminati Ruling Class Conspiracy's Pied Pipers of drugs, sex, and death.

The only way to defeat the narco Goliath is for people not to buy and use drugs and to empower your children with loving, positive minds to ward off the singing devils. We must educate ourselves as to how the Conspiracy's plan to kill as many Americans as possible works. Every citizen has a moral obligation, after learning the truth, to act on it intelligently. At that point, anyone who takes drugs, in effect, wants to commit suicide (the embedded death wish) and blame the social disaster on others. They are determined to cooperate with the enemy and kill themselves; they are, for all intents and purposes, Conspiracy accomplices.

A national "Stop the Drug War Against the U.S." campaign can teach young people how to detect the hidden narco suicide messages that seduce them into the world of drug addiction, failure, and death. Together, we can arm our children with knowledge and power and put their souls beyond the reach of the Illuminati.

PART TWO

# SELF-
# EMPOWERMENT

# 9

# THE CHOICE: GOOD
# VERSUS EVIL

*It must be of the spirit, if we are to save the flesh.*
—GENERAL DOUGLAS MACARTHUR

Part I of this book examined the Illuminati Ruling Class Conspiracy and its agenda to establish an evil dominion over the
world. Undoubtedly, much of what you read made you angry
or resentful. It is now time to sublimate that anger or resent-
ment into a plan of action. Part II of this book, therefore, is a
call to action. As I said earlier, this is a book with a mission.

In the following chapters, I offer a plan for spiritual and economic recovery—for total self-empowerment. My plan is to restore the original system of Americanism that guaranteed our
human rights. For this plan to work, however, we must acknowledge and address the inner as well as the outer realms of
the Conspiracy that steals our money and our right to live life
the way we want to live it—in freedom.

The struggle against the Illuminati Ruling Class Conspiracy

has to be waged in the inner realm of conscience as well as in the outer realm of economics and politics. It is impossible to overthrow the Conspiracy without breaking its hold on our souls. This battle has both a materialistic and a moral reality, and I hope that you will join it on both levels.

## THE PLAN

My plan for fighting the oppression of the Illuminati Ruling Class Conspiracy hinges on a return to the spirit of Americanism, a belief in the fundamental principles of the Constitution of the United States and the Declaration of Independence. Americanism inherently defines a Republic whose citizens are equal in the eyes of God and who enjoy the fundamental right to life.

The Declaration stresses God's role as the source of our human rights, a form of property rights, and our civic obligation "to alter or abolish" tyrannical government.

> We hold these truths to be self-evident, that all men are created equal, that they are endowed by their Creator with certain unalienable Rights, that among these are life, liberty, and the pursuit of happiness. That to secure these rights, governments are instituted among men, deriving their just powers from the consent of the governed. That whenever any form of government becomes destructive of these ends, it is the right of the people to alter or abolish it.

As we have seen, statist America has usurped God's place as the source of human rights. Statism, which is, in effect, the creation of the Illuminati Ruling Class Conspiracy, has replaced Divine guidance; secular humanism has replaced moral responsibility; and the government of the United States has become the enemy of its people's "pursuit of happiness." In America's statist society, we live by deception and chicanery. A good politician is one who lies, steals, and brings home the bacon. Living within our means is a politically incorrect concept in such an environment. And Big Brother routinely cooks the books to make the budget numbers come out right.

The questionable character of our President, his habitual lying, and his background of alleged criminal activities are absolutely irrelevant to most Americans as long as the economy is strong. What I see in Bill Clinton as sociopathic traits, I now see in the national character. Even after his latest alleged paramour, Monica Lewinsky, was exposed and leaks of a tape-recording on which she supposedly described an affair with President Clinton, including her claim that he asked her to lie to the court, were made public, 58 percent of Americans in a Time/CNN poll felt his possible involvement with women had no effect on his job performance.[1] How can I believe a President who tells a twenty-one-year-old White House intern that their practice of oral sex over a period of sixteen months is not adultery, not sex at all when he says it's time to go to war?

The fact that a married man like Bill Clinton with a reputation as an indefatigable womanizer can get elected President and then reelected, notwithstanding the rationalization about economic prosperity, has diminished my respect for the American electorate.

If only money is important to Americans, America is not worth saving or defending. Ironically, the economy really is not very sound, and, on some level of consciousness, Americans must realize it. They are living in the ever-present shadow of an economic disaster that could erupt at any time, the result of a mountain of federal and personal debt and the financial—and moral—implications of running up a $7 trillion tab and then leaving it for their children and grandchildren to pay. The Baby Boomers now eat "the forbidden fruit," narcotics, and many have developed a sociopathic personality that has begun to characterize their entire generation. Others name themselves the Lost Generation and Generation X. With increasing frequency, teenagers are baby killers, sexual perverts, and Devil worshipers who wear their appellation—"Beast 666"—with pride. These are the "blessings" of statist America.

## GOOD VERSUS EVIL

Good and evil in the world generally apply to two flawed groups of people: those who believe the revealed word of God and those who believe the Luciferian dogma that human reason is the true religion and that mankind, without any guidance from God, is perfectly capable of using the mind to understand the difference between right and wrong and to attain happiness. This is the doctrine that ran God out of the United States government. This concept is reflected by Zev ben Shimon Halevi in *Kaballah and Exodus:* "The Secret of Existence is that it is a mirror in which man reflects the Image of the Divine so that God may behold God."[2] The Great Deceiver—Lucifer, Satan, the Devil—sowed the seeds of evil in the souls of men when he tempted Adam and Eve with the narcotized promise of "illumination," of the power to behold the gods within themselves. This original sin of striving to be equal to God is echoed within each of us, even among some of the deeply religious who judge others in defiance of God.

We all carry the duality of good and evil in ourselves. Whichever way we turn on the inner and outer journey, we are challenged by the temptation of illumination and "the Illuminated One"—another name for the Devil. For instance, racial prejudice, the progeny of Illuminism, must ultimately be resolved on an inner level as a sin committed by the soul. Therefore, we struggle with evil as an inner force as well as the temptations that arise from the external opportunities for dominance over others, and advancement and profits.

Illuminism, as we have seen, leads to elitism, the belief that the chosen few are superior to everyone else. The form that that elitism takes may be race, class, intelligence, education, wealth—whatever attribute one can use to justify the innate sinful human desire to make oneself equal to God by placing oneself above the rest of humankind. The struggle is truly against "evil in high places" and "principalities" of the soul, although it manifests in the flesh. The need to feel superior, to be mentally illuminated, in order to dominate others is in each of us. On the inner level, the Illuminati Conspiracy manifests as one part of us (our conceit or spiritual pride) acting against the rest, and against humanity, against God's will.

The struggle in the flesh takes on other forms in a secular society, however. Class bias is the most conspicuous example. Racial and sexual biases especially indicate an ignorance of God's plan—and are therefore evil—if you believe, as I do, that each successive life places us in the circumstances and milieu necessary for the correction and advancement of the soul. In other words, the venom you spew toward people who are different in this life will come back to bite you hard the next time around. And, of course, the love, kindness, and compassion you show during this trip will bless you tenfold on the next one.

Life is a game with rules. In *The Game of Life and How to Play It,* Florence Scovel Shinn explains:

Most people consider life a battle, but it is not a battle, it is a game. It is a game, however, which cannot be played successfully without the knowledge of spiritual law, and the Old and the New Testaments give the rules of the game with wonderful clearness. Jesus Christ taught that it was a great game of Giving and Receiving.

Whatsoever a man soweth that shall he also reap.[3]

In other words, whatever man sends out in word or deed will return to him; what he gives, he will receive. In my opinion, this is God's law.

## THE CHOICE

Often, what we fear most in the world is what we ourselves have become. As above, so below; as within, so without. We conspire within; therefore we conspire in the world. It is our evil nature that conspires against our human race. We are more comfortable in the presence of evil than with goodness. These are harsh words, but they are not belied by our history and behavior. In man's current earthbound state, it is easier for the Devil to overcome his soul than it is for God to save it.

Life returns love to us when we have given love. It is charitable to us when we have been charitable. In America, the presence of evil has become so gross and ubiquitous that everyone is almost continually confronted by it, and forced to choose between good and evil. This inner discovery also becomes a collective reality. A nation too must recognize the existence of God and the Devil, good and evil, as its central paradigm, and choose between them. Modern America denies this reality, but we are still confronted with the choice of good and evil.

We have turned our backs on the compact with God made in the founding documents of our nation and embraced the secular religion of rationalism as the basis of our political and educational belief systems. Our government has been seized by the corrupting influence of the ruling class of economic elitists. Greed and selfishness are bred in the hearts of the people by statist entitlements for rich and poor alike. And cynical science, led by a priesthood of cosmologists, with its untested theories, "would exclude God from the universe, and with him all mystery."[4]

Where in this country can an honest man or woman be rewarded without compromising principles? There is nowhere that you are expected to be better than amoral. America's new definition of virtue is: It is better to succeed than to be honest.

Bill Clinton's presidency is a benchmark of America's moral decline into a nation of sociopaths. Only 16 percent of Americans rate personal moral traits as the most important factor in evaluating a president. Compare this nation's president, a moral midget and serial sex artist, to an inspiring giant like Pope John Paul II, who courageously marched into Cuba in 1998 and assailed its system as a godless, morally rotten Communist product of Illuminist statism: "No ideology can replace His [Christ's] infinite wisdom and power." And he included Capitalism and the American worship of materialism as well.

In fact, there is not one major institution in our prevailing American system that is not controlled by the forces of evil, including several Christian denominations where over 50 percent of the ministers have not accepted Jesus as their unconditional savior, but fully embrace the religion of Freemasonry.

Overall, it is a world of chaos and irrational behavior that has become increasingly evil and unworthy of God's gift of life. If God ends this collective existence, it is because we are not worthy of it, as a human group. Therefore, we will collectively lose this precious gift unless we are willing to pay for it with our spiritual growth. How do we do that? By resisting the forces of evil: first, the conflict between good and evil within ourselves; and then, the Illuminati Ruling Class Conspiracy's system of political and economic materialism.

Victory in our inner battle against our sinful nature will come from a genuine love of humanity. We will overcome this nature when we conquer the need to love ourselves more than others. This spiritual consciousness manifests itself in the world as the ability to fight the money lords and their spooks on behalf of those who are less fortunate.

When Jesus Christ came to earth, he exposed the church of Satan. Jesus taught us how to fight evil: Teach the truth about the Devil's conspiracy.[5] History indeed repeats itself, and we must again educate ourselves and each other about the inner and outer conspiracies.

Christians are instructed to oppose the Great Deceiver's "spiritual wickedness," and his human agents and their counterfeit teachings, even when these are hidden behind the mask of Christianity itself. The Spirit of Christ lives not in the world; it dwells through His word only in the hearts of the sincere Christians who comprise God's church on earth. Therefore, Christians believe, if the word of God is spoken from the heart of a sincere believer, it becomes a judgment of God, as when Elijah pronounced the death of Jezebel.

Therefore, the Christian's weapons are not temporal might or power, but the spirit and the word of Jesus—not the things that are created, but the Creator. The two great Witnesses of the truth of God are the Old Testament and the New Testament in the Holy Bible.

They are both witnesses, or testaments, to His glory. Whatever our religious faith, each of us must choose our soul's path to happiness with the Almighty God or eternal damnation with the Devil. My paradigm in this book is a parallel choice between conspiracy and empowerment, or evil and good.


## EMPOWERMENT

To combat the Illuminati Ruling Class Conspiracy, we must develop a spiritual and moral vision that is accompanied by an economic strategy with which to alter pragmatically our compromised government. "It must be of the spirit, if we are to save the flesh," as General Douglas MacArthur said in a speech given aboard the U.S.S. *Missouri* after the Japanese surrender ceremony on September 2, 1945.[6]

In order to survive the turbulent days ahead, we must realize that God is still the ruler of this world and everything in it and that at an appointed time He will destroy the Devil and all of his agenturs, including the network of the Antichrist called the Illuminati Ruling Class Conspiracy. Satan may deceive you and me, but not God. God is exploiting the Devil to fulfill His plan to give human beings a clear choice between good and evil. The Devil does not tolerate freedom of choice; God demands it. God cannot lie; the Devil is a lie. God does not want you as a slave; He wants you to see Him for what He is, the Truth.

My form of order is faith in God, the phenomenon that is called "a curious superstition" by those in the intelligentsia who consider themselves rationalists. I am not a rationalist, I suppose, because I have rarely found life to be rational. People certainly aren't. People in one part of the world throw food away while people in another region die of starvation. And those who eat the most are starving because they did not feed the hungry. The good suffer, and the evil prosper, on the average. Faith in God is rational because it's based on the truth.

In my life paradigm, I have found that giving and receiving is the only practical formula for a bountiful life. Therefore, by offering in this book the knowledge of evil and its earthly hierarchy, the Illuminati Ruling Class Conspiracy, I am hoping to give the people of the United States and the world the key to self-empowerment. Illuminists, agents of the Devil, such as Carroll Quigley, from the economic and policy wing, and Albert Pike, from the Illuminati Freemasonry religious arm, through their writings have revealed to us the conspiratorial and evil threat that is engulfing our nation and our world. We are just not listening. Obviously, few of us have paid much attention to the age-old wisdom found in the Scriptures. The Holy Bible prophesied this ungodly conspiracy thousands of years ago and explains that to understand evil, we do not need to know who it is, only *what* it is.

> For we wrestle not against flesh and blood, but against principalities, against powers, against the rulers of the darkness of this world, against spiritual wickedness in high places.[7]

We can only receive the light of illumination through faith in the Almighty God of the Christian Bible, the Koran, the Torah, and the holy books of all religions that fight evil. God is good and the Devil—aka Satan, Lucifer, and the Baphomet—is evil. We possess the knowledge of good and evil when we know the truth and use it to worship God and to develop moral virtue. In turn, this moral virtue, or character, produces correct emotions, thoughts, words, and actions. This new consciousness brings us closer to God. He only lives in goodness.

In truth, the only "dominion" the Devil has is in the minds of the people he has deluded into joining him in his eternal damnation. The condition of the world today can in no way be used to conclude that the Devil has any chance of victory. But it does confirm the fact that everyone in the world is deluded to some extent by the Great Deceiver. Statism is his most recent illusion. And it is now time to make the choice between the evil of statism and the good of Americanism.

The solution, of course, is right there in the words of the Declaration of Independence: "Whenever any form of government becomes destructive of these ends [securing our unalienable human rights], it is the right of the people to alter or abolish it." Since the Conspiracy has subsumed the system, we cannot simply abolish it. Nor would a superficial public exposure of the members of the oligarchy, no matter how titillating, result in any substantive change. The only way we can alter the conspiratorial system in which we live is by realizing that God is the only source of our human rights and heightening our sense of spiritual consciousness. This solution requires that we empower ourselves spiritually by making a conscious choice between God and statism, faith and rationalism, good and evil.

Without God and with statism, there is no chance for prosperity or happiness, or for the United States or any other nation, especially England. As the next chapter will show, it is already too late to avoid a serious, 1930s-style Depression. But it is not too late to ask God for His guidance. With God in the equation, the nation may have true prosperity once again. Without Him, we may come to know why there is little reference to the United States in the Bible's prophecy of the last days. I do not believe that God has shut the door in America's face yet, but I do believe that He is considering it.

# 10

# THE COMING CRASH: CHAOS AND OPPORTUNITY

THE GOVERNMENT IS PREPARED FOR MARKET CRASH—
headline, *New York Post*, July 21, 1997

Nostradamus, the famous sixteenth-century seer, predicted that the Third Antichrist (he forecast the first two as Napoleon and Hitler) will come in July 1999.[1] In my opinion, the Antichrist is already present and accounted for as the Illuminati Ruling Class Conspiracy. Perhaps the world will realize it in 1999. Many of those who read this section will reach that awareness before then.

The state of America near the end of the millennium reinforces that opinion. Here are the facts: The government has run up $7 trillion in debt in the name of welfare statism and continues to sell $200 billion in Treasury securities every month. At this rate, by the year 2012, the cost of entitlements and interest on the debt will consume 100 percent of all taxes collected by the government. Unless the American people wake up to the

Anglophile conspiracy that has claimed our country, rein in our unbridled appetite for welfare statism, force the ruling class to relinquish control of the money supply and credit, and stop inflation by producing "lawful money" (gold- and silver-backed currency), the government will eventually go bankrupt and send the country into Third World Oblivion.

## TOO FEW, TOO RICH

The United States is not the first nation in history to face this man-made disaster. In *Lincoln Money Martyred,* Dr. R. E. Search explains that when the Egyptian government fell, "four percent of the people owned all of the wealth." In Babylon, it was 3 percent; in Persia, 2 percent; in Greece, one half of 1 percent. And when the Roman Empire collapsed, "only two thousand people owned the wealth of the civilized world."[2]

Describing the economic condition of this country in 1935, Search writes: "Less than two percent of the people control ninety percent of the wealth of America."[3] In 1998, it is 1 percent. He blames this phenomenon on "power in the hands of individuals or private groups to issue and control the value and volume of the money of the nation. This right, of course, being obtained by bribery, corruption, trickery, treason, murder, etc."[4] That is a very explicit reference to the Illuminati Ruling Class Conspiracy's takeover of America's money supply through the Fed.

## THE MONEY LORDS

At the center of the British-led Anglophile conspiracy is Illuminati Freemansonry, which has allegedly evolved into a secret core group of an estimated twelve hundred occult family empires. It represents a considerable portion, perhaps most, of the money power in the world.

My source for this contention is *The Occult Technology of Power,* a fictional albeit extremely accurate document that is purported to be a transcript of a transgenerational initiation ritual, in which a paterfamilias of an Illuminati empire passes the reins of power on to his son. Even if the tome is fictional, it contains a logic that is consistent with the investigative reports I have studied.

To understand "the secrets of the finance capitalist money cult," explains the Illuminati money lord to his initiate son, it is essential to understand "occult astronomy, the oldest source of stable rule known to man."[5]

At the dawn of history, in the countries of the Fertile Crescent—Chaldea, Babylon, Assyria, Judea, and Egypt—astronomers were a very small, elite, and powerful group because they could predict the seasons by observing and calculating the positions of the sun, the moon, and the planets. The people needed this information to know when to plant crops, and how to avoid the droughts of summer and the floods of the rainy season. Otherwise, they would starve to death, since in those times, the average person could not count and had no idea of the number of days between seasons.

The ancient astrologers, who used astronomy and who could presage the seasons, had a valuable commodity to sell and they milked it to the fullest at the expense of their credulous fellowmen. "The occult priesthoods of early astronomers and mathematicians, such as the designers of Stonehenge, convinced their subjects that they alone had contact with the gods, and thus, they alone could assure the return of planting seasons and weather favorable to bountiful harvests."[6]

The ancient priesthood's power lay in its ability to make successful predictions about the seasons; and all "knowledge of seasonal regularities was discouraged" among the populace. "The

power of our finance capitalist money cult rests on a similar secret knowledge, primarily in the field of economics," the Illuminist explains to his son. "Fortunately, the public at large and
most revolutionaries remain totally ignorant of economics."[7]

In short, the Illuminati Conspiracy realizes that the public's
ignorance of basic economic principles is the key to robbing and
controlling the population. The Illuminati economic royalty's
greatest fear, along with public exposure, is of a general public
that is aware of the laws and principles of economics. The people, if properly schooled in this field, could not be scammed,
but as the situation now stands, the opinions of one handpicked
man, John Maynard Keynes, constitute the only economic theory that most educated Americans ever receive in our Illuminati-
controlled education system.

Statism, the Illuminati capo instructs his son, as it is taught
through our institutions of higher education, is the cement that
holds the Illuminist scheme of world domination together. To
augment this claim, he points out that for the last fifty years
virtually all American college students have been exposed to
only Keynesian economic theory in a textbook by Paul Samuelson entitled *Economics*. Just think: In a Capitalist and democratic system, every university student is taught, from a Marxist's
viewpoint, the principles of economic science. As noted earlier,
John Maynard Keynes is the British Marxist Illuminati Freemason who allegedly helped confiscate America's gold from Fort
Knox. Samuelson's theoretical mooring is income redistribution, deficit spending, and an aversion to big business—in a
word, basic Communism.

For fifty years, American education has also offered statism
as the only possible environment in which this economic system
can flourish. And for the majority of students, this "Illuminati
101" course, which serves as a primer on basic economic features such as jobs, wages, investment, and growth, will be their
only brush with economics in their entire lives. Ludwig von

Mises, whose economic principles of wealth creation Americans should be studying, said: "Even the opponents of Socialism are dominated by socialist ideas."[8] "I don't care who writes a nation's laws . . . if I can write its economics textbooks," Samuelson boasted in an article in *The Economist,* appropriately entitled "The Puzzling Failure of Economics."[9]

"Our power is weakened," the Illuminati leader explained, "by real advances in economic science."[10] To protect this Achilles' heel, "we money lords have . . . systematically . . . through our power in the universities, publishing and mass media . . . corrupted economic science with fallacious and spurious doctrine." The Illuminist cited "Keynesianism" as "the highest form of phony economics yet developed to our benefit."[11]

He is referring to the "phony economics" of Marxist John Maynard Keynes, "Keynesianism rationalizes this omnipotent state which we require," the evil Illuminati capo concluded.[12]

## THE BASICS

Your ignorance of the basics of economics is essential to the Illuminati financial cult's success. Official government corruption, the theft of your income, and the very existence of the Illuminati depend on that ignorance. Self-empowerment depends on your grasp of these basics. Before you can truly comprehend the world in which you live, you must understand some essential principles of money.

Since the beginning of recorded history, the world has been controlled by real money. Real money is valuable because of what it is: rare, durable, uniform, and exchangeable. Gold and silver are universally accepted as real money, and the Coinage Act of 1792 specifically identifies gold and silver as "money in the United States." The note for a dollar that is now circulated is not real money. It is artificial money—a "promissory note" that can be exchanged for real money (like an IOU, it represents an obligation or promise to repay a loan). It is the scrip of "our" privately owned "Federal" Reserve Bank.

The Constitution declares, in Article I, Section 10, that only gold and silver coin can be a tender in payment of debt. Between 1913, when it unconstitutionally became the bank of issue in the United States, and 1963, this central bank promised to redeem its scrip money for lawful money—silver and gold coin. However, since 1963, the money lords of the private banks have dropped all pretense and made their scrip the "legal tender" of the nation. It is this artificial money that causes inflation, and inflation confiscates our income and savings. As you can see, the fundamental principle of slavery—"You work, I'll eat"—is still in effect in America.

## WHO KILLED THE DOLLAR?

Dollars are more like "bills of credit," which is what notes were called in the American colonies. Imprudent policies followed while managing our country's finances and national currency have resulted in the current federal deficit and the trade deficit and have caused our nation to be weaker politically, economically, and socially. Today, the government's IOU dollar note suffers from a dramatic loss of value, and the trend line is in a perpetual decline.

President Lyndon Johnson started the ball rolling toward the inevitable collapse of the dollar currency and national bankruptcy when he conned the American public with what he called "a unified budget." This act of fiscal manipulation, repeated by every President and Congress since, brought the Social Security program and its enormous surplus into the federal budget so that Johnson could finance two wars—the war in Vietnam and the so-called War on Poverty. The inclusion of the Social Security surplus produced the illusion of a balanced budget.

The American taxpayer was fooled, but the financial markets were not. Although gold was pegged at $35 an ounce, American banks and citizens were not allowed to buy it and other nations, out of fear of destabilizing the U.S. economy, would not convert dollars into gold. In my opinion, benign paternalism among sophisticated investors replaced confidence in American money.

As we have now learned from the Establishment media, this loss of confidence in U.S. currency among international investors—rather than the public's opposition to the Vietnam War—was the main reason for Lyndon Johnson's "sudden decision" not to run for reelection as President in 1968. He knew that he had set this country on a certain course to destruction. By 1971, the dollar's precipitous decline forced President Richard Nixon to abandon officially all pretense of a gold standard.

Today, not one dollar in real money—that is, backed by gold or silver—remains in existence. We now circulate what is essentially evidence of our national debt. And monetary policy, as a result, is now outright evil. Official government economic policy, based on the Fed's propaganda that too many jobs raise the risks of "unacceptable wage inflation," is to curb the very inflation and high interest rates that it creates by printing more fiat money. Inflation is simply too much money chasing too few goods and services. Inflation, as economist Thomas McAuliffe explains, is also the sole product of debt, and debt has created the fiat money that is driving the stock market over the cliff of solvency.[13] Another way of putting it is that the government finances its debt with high unemployment rates created by the Federal Reserve's manipulation of inflationary cycles and subsequent interest-rate increases. Our incomes and wealth are being virtually eaten up by the Fed's debt dollars, as well as by taxes.

And just think, this is the official economic plan of our government to improve the welfare of the people.

As international investors come to understand that future dollars will be worth even less, they will demand higher and higher interest rates to compensate for their risk. If Treasury sales securities increase by only one tenth of 1 percent for six consecutive years, taxpayers will pay—before losing our jobs and businesses and going bankrupt—an extra $25 billion in interest on the $7 trillion national debt. And that scenario is based on a conservative projection.

Because we refuse to cut spending and/or increase our productivity sufficiently to live within our means, our debt and interest on the debt (already over 20 percent of our federal budget) will bankrupt us. The national debt is eating us alive. And it can never be retired. The major media characterize this concern as an obsessive Republican trait, and politicians refuse to do anything serious about this predicament, other than throw impotent and proposed "balanced budget amendments" at it that never become law. Change is fine with the American people, as long as they do not get it and the entitlement checks keep coming. Decades of statist political pandering and free-lunch politics by both major parties have convinced us that you can have smaller government with bigger entitlement checks. The voters have become so confused that they think gridlock—one party in the White House, the other in control of Congress—is a viable political solution to their declining standard of living.

## AN AMERICAN PREDICAMENT

It does not matter which political party controls Congress or the White House. The English Illuminati bankers in "The City" still call the shots, especially with an English-trained puppet like Bill Clinton as President. As a result, there is consistently bad economic news for high school graduates as well as dropouts, men who graduate from college and those who do not, and the employed poor as well as the poor who are looking for a job. Despite the fact that employment and incomes are rising for 5 percent of American families, 95 percent of American families in 1994 had incomes below their 1993 level. Male workers lost 6.3 percent of their income between 1989 and 1995. Wages declined in the 1980s under two Republican Presidents, and continue to do so in the 1990s under a Democratic President. Fewer than 30 percent of Americans are benefiting from the temporary gains on Wall Street, a report by the liberal Economic Policy Institute (EPI) revealed. The 400-page report, *The State of Working America: 1996/97,* also states that the Clinton administration "has done little for the average American worker." And, it concludes, things are only going to get worse.[14]

The Pinocchio race for President in 1996 involved promises as usual. Bob Dole promised a 15 percent tax cut—a good idea in light of the much-needed tax relief, but a bad idea if the President and Congress will not also cut entitlement or defense spending, which Dole himself opposed. Bill Clinton, for his part, bought the votes he needed to remain in the White House with a promise of his own tax cut and a voodoo recipe for debt reduction that was nothing less than disingenuous. Amazingly, after his reelection, Illuminati spooks in both parties made his occult economics plan the law of the land. When the stock market loses 50 percent of its value, don't say I didn't tell you so.

Now President Clinton takes credit for "the best economy in decades," as he calls our debt-burdened system. And the government's agents in the mainstream media chastise the American public for suspecting otherwise. Reality, of course, is on the side of the public's perception of America's decline, as the EPI report confirmed. Another economic report that everyone can

understand was cited recently in *USA Today* under the headline CITIES REPORT MORE HUNGER, HOMELESSNESS.[15]

The main reason the value of the dollar note has not sunk to zero is that many foreign countries use it as the key international currency to contain their domestic inflation rate. This international demand, however, is being jeopardized by a debased dollar note, caused by the inflationary debt created by the printing of fiat money by the U.S. government. At a certain point in the not too distant future, these nations will not be able to afford to hold our debased currency. Sooner or later, these countries will take dollar notes out of circulation and the entire world will see that the U.S. emperor wears no clothes. At that point, the world will unmask this "superpower" as a beggar nation unfit to govern itself, and the United Nations will become our governing body. How can a nation that can't pay its bills call itself the most powerful nation in the world.

What happens when the government cannot pay its bills and faces a $12 trillion debt? The privately owned Fed prints more dollar debt notes and hyperinflates the economy. That robs everyone of their wealth, and $10,000 in the bank becomes $1,000 or less in hours. The Illuminati Communists did it intentionally in Russia to destroy the middle class and transfer the income of the people to the ruling oligarchy. Germany hyperinflated its money supply after World War I, when it could no longer raise taxes. After only three years of printing-press money flooding the country, the German mark was pegged at 2.4 trillion to the dollar. It took a basket of money to buy a loaf of bread.

History is instructive about the consequences of printing-press inflation. Invariably, it wipes out savings and investments, resulting in a massive loss of homes and businesses. Why would the same phenomenon spare America when it crushed Germany years before? You've been fed the propaganda about new government safeguards to prevent a recurrence of the 1929 crash.

No government can reverse the law of compound interest on its debt.

## THE GROWTH TUNNEL

Investors are rational people, and they are not fooled by the government's printing-press scam. They simply do not want to be paid back with weaker dollars. Therefore, they only have confidence in the U.S. economy when unemployment is high enough to offset the debasing effects on the currency of the circulation of more dollar notes of debt.

In my opinion, this policy has placed our country on an unsustainable path because it ignores the mandate to invest in the future. Officially, the government strives for a sluggish 2 percent annual growth.

Why is the government deliberately stunting the growth of the American economy? "Because we're in a growth tunnel," says economist Lester Thurow. And the ceiling and the floor of this growth tunnel are bounded by federal debt. For example, if output continued to grow at 4.8 percent annually, the hidden structural flaw in our economy would become apparent to the public. The process of inflationary printing would be exposed, as would maintaining enough joblessness among the poor to protect the investments of the wealthy. Also, if the output of the rest of the world is growing at about 2 percent, the United States would suck in so many imports that our trade deficit would soar. Professor Thurow says that with that kind of trade deficit problem, at some point "the dollar falls out of bed" and causes hyperinflation of American assets. Therefore, our debt limits us with a growth *ceiling*.[16]

The *floor* is made up of another kind of debt problem, Thurow says. For example, if our overdue recession occurs in 1998, Latin America, which sells most of its exports to the

United States, will not earn enough to pay the interest on its debt. Latin America would default and, as a result, the ten largest banks in the United States would be technically bankrupt.[17]

America's dilemma: Both the ceiling debt problem and the floor debt problem in our economy's growth tunnel lead to hyperinflation and ultimately a national disaster.

We lost 28 percent of our standard of living during the Great Depression of 1929. The loss I am describing will be four times as big as the biggest recession since World War II. Poor and marginal families will be hit even harder. To put it mildly, it will be an industrial-size mess. And that mess is being intentionally created in the name of fighting inflation.

## BILL CLINTON'S BIG LIE OF PROSPERITY

In the course of writing this book, I have come to the opinion that the forty-second President of the United States has cast his lot with the power elite. Clinton is, depending on who you talk to, a former member of the Trilateral Commission and the Council on Foreign Relations, a Freemason, a Rhodes ("British Race Patriot") Scholar, a CIA asset, and a Bilderberger. Somewhere in *that* woodpile is the Illuminati Ruling Class Conspiracy.

Two other factors shape my opinion: his racist attitude and pattern of scolding Blacks who resent his arrogant, British-style paternalism (the Jesse Jackson–Sister Souljah syndrome), and his cynical alliance with the Federal Reserve system to drive the country into inflationary chaos.

Clinton's first four years in office were unencumbered by high inflation rates, the Illuminati's weapon of choice to destroy a President. That makes me even more suspicious of him, because I believe that Jimmy Carter's performance did not please the private owners of America's money supply, and, as a result, they inflated him out of office. However, pleased by Clinton's sycophant economic performance and his charismatic ability to sell bankruptcy with a smile, the money lords temporarily restrained their confiscation greed and monetizing of the debt by reducing inflation—printing less scrip—to make the economy look good. The "economic miracle" bought Clinton a second term.

Meanwhile, as Clinton and Greenspan increase unemployment with Nairu, the alleged rate at which unemployment does the most for the economy, to maximize the Illuminati bankers' profits, a new wave of inflation is under way to confiscate more of Americans' income and property. Clinton is feeding inflation. He knows that "real," inflation-adjusted, earnings and family incomes have been declining for several decades. A Teamster who won a 5 percent wage hike, amounting to 17 percent over the next four years, saw his hourly wage shoot up to $8.96 an hour. But in real terms, after adjusting for the inflation that Clinton is inciting, this Teamster and millions of other Americans like him are making less than they did in 1988.

I am not blaming Clinton for Ronald Reagan's deficit-driven economy or the horrendous inflation rate that Reagan inherited from Jimmy Carter. I am blaming him for using unemployment to curb the inflation he creates that is taking 5 percent of that Teamster's salary every year. Clinton is employing Illuminati high finance: deliberate inflation by means of floating scrip money that destroys the middle class and allows the government and the banks to confiscate workers' savings.

As a Rhodes Scholar loyal to British imperialism, Clinton knows that when the government steals the income of the people through a debased currency, the people become more dependent on government. Control becomes centralized and allows the Karl Marx Illuminists like the horde of Rhodes Scholars in the White House to ravage the hated middle class and its ownership of property (income and home). People are forced to work harder and keep less, and in return they are offered welfare statism, which inevitably brings totalitarianism and an antireligious society.

In the meantime, the economy, according to Dr. Stephen Leeb, editor of *Personal Finance,* is, in technical terms, reaching its outer limits, and the demand for products and services is putting "pressure on loan capital, wages" and products and services. "Any Economics 101 textbook will tell you that increasing demand plus dwindling resources equals inflation."[18]

Under the circumstances, Leeb argues,

> The only way to avoid inflation is to try for a so-called "soft landing" by raising interest rates, lowering the money supply and reducing government spending. But Clinton knows full well that a growing economy, with low unemployment and rising wages, will help put his agenda in place. . . . He's not about to take a hard stand on inflation.[19]

A politically motivated Clinton knows very well, as Leeb explains, how to stop inflation, but he will not. According to Leeb, Clinton is encouraging it with "growth-oriented policies that will lead to rising commodity prices, put upward pressure on wages and allow banks to raise lending rates. The net result: higher inflation and interest rates."[20] I think it is fair to say that our character-impaired President is doing his part to cause an economic crash.

## A CRASH

Expect higher inflation and a "stock market crash of possibly historic proportions" in late 1988, predicts Dr. Leeb.[21] Accelerated inflation, he says, "cannot be stopped or avoided," and a stock market crash will shortly follow. Greenspan has taken the unprecedented step of warning the public about its "irrational" investing in the stock market, Leeb says, "because he wants you to get your money out of the market now, before you get slaughtered."[22]

Since Greenspan knows the market, Leeb concludes, it is prudent to follow his advice, and invest "with him" if you want to "get rich." In spite of Greenspan's wisdom, however, inflation has returned because "the factors that caused disinflation have ended," Leeb reports. Corporate downsizing has bottomed out and wages are rising at the fastest rate since the 1980s, despite the Fed's Nairu policy to keep millions unemployed.

Leeb, who has also authored *The Agile Investor,* says that this fast growth in wages is "not being matched by productivity gains. For the first time since the Industrial Revolution, productivity for most corporations is flat—zero."[23] Greenspan knows this scenario is playing itself out but is afraid to "hit the brakes" by increasing interest rates and killing demand for mortgages, loans, and other consumer needs because that "may trigger a stock market catastrophe,"[24] the effects of which will be more widespread than ever because a record 63 percent of Americans now own stocks. This will not be a sophisticated investor catastrophe; it is going to be Ma-and-Pa-driven panic, followed by a recession and/or depression. Our recent penchant for making money with paper instead of productivity has come home to roost.

At this stage, it really does not matter whether the Fed decides to increase interest rates or not. They will go up automatically because lenders are aware that they will be repaid with dollars of less value. Higher interest rates, of course, will attract investors into the bond market. When rates get high enough, as John Crudele, syndicated business columnist for the *New*

*York Post,* explained on *Tony Brown's Journal,* people are not going to sell their homes to buy bonds, "they are going to sell their stocks to buy interest rate bonds." At this stage, "you're looking at a slowing economy and a Federal Reserve Board that has no control over the economy," Crudele says.[25]

"But the greatest danger will come in late 1998. By then inflation will have built up a head of steam and interest rates will have been raised sharply by the Fed," Leeb adds. "This, in turn, would likely push the stock market over the nearest cliff, and could easily trigger a decline of historic proportions."[26]

## GOVERNMENT WARNING

Amid a general euphoria about the health of the economy, Treasury Secretary Robert Rubin, former Vice-Chairman of Salomon Brothers, announced that the federal government was "ready to handle the economic and financial fall-out if the high-flying stock market collapses." Rubin advised investors "to take account of the economic outlook," as he joined Federal Reserve Chairman Alan Greenspan in warning naive stock market investors of "irrational exuberance."[27]

Paul Volcker, Greenspan's predecessor at the Fed, was decidedly not exuberant when he told *Forbes* magazine that the current expectations in the stock market are excessive and that a 15-percent-a-year growth "cannot be met."[28] Volcker explained that "15 percent compounded doubles in 5 years. The stock market in 15 years would have to be 60,000."[29] He warned against American "arrogance," and predicted a downsizing in stocks and "five years of no increases."[30]

Prognosticator and Wall Street icon Robert Precter forecasted the 1982–1987 bull market. In 1997, he predicted that the market would fall by more than 50 percent over the next two years. It will be followed, he said, by a 1930s-style Depression.[31] I asked John Crudele about Precter's prediction.

The stock market of "irrational exuberance" (Greenspan's term), Crudele explained, is a liquidity-driven market, just as a "Ponzi scheme is a liquidity-driven scheme, when you pay back your first investors with new money coming in."[32] At the time of Crudele's statement, there was so much money coming in that the market could only go up. That has created the unsustainable 15-percent-a-year growth rate in an economy that is only growing in real terms at a little more than 2 percent. That worries Paul Volcker.

That unsustainable growth is the magnet that drags new investors into the scheme. As long as there is fresh money coming in, the market continues to rise and build in "irrational exuberance." That brings us back to another Volcker worry: the low savings rate, which means, according to Crudele, that the amount of money coming into the stock market cannot be sustained. In fact, it has already diminished, and although still large, it is slowing dramatically.[33]

As a result of the diminution of new capital, the Ponzi scheme (those at the top of the pyramid get paid as long as enough new suckers are recruited) ultimately collapses, and along with it the market. When that happens, expect the 1929 investor psychology to take over. Crudele explains that when the market starts going down, the same people who came into the market thinking they would make a fortune panic, and all of them try to get out at the same time. If enough people lose their retirement income and investments, the Precter-predicted 1930s-style Depression will be a reality.

Of course, the real threat to a debtor nation that would rather lose its sovereignty than live within its means, increase its productivity to accommodate its spending, or increase its savings to eliminate the need to borrow is always foreign control. When you allow "foreigners into your house to essentially buy your furniture," Crudele says, "you lose control over your house."[34]

"Increasingly the gains are going to the people who lent us the money," an obviously worried ex-Fed Chairman told *Forbes*. No one in government will do anything, "nobody pays any attention. . . . It's really sad. Everyone agrees we need change, yet nothing gets done."[35] With those words, Paul Volcker clearly meant that President Clinton's administration is asleep at the switch. And Congress, having learned during the "Republican Revolution" of 1994 that any attempt to genuinely balance the budget is political suicide, has seen Republican revolutionaries turned into Illuminati spooks and Congress itself become coconspirator with the White House in doing the Illuminati Ruling Class Conspiracy's dirty work, the Hegelian Shuffle.

## A WEALTH OF OPPORTUNITY

The prediction that the United States economy will collapse in 1998 may be off by a few months or even years, but a total economic collapse is inevitable. It is just a matter of time. Facts, such we have seen, do not lie and cannot be legislated out of existence.

Out of what will be a horrible period for the world will come great opportunities for the accumulation of wealth and for spiritual growth. Wealth will not disappear; it will just change hands.

The new factor in the global economic equation is competition by an increasing number of nations for a finite amount of commodities: steel, copper, tin, and oil, among others, Dr. Stephen Leeb believes. For the first time, developing countries, especially in Asia, need large amounts of these natural resources to fuel their economies and accommodate a burgeoning middle class. The growth of demand in China, with 20 percent of the world's population, for many raw materials will cause a price surge in commodities, especially gold and oil. China's imports of oil within fourteen years will quintuple to 15 percent of total global consumption.[36]

America never did anything about its energy crisis of the 1970s. In fact, we are now driving bigger gas guzzlers at faster speeds. While demand for oil is skyrocketing, supplies have not kept pace and it takes years to start up production again. As a result, there will be no immediate increase in supplies, which means a dramatic and sustained increase in the price of oil, perhaps to as high as $50 a barrel, Leeb predicts.[37]

The coming years will be a replay of the period between 1965 and 1981 when the "buy-and-hold" strategy proved disastrous for investors in stocks, bonds, and mutual funds. And Leeb believes that if you listen to today's "media darlings" and put your money in mutual funds with a long-term outlook, you will relearn the lessons of 1965–1981.

*Business Week* called Leeb "one of the most prophetic newsletter writers."

Here is an overview of Leeb's four suggested investment opportunities from his newsletter, *Personal Finance*:

1. *Massive Profits From the New Oil Shortage: Toward $50 Oil—How to Profit Richly From the Classic Supply-Demand Squeeze Now Building in Oil.*

Long term, rising oil prices are as certain as death and taxes. Since oil became a commercial commodity in the last century, oil prices have followed fairly regular cycles, with prices rising for about a decade and then falling for a decade.

At this point we're in the early stages of a sustained period of rising prices that will ultimately take oil prices well past their previous peak in the early 1980s. They could go as high as $50 per barrel. . . .

Currently the world's oil producers, save for Iraq, are operating at close to full capacity. This means the growth in demand has to be satisfied by added capacity.

Over the next decade, even assuming Iraq comes back full force, growth in demand promises to far exceed the ability to add capacity. Oil is a finite commodity, so even new technologies will have limits in bringing along new capacity. . . .

China's per capita oil consumption is only one-tenth that of Korea and one-thirtieth that of the U.S. When you multiply gains in per capita consumption by a huge population you get a monstrous increase in demand. Add to that the precarious stability of the Middle East and the region's inability to add to its production capacity, and oil prices have nowhere to go but up.

Not only is international activity heating up, but the domestic economy is on a roll as well. This rare occurrence of simultaneous worldwide expansion will pressure energy prices no matter what the cartels and heads of state attempt.

2. *The Single Best Investment of 1998: Why Small Stocks Will Run Rings Around the S&P 500 in 1998 . . . and for the Next Several Years.*

The economic conditions of the last ten years—declining inflation and slow growth—favored large companies that dominate markets through efficiencies of scale. But during periods of high inflation, the right small company can double in size much quicker. Small stocks even outperform gold stocks, the number one inflation hedge, during times of rising inflation.

You hear it all the time: Small stocks outperform their big-cap brethren. But in the past decade the reverse was true. How did this happen?

Over the past 10 years the economy was marked by

slow growth and declining inflation. These are conditions that reward large companies, which can dominate their markets through efficiencies of scale. Then, because of their dominance, they control how products are priced.

But if, as we expect, inflation picks up over the next five years, small companies will once again have the edge. In an inflationary economy, small companies turn in much faster rates of growth. For example, it's easier to go from $1 billion to $2 billion in sales than from $10 billion to $20 billion. When growth is rapid and inflation rising, small stocks and mutual funds shine.

3. *Bargain Hunting Abroad.*

"International stocks" performance and investor interest may have lagged the U.S. market in 1995, but the tide is changing. . . .

First, economies around the world, especially in emerging nations, have higher rates of growth than the U.S.—often with very low rates of inflation.

In Southeast Asia, stock markets have been growing stronger since their poor performance over the last two years. In Japan, the economy continues to recover slowly but surely. The yen is lower but consumer expenditures have finally shown some signs of life, and the Bank of Japan is pursuing a supportive monetary policy without accelerating inflation.

Europe's major markets are outperforming many of the world's robust developing markets. And there are many European-based multinationals that are going gangbusters as they expand into other economies that are growing quickly.

Latin America is on the comeback trail. After having its currency and bolsa [stock market] decimated in late

1994/early 1995, Mexico has seen some economic recovery and the peso has finally stabilized. In South America, Chile has slowed but Argentina, Venezuela, and Brazil are all brimming with confidence and economic activity.

A second impetus for looking beyond our borders is that international mutual funds allow you to remain fully invested in a broad portfolio of stocks while reducing the risks of being in the domestic market, which is fluctuating around record highs.

4. *The Right REITs—Doubling Investors' Money Every 4.2 Years.*

Real Estate Investment Trust (REIT): The investment is both safer and better-performing than stocks. At 17 percent a year, your money doubles every 4.2 years.

Which sounds better: a long-term bond that yields about 7 percent but falls in value whenever inflation appears, or a stock with a dividend yield of 7 percent that rises faster when inflation picks up?

Real estate investment trusts offer everything bonds do, and more. The only problem is that if we're half right on inflation, REITs won't remain in the bargain bin forever. . . .

REITs are professionally managed collections of real estate properties. They're to real estate what mutual funds are to stocks, with one critical difference. While mutual funds have a tough time outperforming the overall stock market, REITs in general far outdistance the overall real estate market.[38]

Along with oil, small stocks, real estate, and select international funds, the editors of *Personal Finance* say that "gold is poised to be one of the top performers of 1998," and "All five of these investments are tied to rising U.S. inflation and the enormous economic growth of Asia."[39] When inflation rises, gold prices also go up because of its intrinsic value.

Leeb further ties gold's increased value to the economic growth of Asia and Asians' demand for gold jewelry. In one year, China and India alone purchased 55 percent of the world's supply of gold.[40] In 1995, gold consumption hit an all-time high, an event that was underreported in the media. Since 1995, unlike the previous five-thousand-year history of gold mining, demand for the precious metal has outpaced the supply of newly mined gold.[41]

Leeb says the world's central banks presently do not have enough supply to meet the increased demand. Add the inflation factor, he says, and

> the case for gold becomes exceptionally strong. . . . Over the last five years, one of our favorite gold funds, The Midas Fund, has risen 18.9 percent annually, eclipsing many other types of mutual funds. And that's without much movement in the price of gold! As inflation moves higher and Asian demand keeps growing, gold prices will rise and gold funds will skyrocket.[42]

In Part I of this book, we explored the Illuminati Ruling Class Conspiracy's use of government debt creation, currency debasement, monetary supply inflation, taxation, and importation of illicit drugs to destabilize the U.S. economy and drive the country toward totalitarian statism. In the previous chapter, we saw how imminent the economic disaster is and how relentlessly the government is speeding it along.

The President and the Conspiracy agenturs of both parties in Congress "balanced" the budget in 1997, using false and occult economic assumptions, only to leave in place a shortfall of $50 billion to $150 billion.[43] The two major entitlements were left to grow and gobble up the national income, and the $7 trillion national debt was entirely ignored.

Knowing full well that the United States can never hope to retire the "national" debt, Bill Clinton and the bipartisan welfare statists in Congress put on a cynical public relations show of signing the "balanced budget" accord, whose supposed goal is the *eventual* elimination of the deficit. The deficit is the annual shortfall between what we take in and what we spend. In other words, the deficit is the amount we steal each year from future generations of Americans. The debt is the nation's total obligation, the sum total of the accumulated yearly deficits, including the interest that has compounded.

The new Big Lie told by Congress and the President is that there is for the first time in thirty years a budget surplus. A declaration by House Speaker Newt Gingrich that we are near $100 billion a year surpluses is simply untrue, and if a business computed its income the way the government does, it would commit a criminal act. The government accounting counts the huge Social Security trust fund in computing the annual deficit, thereby hiding the true size of the federal deficit.

*Newsweek* magazine explains that the government claimed a deficit for fiscal 1997 of $22.6 billion. But in reality, it was $103.9 billion.[44] The political class also hides the interest we must pay on the fund's holdings, which adds billions to the deficit. Were the federal government to account for its unfunded Social Security liability "the way federal law requires corporations to account for their pension liabilities, this year's [1998] deficit would instantly rise by over $500 billion," The Concord Coalition reports.[45]

No matter what Congress does, it cannot repeal compound interest. We owe foreigners and the stockholders who own the private central bank so much that by around the year 2012, the *interest* alone on the debt—already over 20 percent of all taxes collected, or $650 billion—will be more than 100 percent of all personal and business taxes collected. That is bankruptcy, and what will follow is the unavoidable chaos of hyperinflation and a likely takeover by the one-worlders at the United Nations and its economic instruments, the International Monetary Fund (IMF) and the World Bank. And that will lead to an Illuminati Ruling Class Conspiracy dictatorship.

The money lords and the politicians know this scenario better than anyone. Their response to our current economic crisis is to hasten the inevitable by continuing to borrow $1.1 billion every day. There is only one conclusion that an intelligent person can draw: Some of America's "leaders" are members of the Illuminati Ruling Class Conspiracy, which aims to destroy the United States.

Whichever way you look, there are very few in authority who can really be trusted. The solutions to our problems must come from us, the people. To protect ourselves and save the country, we have to rely on ourselves and each other. If you can identify one institution in this country that is not corrupted, you have defeated the premise of this book.

## IT HAS STARTED

Friday, August 8, 1997, just as I was completing this chapter, there was a dramatic drop in the stock market. The dollar "fell sharply against the yen and the mark, raising fears that foreign buyers might pull back from the U.S. debt market," *The Wall Street Journal* reported.[46] "Two weeks ago none of this seemed possible," the *Journal* commented; the economy was fine and "inflation was in check." The economy, in fact, was not healthy two weeks before, nor was inflation "in check."

*The Washington Post*'s take on the August 8 minicrisis was that it might have to drop "Nirvana" as a description of financial market conditions.[47] This was the second end-of-the-week

plunge in a row and inflation, they had to know, was back because the Fed would print more fiat paper to cover Japan's
shortfall and raise interest rates at the same time to fight the
inflation it created. *The New York Times* said it was "a bad day"
for bonds, stocks, and the dollar.[48] The Ponzi scheme is on its
last leg.

"What If Wall Street Crashed," the *New York Post* asked
without a question mark in a front-page story. "After Friday's
156-point plunge, the chilling scenario that could happen . . ."
In the *Post*'s what-if futuristic scenario, the stock market crashed
by nearly 25 percent or 2,000 points in one day. My sources
believe that the real thing will be closer to 50 percent. "Of
course," the *Post* continued, "they say it can't happen. But
that's what they said in 1929," and in 1987. "In both cases,
the downturns came after weeks of slow but steady declines—
such as Friday's 156-point dive—which should have served as a
warning to investors."[49]

I include this dated material because the same phenomenon,
only worse, is likely to happen any day. The impending crisis is
candidly reported in the European press. The July 27, 1997,
*London Sunday Times* headline advised readers BRACE YOURSELF
FOR THE CRASH,[50] and columnists are offering advice on survival
methods in the event of a depression. "If you look at the big
crash in 1929," the July 26, 1997, *Frankfurt Allgemeine Zei-
tung* reported, "there are certain striking similarities: the overall
euphoria, the growing wish today to buy financial assets, the
run-up on new stocks, the utilization of the favorable market
climate to issue new stocks, the takeover speculation." And this
"high-altitude ecstasy" is driven by huge liquidity.

Of course, "free markets do not always warn," as Beth Piskora wrote in the *Post*.[51] There is nothing we can do to prevent
the looming economic tragedy, but we can prepare for it. Empower yourself and others in your community by learning to
build and protect real wealth—spiritual and material.

# 11

# THE SEVEN STEPS TO EMPOWERMENT

*I manifest character and genius, with which I create and cleanse
wealth. By applying critical thinking and the active principle,
my role is to help build self-empowered families, train cyberleaders
for the twenty-first century, and teach twelve others for the
perpetuation of the work. Brother to brother, sister to sister, in God
we trust.*
—THE INNER CIRCLE CREED

The American people have been fed the assumption that since
politicians and central bankers are inevitable features of our society, we can only improve things by getting better central bankers and politicians. In fact, we would be better off without
either. These elites exploit human misery and practice deception
in order to dominate the citizens of this Republic. Our government is not "for the people," neither as prescribed by the Constitution nor as advertised during July Fourth celebrations.

## SELF-EMPOWERMENT TO THE PEOPLE

You and I, Joe and Jane Taxpayer, are on our own. Our government has failed us and has turned its back on God. The country

cries out for honest leadership and action from people like you and me. If we, the people—all of us, Black, White, Red, Yellow, and Brown—do not unite on our own behalf and for our own welfare, we will all share a sad fate.

The first step in the process of self-empowerment is realizing our own responsibility and establishing our authority within our local communities. The trick to dealing with conspiracies that dominate our lives is to take control of our own lives. An awareness and knowledge of our own power will lead to freedom and prosperity.

The Tenth Amendment to the Constitution states that all powers not delegated to the government belong "to the people." But to take the country back from the ruling class, we will have to work within the boundaries of "the system." To step outside of it is only to provide a convenient opportunity for the Illuminati Ruling Class Conspiracy to flex its "legal" muscle to enforce its dominion. It is essential that we recognize our limitations in this conspiratorial system, yet move to create our own reality, identity, purpose, and destiny.

Our identity, purpose, and creativity are the major weapons we will use against tyranny. Life and reality become what we make of them. We can either conspire to fulfill ourselves or live vicariously through those we criticize for running the world. Why not dominate and run your own world? With simple and inexpensive technology, we all can, for the first time, create our world.

## BECOMING A RULING CLASS

The Illuminati money lords have developed a system of tried-and-true measures to control and dominate us. The Illuminati Ruling Class Conspiracy has: (1) its own money system and control of the money supply; (2) control of an economy that hires talent and buys influence; (3) products to sell; (4) a network of alliances with like-minded people who also control wealth and their own spheres of influence; (5) a strong commitment to achieving specific social, economic, and political objectives; (6) the use of cutting-edge technology (capitalism is essentially a system in which employers provide tools for workers); and (7) the intergenerational transfer of money, power, and philosophy.

The way to defeat a ruling class is to become one—a power bloc that eliminates the elite's advantages and serves the interests of the people. The focus must be on organization and money. We must deal with earning a living and fighting an oppressive system at the same time. Therefore, our solution must be synergistic. We need to make personal progress in a way that also addresses our national predicament. That is the unique feature of my proposal. In my self-empowerment plan, when Tony Brown solves his predicament, he takes a chunk out of the nation's predicament at the same time, because my neighbor also benefits.

My plan will not just show you how to make more money while ignoring your social and political environment and the plight of others. Being rich will not protect us from the perils of an economic crash or a race war. We will need to use our numerical and moral advantage to organize local community-based networks to generate money by marketing products that are routinely consumed and needed by members of the community and to empower members of the community to use their talents and skills. Such a networking system not only creates wealth for its members but also frees them from dependence on the ruling class.

## SEVEN STEPS TO EMPOWERMENT

The basic premise of my seven-step plan is that we must protect ourselves from the Illuminati Ruling Class Conspiracy in order to guarantee justice and equality for all in an information-driven, litigious society. My plan is for the people to compete directly with the ruling class for the monetary and intellectual control of the country. Furthermore, I propose that we use the tools and instruments of the power elite to restore power to the people in the spirit of egalitarianism.

Americans can do this with root economies, a local money system, computer intranets, and faith in one another. In addition, since in the new millennium, information will become the currency of power, we must prepare ourselves for technological self-empowerment with a nationwide online computer network and computer training capability.

I am convinced that this plan will reduce the size of welfare statism and its authority. Using our brains, not violence, is the only viable way to wrest our freedom from the Illuminati Ruling Class Conspiracy. Its hold on the United States is based on the central bankers' control of our money and the citizens' pro-grammed ignorance of economics. The only force we need in order to stand up to this encroaching slavery is willpower and awareness. Besides, the pen has always been mightier than the sword.

I have organized the Inner Circle, a prototype empowerment network with its own money system (with scrip called Freedoms), a Work Force 2000 training component, and a nationwide online computer system and internet service provider (ISP) that links members of the network together in a root economy, along the principles of my seven-step plan. The experience of the Inner Circle along with the following step-by-step approach will show you how to empower yourself and your community:

Step 1: Organize a Marketing Network

Step 2: Create and Cleanse Wealth: E=CLP+FSI

Step 3: Start a Root Economy and a Money System

Step 4: Make Sure Every Home in Your Network Has
       a Computer

Step 5: Reach Out and Stop Civil War II

Step 6: Start a Public Awareness Campaign to Fight
       the Drug War Against U.S.

Step 7: Justice: Make the Government Work for U.S.

## STEP 1: ORGANIZE A MARKETING NETWORK

Local communities can empower themselves by marketing within their own borders in order to retain their incomes and create wealth. For example, in the 1960s, Blacks talked up Black pride and thought up dashikis but bought them from Whites, Yellows, and Browns. They created a market that other ethnic groups exploited. Today, Blacks are exchanging only 3 percent of their annual incomes—$15 billion dollars a year out of $500 billion—with each other.

Wealth is the source of power, and communities of interest must be astute enough to create empowering structures among their own members. In addition, when members of a community cleanse wealth by helping each other, they create more wealth in the form of social capital and are spiritually empowered.

Each of us belongs to several communities of interest: ethnic, religious, professional, and so on. All of these groups control money, comprise educated, skilled people, and help their members; in other words, they are wealthy. They are alliances, networks with a major common interest.

Among the members of these groups, find the doers. I call my doers the Inner Circle. Use the information from Part I and the Y2K Corps opportunity described later in this chapter to motivate them to understand why they must act—now. Find nondoers, those who have stopped trying because they have never had good leadership, a structure, and a plan to get things done. Get them to read this book and join your network as consumers, if they do not want to play an active marketing role and/or if they do not need more money. We cannot afford to leave anyone behind. Once they see the big picture and become more convinced of their own worth, they will become indispensable to what we are trying to achieve and our ultimate victory. Everyone has a role to play, and everyone should be treated with dignity.

THE INNER CIRCLE: A SELF-EMPOWERMENT MODEL

The Inner Circle is my prototype for an empowerment project. The goals are self-empowerment and community empowerment. It is based on the theory that only a core group will work and get things done. I encourage you to use this prototype to set up your own empowerment network. This chapter will show you how to accumulate money and cleanse your wealth, create your own money system, find products that literally sell themselves, ally yourself with people of character and genius, access self-improvement and training, and use computers and online computer services to connect you to everyone else in the network nationwide and over 50 million people on the global Internet. You may add to the model of the Inner Circle or subtract from it to fit your needs in designing your local empowerment network.

The Inner Circle began as a pilot project in the Tri-State area of New York, New Jersey, and Connecticut. Within six months, it grew to five thousand members, primarily from the audience of my radio program on WLIB-AM. It is now a nationwide program devoted to community empowerment—a network that produces financial, social, and human capital and builds character and genius among its members.

The Creed of the Inner Circle is: "I manifest character and genius, with which I create and cleanse wealth. By applying critical thinking and the active principle, my role is to help build self-empowered families, train cyberleaders for the twenty-first century, and teach twelve others for the perpetuation of the work. Brother to brother, sister to sister, in God we trust. Yours in the Truth." The seven principles of the Inner Circle are: (1) Character and Genius, (2) Wealth Building, (3) Wealth Cleansing, (4) Critical Thinking, (5) Self-Empowered Family, (6) Cyberleader Cadet Corps, (7) Each One Teach Twelve.

The Inner Circle fosters the creation of wealth by providing various opportunities through a multilevel marketing distribution network. To facilitate retention of our collective income, I encourage the use of a mix of Freedoms, our barter currency, and U.S. dollars for trading among the members of the network and their friends. Each member is expected to empower a minimum of twelve people by bringing them as members into this academic, technical, and economic network. Networking is on a quid pro quo basis: something-for-something empowerment.

At the end of its first year, I project that the Inner Circle will have between 50,000 and 100,000 members in the United States. In five years, it could approach over a million members in one of the largest network marketing groups in America, handling billions of dollars. That would constitute a major economy in its own right. This geometric expansion will create an Inner Circle market capable of supporting a local root economy whose paper scrip (Freedoms) will be as valuable as the Fed's private scrip (dollars). There is no other possible model for empowerment that can reach so many, at such distances, in so little time, with so little capital investment required. Our greatest assets, of course, are our numerical strength and our talents.

The overall goal of the Inner Circle is to uniquely empower

as many people as possible. The Inner Circle organizes people of character for the simple purpose of self-empowerment, while offering specific opportunities to create additional income and participate in an economic alliance with thousands of like-minded people nationwide. I say uniquely empower because nontraditional tools, such as computer networks and information technology, are utilized along with the traditional instruments of human and financial capital to exploit business opportunities in cyberspace and develop twenty-first-century solutions.

Any serious empowerment program today requires rapid communications. We employ our own online computer network and internet service provider (ISP)—*Tony Brown Online*—because we are prepared to operate in the technological millennium. In the fading Industrial Age, the main source of wealth was physical. We bought and sold things. That age is gone, replaced by the Information Age. Knowledge—not just scientific knowledge but also news, advice, entertainment, communication, and information services—has become the recognized primary ingredient of what we make, do, buy, and sell. Today, knowledge is more valuable and more powerful than natural resources, big factories, or fat bankrolls. Knowledge assets are the key to creating wealth.

And as personal income for Blacks jumped 13 percent from 1995 to 1996, a sharp increase in purchases of personal computers by the Black middle class demonstrated a keen awareness of the importance of technology to the education of its children, according to a study on the *Philadelphia Inquirer*'s web site. Blacks, who are now closing the technology gap, are beginning to demonstrate this same growth in the arena of network marketing.

ANYONE CAN DO IT: E=CLP+FSI
You're probably thinking that in order to take advantage of

these opportunities, you need a storefront, an inventory of products, an advertising budget, and a ton of money to pay for it all. Not anymore you don't. In fact, you can, in some cases, start with no money, run the business out of your home, and build it to almost any size you want. The Inner Circle can assist you in getting a web site, a storefront on the Internet with a virtual office, and supply the inventory for your business, plus a specific marketing plan for each product.

There are good, better, and best marketing strategies: *Good* involve selling one or more of the Inner Circle products to your friends and relatives; *better,* selling the products also to churches, mosques, synagogues, and civic groups; *best,* selling the products of the Inner Circle on the Internet to fifty million people worldwide, as well as friends, relatives, churches, mosques, synagogues, and civic groups. Your choice will be dictated by your personal circumstances and financial goals.

## TBOL: INNER CIRCLE ON THE INTERNET

If you choose to become the *best,* you will need access to the World Wide Web on the Internet in order to recruit a national and international downline and sell worldwide. To get there, you can sign up with *America Online* (AOL) and frequently spend hours listening to busy signals and waiting for Internet access or you can join the family on *Tony Brown Online* (TBOL) for an instant connection and reach the Internet whenever you want without wasting valuable time—and time is money. Both AOL and TBOL cost only $19.95 a month and both online services provide local access telephone numbers.

But if you choose TBOL, you will get a speedy connection and a *free* web page as well. This one simple, inexpensive act will put you in the Inner Circle on the Internet with your own personal store on the World Wide Web (free advertisement to fifty million people), as well as the availability of Y2K online (at-home) training. The Inner Circle will also offer you nine opportunities to stock your Internet store with top-of-the-line products that can be electronically ordered from you from anywhere in the world—even while you sleep. The Inner Circle products were carefully selected. Because they are used by virtually everyone, they are beneficial to the individual and to society (including the environment) and therefore they sell themselves.

## SUPER-MARKET NETWORK MARKETING

The Inner Circle business opportunities are as follows:

1. Exquisite Wittnauer watches, at distributor prices (no inventory required). The NEW Wittnauer, a Black-owned company and Inner Circle member, is the new sponsor for *Tony Brown's Journal* on PBS. Therefore, if you wear a Wittnauer Inner Circle watch you'll know what time it is—in more ways than one—and you will be empowered.

2. A chemical-free and environment-friendly Laundry System (cleaning disc), with a seven-year warranty, that cleans your clothes—for pennies a wash. A New Yorker named Nuriddin Muhammad earned approximately $30,000 during his first month as an Inner Circle distributor of this system. Lynda Howard earned $924,413 in 8 months by showing people how to clean their laundry without laundry detergents. In fact, here's a message from Lynda, a Carlsbad, California, single mother of two:

"In April 1997, I was introduced to an incredible opportunity. At first, I couldn't even imagine that anyone could be interested. Skepticism was my first knee-jerk reaction to something different and unique. But I was in a financial situation that gave me no choice other than to listen with an open mind.

"I sure am glad that I did! Amazingly, my first check for April 1997 was over $51,000, my second check was $78,700.03, my third check was $91,492.77, my fourth check was over $119,000, my fifth check for August sales was over $138,000, and my sixth check for my September sales was over $175,000!!! And I did all this from the comfort of my home." (Verification of her income is available.)

Although the average income in network marketing is $200 a month, Lynda Howard has proved that no one is limited to $200 a month. In fact, if your group or church became a distributor and Lynda Howard was in its network marketing downline, your church or group would automatically receive an additional $150,000 a month in compensation!

3. A legal protection service that provides a $300-an-hour lawyer for only $200 a year.

4. Helping other people eliminate *all* their debts while they get a guaranteed, no-risk return on their money of over 25 percent. Available to Inner Circle members: A list of eleven million prospects who need this service.

5. Your own promotional travel agency, with personal discounts and commissions for hotels and airlines.

6. Tony Brown Tours around the world, with Empowerment Seminars.

7. *Empower the People,* Tony Brown's new book and the road map to self-empowerment plus a seven-step plan to fight the conspiracy that is stealing your money and freedom.

8. Low-cost Inner Circle computers to get you on the Internet, via TBOL, with its fifty million potential customers and connected to your downline organization in many countries.

If you cannot take advantage of this opportunity because you do not own a computer, the Inner Circle can provide a computer for under $1,000. Our cyberleaders can teach you how to use it to run your business on the Internet or train you for a twenty-first-century job. This is also the key to free E-mail (electronic mail), audio and video presentations, and an exclusive area reserved for network marketing meetings for you and your downline across the country and around the world—free.

9. Training for a twenty-first-century work force. Learn how to become a COBOL programmer in six to twelve months and start out at $63,000 a year or in three months become a PC tech (personal computer technician) and build and repair computers, among many job options.

The Inner Circle program emphasizes the acquisition of information technology training such as the Y2K Corps and the Cyberleader Cadet Corps that leads to high-skilled jobs in the new information-based work force, computer-based self-employment, college and university study, advanced technical training, and job retention and advancement.

## YEAR 2000 (Y2K) DATE PROBLEM

COBOL.com on the Internet describes New Year's Eve, January 1, 2000. Dick Clark is in New York counting down the seconds before the ball drops celebrating the arrival of the new millennium. The next minute your car might not start, your bank is out of business, your job has disappeared, and planes fall from the sky—if they can get off the ground. "A series of 40 crucial air traffic computers controlling flights to and across America will not work beyond December 1999," IBM has already promised according to *The Electronic Telegraph*.[1]

Come New Year's Eve, January 1, 2000, most computers will think it's January 1, 1900. From that moment on, your life could become a Y2K nightmare. Whether it's the computer that tracks our nation's money supply or controls our missile defense system—if it hasn't been reengineered to recognize Year 2000 (Y2K), it will crash—or "continue operating but spin out inaccurate information"[2] Months later, glitches, called "sightings," may continue to plague the system. Approximately 180 billion lines of source code have to be rewritten, with enough time to spare for testing. This is what has become known as the Y2K (date) problem or bug.

What is wrong is very simple to understand. More than two decades ago when computers were very expensive ($600,000 a megabyte vs. 10 cents today), the information managers conserved expensive digital space dates in billions of lines of computer code by storing the year in two digits instead of four. For example, "8-2" was used instead of "1-9-8-2" for 1982. Up to now that has worked because the computers assumed that year data were always prededed by "19." This assumption breaks down, however, at midnight, December 31, 1999, when the computer reads "00" and puts "19" in front of the zeros, assuming the year to be 1900 instead of 2000.

Decades ago, the information systems experts used COBOL—an acronym for Common Business Oriented Language—to write mainframe-based applications that are still used today by large institutions. It was a deliberate decision. However, the future is now and the time has come to pay for the short-term profits. With less than seven hundred days left before the year 2000, with some computer systems already crashing when they read "00" as the expiration date, five out of six businesses and government agencies are still not millennium-compliant. As the situation now stands, fourteen of twenty-four major federal agencies are not on track and will not finish fixes to their mission-critical systems until 2012, some as late as 2019.

That represents twenty years of program failure and logic errors that, in an automated society, will cause economic recession, massive loss of jobs, and social upheavals, including racial tension. On a more mundane level, elevators cannot find the correct floor, the airplane traffic control system will be inoperative, government checks will not be processed, banks will fail, a collapse of the credit system will ensue—overall chaos.

## INNER CIRCLE WORK FORCE 2000

The articles listed in the Bibliography will explain the shortage of programmers; the inability of universities to train the one million programmers needed between now and 2006 (exacerbated by elitist college sutdents who can afford to reject programming jobs because they feel the hard work is "boring"); the fact that most women, as well as most Blacks and Hispanics, are being automatically excluded from the twenty-first-century technical ruling class by their miseducation; the plethora of starting salaries of $54,000 and typical programmer salaries between $75,000 and $125,000; and 346,000 unfilled information technology jobs.

A *New York Times* article, "Software Jobs Go Begging," noted that the talent "shortage is contributing to a looming crisis known as the year 2000 problem. . . . Unless all date-sensitive lines of computer code are tracked down and fixed, many businesses and institutions, from banks to government agencies to research labs and air traffic control centers, will be thrown into chaos or simply cease operating on Jan. 1, 2000."[3]

The Year 2000 (Y2K) Problem should more appropriately be called the Y2K Nightmare because the pain of business bankruptcies, unemployment, racial stress, and riots could accompany it. In fact, *Money* magazine suggested that you find out whether your bank is year 2000-compliant by the end of 1998; if not, it recommends that you move your money to a national bank where the Fed will support a bailout if "sightings" occur. *Money* names two banks that are ahead of the game: Bank of Boston and First Union.[4]

You should act now, *Money* recommends, to "protect your

finances" because in addition to a computer disaster, there is a "40% chance" that the cost of rejiggering and the "business interruptions will trigger a recession in 2000." Another investment tip, per an investment attorney: Year 2000-compliant companies "are going to eat the lunch of companies who aren't."[5]

On January 11, 1998, the Clinton administration announced that it was bowing to pressure from government and business leaders and investing $28 million to combat the critical shortage of skilled technology workers. Even some Republican governors are supporting government-sponsored training programs to expand their states' high-tech work force. Despite this political support, the shortage of computer programmers could lead to the collapse of our automated society and our economy within the next seven hundred days because of the Year 2000 date problem.

## HELP REALLY NEEDED

At the heart of the Year 2000 crisis is a shortage of computer programmers, people with cutting-edge skills. For some banks, hospitals, consumers, and retailers the next millennium has already arrived: credit cards expiring in 2000 or later are not acceptable to businesses' computers (and even if they are, you risk an inaccurate bill, so keep paper records); computer systems are crashing because they cannot read a couple of zeros in three-year contracts; and insurers refuse to sign policies longer than one year "for fear their computers can't process them."[6] Most large businesses and organizations have an average of 50 million lines of source code that needs to be modified by common business oriented language (COBOL) programmers. And correction plans for the Year 2000 date problem in COBOL programs will cost about $1 for each line of code (as compensation for scarce programmers intensifies, $2 per line will be more common). That's a cost of $50 million (or $100 million) to each large company and $600 billion (to over $1 trillion) worldwide. Military applications have been estimated as high as $9 a line, almost ten times the cost of a large business. The Social Security Administration, the most prepared government agency— "scheduled to be year 2000 'compliant' in 1999—discovered in 1997 30 million lines of code in its disability benefits computers that still need fixing."[7] As of now, on average we are 5 percent done, with 95 percent to go.

## Y2K JOB BONANZA: NO EXPERIENCE NECESSARY

But the Inner Circle has a practical remedy—recruiting people in the general labor pool who have no experience as information technology workers (people who can't afford to be bored) and training them quickly—to help lead the assault on the global software crisis.

We are using software high-technology in classrooms or in people's homes through an interactive online learning program on *Tony Brown Online,* a computer network and internet service provider (ISP), to train and empower an Inner Circle Year 2000 Work Force in Y2K problem solving. Practically anyone with basic personal computer skills and no programming background can be certified as a Y2K COBOL programmer.

A student in Y2K Corps needs only a basic knowledge of Windows and high school Algebra I skills. If you can use a mouse, possess the ability to browse the Internet, have good organizational skills, especially attention to details, and operate word-processing programs, you can do the job. A personal interview and testing are provided to determine job placement potential for adults. An applicant must be neat, polite, capable of working within a culturally diverse and racially mixed work-place, and demonstrate a respect for authority. Relationship skills are stressed. All certified adult graduates receive job placement and entrepreneurial assistance.

Although two million professionals work in computer programming and related fields in the United States, 346,000 jobs in the field remain unfilled every year. Because of the impending year 2000 business pressures and technical-labor shortages, Y2K paratechnicals can readily be placed in well-paid positions. The number of computer-science graduates inexplicably has declined by almost 50 percent. "We're in a situation that is similar to running out of iron ore in the middle of the Industrial Revolution," says one expert. "We're running out of our primary resource—people." This is not just a technological revolution, as most people think; it is essentially a revolution in human resources—a new paradigm for the kind of worker now in demand as a result of technology advances.

Large companies are taking over smaller companies, not for their profits but for their computer-trained personnel. Employers are going to extravagant lengths to attract talent, and as a result, wages are soaring for skilled computer operators as technology advances. One American company is hiring scores of graduates from Finland's technology institutes. "Virtual immigration" of Indian software programmers who work in American firms from their desks in Bombay and Calcutta is already a reality. Companies do not care if employees are Finnish or American, Black or White, man or woman. Due to the acute shortage of workers who can handle the computing requirements of businesses in the information age, businesses simply are desperate for workers trained in information technology, specifically in software programming.

America, in my opinion, is also on the verge of a severe economic crisis because of the national debt. And although this can result in catastrophic unemployment in the nontechnical service sectors, such as consumer-dependent retail sales, $600 billion will still be available to hire as many computer programmers as the system can produce to fix the Y2K bug. While the retail sector will be hit hard, the explosion in demand for computer programmers who can solve the Y2K problem will be unprecedented.

## JOB BONANZA: THE SILVER LINING

Tracking year 2000 date-field problems, the Inner Circle's work force supplies the missing human resources to resolve the global software crisis and set higher software engineering standards in the twenty-first century. In effect, software programs make it possible and cheaper to complete the conversion process with a lesser skill level of paraprofessionals.

The rapid training via Interactive Online Learning on *Tony Brown Online* computer network will also provide the graduates in the Inner Circle Y2K Corps (adults) and the Cyberleader Cadet Y2K Corps (fourteen to seventeen years old) with the knowledge and experience to go on to other data-related responsibilities with the computer industry, especially with additional training in computer skills. Therefore, the Inner Circle technicians will be not only prepared for the year 2000 conversion efforts but equipped with a new skill set that qualifies them for software maintenance beyond the year 2000.

## INNER CIRCLE CERTIFIED TECHNICIANS:
## WIN-WIN

There aren't enough trained and available programmers to even begin to assess, much less solve, the Year 2000 Problem. Therefore, we must train people in the general labor pool—quickly—equip them with state-of-the-art tools that find the code that needs to be fixed, flag the code for programmers and testers, and then audit the fixes.

Inner Circle graduates, most of whom will begin with minimal computer skills and no programming background, are certified. When placed on the job, they are capable of Y2K work. Hourly rates vary in different regions of the country. But on the average, after the training phase, Y2K entry-level graduates' hourly earnings are above the paratechnical wages. Their services are performed in the following areas:

- HTML Documentation Specialist (Rate: $12/hour)
- Date/Data Analyzer (Rate: $15/hour)
- QA (Quality Assurance)/Audit Technician (Rate: $20/hour)

Although these are high-paying jobs for people with little or no experience in programming, it is an inexpensive way for the employer to acquire date-field finders and get a large number of lines of code scanned for below the $75 to $150 an hour paid to programmers and analysts. It's win-win. That's why Y2K paratechnicals provide a great savings and a unique business opportunity for companies and government agencies. In fact, these specialists, with a little experience and support, can also become entrepreneurs and earn larger amounts by charging by line of code.

An HTML Documentation Specialist who is certified as a paratechnical utilizes a state-of-the-art code documentation tool set that generates output. Documentation Specialists surround and support managers, programmers, analysts, and auditors, enabling them to work in a more coordinated fashion, from a deep level of understanding of how their systems function. The Y2K paratechnicals enable source code audit and greatly reduce technical and legal risks during the year 2000 testing.

A Date/Data Analyst, certified as a Date/Data Researcher, creates and searches a database of potential Y2K significant elements and other data-related issues. Relieving the overworked and highly paid programming staff of routine analytical duties, the paratechnical increases overall efficiency and dramatically reduces the time of the conversion process. A certified Quality Assurance (QA)/Audit Technician validates each programmer's code change as to completeness, correctness, and any new errors generated in the syntax and functional linkages.

**Marketing Opportunity.** Tony Brown's Inner Circle Work Force 2000 (the Y2K Corps and the Cyberleader Y2K Cadet Corps) is an adjunct to the Inner Circle marketing opportunities and an integral part of the empowerment process. Inner Circle members will also be able to market the Y2K training and placement of Y2K paratechnicals. The children and grandchildren of selected Inner Circle distributors can qualify for a preference for enrollment and a tuition discount.

CYBERLEADER Y2K CADET CORPS
Knowledge can also be the key to cleansing wealth—an indispensable element of empowerment—when it is imparted to others in mentoring programs. In New York and New Jersey, I organized the Cyberleader Y2K Cadet Corps as a prototype of such a mentoring program to train cyberleaders of the next century. The Corps offers youth ages four to seventeen a rigorous four-month program in various advanced areas of technology (telephony, robotics, database, automated accounting, multimedia, computer-aided draft and design [CADD], web-page design, Y2K paratechnical training, etc.). It is a program that rich people cannot find and poor people cannot afford.

"Building Character and Genius" is our motto. In the selection process, we are not focused on the traditional criteria of grades and "intelligence." In my opinion, young geniuses are ordinary children who have learned to perform at a genius level, largely because of economic and social advantages. Moreover, each cadet is required to demonstrate character by helping other cadets. The entire class is held back if one member lags behind—until the others come to his or her assistance. The cadets are recognized for character as well as technical expertise. A "smart" cadet is a cadet who helps others.

Respect for authority and promptness are mandatory, a uniform is required, and no youths with discipline problems are admitted. An indoctrination process stressing these character traits and moral virtues are integrated into the technical training. Futhermore, the Cadet Corps augments and complements the academic school experience; it is not a replacement for it. Parental involvement is required.

## COLLEGE DEGREE NO LONGER A JOB GUARANTEE

A worried mother phoned me during my radio program on WLIB-AM in New York City to seek advice because her son's high school grades were too poor for college admission. "But he does have a hobby," she said. "He takes computers apart and puts them together again." To which I responded, "And you're worried about him going to college?" In the next decade, 70 percent of the new jobs will require computer skills, not four years of college. In fact, 50 percent of last year's college graduates are still unemployed, while a twenty-two-year-old Black man from the Bronx in New York with a high school GED earns $90,000 a year as a computer programmer in Atlanta. Furthermore, a recent study found that "the average total debt" of a graduating college student is $18,800—"a burden affecting their way of life and job choices."[8]

On the other hand, here is an example of what can be done on a mass scale if we adopt my cyberleader model. A high school

graduate this year became a certified "systems engineer" because he graduated from Ford High School in Wilmington,
Delaware, according to *Newsweek.*[9] His job, running computers
at a local bank, will pay $30,000 a year. With a college degree,
which he hopes to receive in night school, he expects to get a job
earning over $100,000. Why? Because between 190,000 and
346,000 high-tech jobs are vacant and 1 million more
information-technology workers will be needed by 2005, *Newsweek* reported.

The need for a paradigm shift at America's institutions of
higher learning—to a system that provides, at an affordable cost,
a combination of academic basics and technical training—is obvious. The realities and demands of attending college demonstrate why over 90 percent of Blacks and Hispanics and 80
percent of the general population will never finish college
anyway.

### STEP 2: CREATE AND CLEANSE WEALTH: E=CLP+FSI

Here is my simple formula for empowerment: E=CLP+FSI
(Empowerment=Complete Legal Protection combined with Financial and Spiritual Independence). According to President
Clinton's mentor, Dr. Carroll Quigley, a confessed member of
an international Anglophile conspiracy of the ruling class that
controls the world, the American people would be crushed if
they tried to resist the power elite that is stealing your money
and freedom.

But as the old saw goes, "If life gives you lemons, make
lemonade." Ironically, the Illuminati Ruling Class Conspiracy
presents a challenge that offers an opportunity for the average
American to make more money and enjoy true freedom—even
if you do not believe there is a Conspiracy. By cleansing your
wealth and freedom, and helping others to do the same, you
will enjoy even more wealth and security. Utilizing the give-

and-receive formula, E=CLP+FSI, the Inner Circle supports the achievement of total and complete empowerment through various programs and opportunities.

### PRIDE AND YOUR OWN WATCH BUSINESS

Inner Circle members are keeping the proudest time they've ever kept. Members of the Inner Circle now own Wittnauer International, the prestigious firm that has been known for over a century for exquisite and sophisticated Swiss timepieces. Wittnauer, a historic brand name in the watch business, was founded in 1880 and has always been a pioneer. It boasted one of this country's first female presidents from 1916 to 1936. The *NEW* Wittnauer owners, Chairman Robert L. Coleman and Vice Chairman Charles D. Watkins, are pioneering Black Americans who have also made history with their acquisition of the most prestigious brand name in the watch business.

Pride in this fact has compelled many members of the Inner Circle not only to purchase a Wittnauer watch, but also to accept the opportunity to start their own home-based watch businesses as distributors of this historic brand name of luxury watches. I'm especially proud to be a Wittnauer distributor and to have this historic company as a sponsor for *Tony Brown's Journal,* the longest-running series on public television (PBS). Empowerment comes in part from the pride you feel in seeing another Inner Circle business succeed.

### TWENTY-FIVE HUNDRED CHEMICAL-FREE WASHES!

Another project the Inner Circle is involved with is a wealth creation program that protects the ecosystem and your health. One Source Worldwide Network, Inc., offers an opportunity to market a revolutionary product: a laundry cleaning system.

Because if you use this product there is no need for detergents, fabric softeners, or extra rinse cycles, you can save hundreds of dollars with the laundry disc and the enzyme solution while helping to protect the environment. The laundry disc lasts for up to twenty-five hundred washes of your dirty clothing. Simply tossing the laundry disc into your washer every time you wash is like pouring in the right amount of detergent and fabric softener. It is filled with a liquid magnetic particle solution and natural bionic enzyme solution. The liquid magnets were developed by NASA technology. No chemicals or detergents means there are no damaging additives that lead to the breakdown of your fabric—or harm the environment.

Dr. Ronald Fountain, a scientist and engineer from Los Angeles, who currently is the National Marketing Director for the Inner Circle has joined Lynda Howard and Sam Kalenuik in marketing the One Source disc. A network marketing specialist, Professor Fountain is training and assisting aspiring individuals to take advantage of this and the many other opportunities in the Inner Circle program. The search for leadership talent throughout the country is under way in an effort to identify enthusiastic participants who want to earn extra income and return their communities to the people.

After explaining my commitment to the social and intellectual development of people, would you believe that my critics say that I am obsessed with making money? That is not true because I recognize that "the love of money is the root of all evil." But I will admit that I rate money right up there with oxygen. That is especially true if you have very little of it or if you want to wield power. If you don't have any money, you don't have what you want and you don't have the power to get what you want. Wealth (in the form of financial, social, or educational capital—including your talents) equals money, which equals power, and power equals freedom. Put simply, you can't have freedom without wealth. And the way to acquire wealth is through training and work. My mantra is, "If *you* work, anything will."

Most communities of interest lack the ability to create money and control an economy. That is primarily true because they do not recycle their collective income within the community, do not have products to sell, and have never considered a money barter system. Nor are they organized for the specific purpose of materially and spiritually empowering their members.

To create wealth, we must use our communities' social capital to build and control local economies. We have an abundance of skills, talents, and dreams. The trick is to turn this wealth into income.

The easiest and by far the most profitable way to do this is by successfully marketing needed products and services within a community. There is no need to reinvent the wheel, however. Without any capital investment or risk, you can market products and services of major corporations that want access to your community's market. Blacks, for example, represent a $500 billion market—the tenth-largest economy in the world.

In the next ten minutes, 165 network marketing direct selling home-based businesses will open—by someone who fits your demographic profile. You want to make big money with very low financial risk while retaining your total independence. How do I know? Because you're reading this book. Some 21,400 network marketers, people like you, will start this week, according to Michael S. Clouse in *Business Is Booming.*[10] Why? Because the home-based business phenomenon is now a $100 billion industry and you can now sell your products internationally, thanks to the Internet. There are 25 million home-based businesses in 125 countries. "Close to 2 million Americans make six figures at home—and so can you," *Money* magazine asserted in its March 1996 issue.

Corporations such as Columbia Records, BMG, and a variety of credit card companies have discovered that direct selling methods are a lot more profitable than maintaining their own sales forces. Personal products companies that successfully utilize network marketing include Procter and Gamble, Colgate-

Palmolive, and S. C. Johnson and Son. The retail giants know how to produce a product or deliver a service cost-effectively, but the costs of generating interest and purchases makes its price noncompetitive. However, if their products are marketed by independent distributors, companies save the cost of advertising, employee salaries and benefits, office facilities, phone expenses, etc. They pass a portion of those savings on to the independent distributors as compensation for selling the product directly to friends and relatives.

This is called network or multilevel marketing (MLM). It is simple and logical: through face-to-face meetings, people recruit friends and relatives to the sales force. In return, you are paid a commission on your own sales—as well as on business generated by those you recruited. MLM should not be confused with "pyramid schemes." A recent Salomon Brothers report on Pre-Paid Legal Services (the legal-service plan members of the Inner Circle are successfully marketing) by analyst David Strasser concluded: "We believe that this form of distribution is a profitable and efficient way to sell product. It results in low-cost distribution due to its fixed selling costs."[11] Multilevel marketing is "a hot concept and growing every day," according to the report.

These legal-service contracts—costing about $200 a year, roughly the hourly fee for most attorneys today—"seem to have struck a nerve" with middle-class Americans, a Furman Selz analyst, Richard Nelson, told *Investor's Business Daily.*[12]

## THE INNER CIRCLE WORKS

I have spent years searching for products that could help the average person without sales experience make money through a good network marketing compensation plan and serve people simultaneously. That's why I am happy to report that, according to a letter from Victor Matos, Pre-Paid Legal's New York provider law firm, Feldman and Kramer, was able to recover

$2,819.68 of his money in only three weeks. Victor and Ada Matos had tried unsuccessfully for ten months to get their money returned to them. Satisfied members such as the Matoses inspire people who sell the legal service, such as Waheebah-Shamsid-Deen of New York, to write: "It is evident to myself and many others that the Tony Brown Inner Circle works. You and your staff are helping our community EMPOWER ourselves and our families."

Most of the time, network marketing products are too expensive, too complex, and too peripheral to the lives of the average person for even an expert marketer to sell them. And rarely do they improve the quality of the people's lives. There are, however, some exceptional marketing opportunities offered by the Inner Circle.

### $200 A YEAR OR $300 AN HOUR

Countless books dealing with making money will tell you that wealth creation depends on personal motivation. While self-esteem and self-motivation are invaluable tools, membership in a network with a product that sells itself is a surefire hit. It is the organization and the product that make the income possible, notwithstanding personal attributes.

Pre-Paid Legal is one of our breakout products and one of the biggest money makers for Inner Circle members. The reason is an excellent product that fills a real need, because Americans sue each other more than any group of people in the world. Only a very few people can afford the legal expenses of either defending themselves or suing someone else. Most people are aware of the potential for a costly legal entanglement and they would rather pay $200 to $300 a year for a legal protection plan than $200 to $300 an hour for an attorney.

Pre-Paid Legal offers people access to legal services through a network of independent law firms. For a low monthly payment, as little as $9.95 in New Jersey and $13.95 in New York,

Pre-Paid's customers purchase the protection of legal services provided by a carefully selected provider attorney firm in their area whom the majority of people cannot afford. The providers average twenty to forty lawyers per firm and are regularly monitored by Pre-Paid to ensure courteous and efficient service to the membership. "Most of Pre-Paid's plans offer unlimited toll-free telephone access to a lawyer, help in preparing a will and document review," according to *Investor's Business Daily*. "They also provide limited legal coverage in the event of an auto accident, trial or audit. Additional services can be purchased at a 25% discount."

The CEO and founder of Pre-Paid, Harlan Stoneciper, told me, "We have an obligation to make the playing field level for all Americans. Our membership goes a long way toward doing that."[13] *Essence,* a magazine for Black women, informed its readers that justice for the average person had finally arrived.

> The next best thing to having a lawyer in the family may be coverage by Pre-Paid Legal Services, Inc., a law insurance plan that offers a wide array of legal services ranging from drawing up wills to representing you in court or at an IRS audit. For about $16 a month, individuals can buy a policy that covers the entire family and essentially puts a lawyer on retainer, giving you unlimited consultations and access to 6,700 participating attorneys around the country whenever you need representation. Services are free of charge under the plan.[14]

During the first O. J. Simpson trial, a judge was asked what he thought Simpson's legal bill would be. His answer was brutally honest: "How much does he have?" Ask a friend if he or she can afford a lawyer, and the likely negative answer you will get will help you see why a prepaid plan for legal services sells itself. That is why an average person can make money marketing it. That has been our experience in the Inner Circle.

In the first six months of the Inner Circle, approximately five thousand members in the New York tristate area became part-time sales associates for Pre-Paid. During that period, they sold nearly seven thousand memberships (average $13.95 per month) and received almost $800,000 in commission advances. In addition, there is an ongoing income stream from renewals (the average renewal rate is 76 percent). When a Pre-Paid associate stops working, they don't stop earning. By the time this book is published, with more intensified training and experience, their incomes should have increased significantly, as will their numbers. Pre-Paid's share will be $1,612,800 over three years even if 20 percent of these new plans are not renewed.

Given its appeal and low cost, the decision whether to purchase prepaid legal protection is a no-brainer. And when you market the legal protection plan, the company pays approximately $34 or $52, depending on the commission level, on every service contract. At the level of Executive Bonus Qualifier, the commission is approximately $95. Provide legal protection for four friends, relatives, or neighbors a week, and you are making anywhere between $136 and $380 a week—$544 to $1,520 a month—of *extra* income.

### THE $25,000-A-MONTH MAN

Reynold ("Ron") Diaz, who heads the New York Eagles group of the Inner Circle, was himself earning $25,000 a month after only six months in 1997. Diaz was made Pre-Paid Legal's Regional Vice President for New York State a month later. During the same period, he also recruited twenty-seven hundred new associates in his downline and produces scores of new Fast Start graduates with enhanced compensations. Diaz promoted twenty-one new directors (average income $4,000 to $8,000 a month) and twenty-one new managers (average income $2,000 to $4,000 a month). After four months, the Inner Circle in New York became number one in both Pre-Paid Legal Services' recruiting and sales.

Ron Diaz is exceptional, but despite his brilliance and tenacity, he has never before earned so much money because he has never had so much opportunity. Desmond Gibson, another Inner Circle member in Diaz's organization, is earning $17,000 a month in extra income, as an Executive Bonus Qualifier (average income for this group is between $5,000 and $10,000 a month). Ron, Desmond, and many others were previously marketing various other products, but with much less success. The average Jane and Joe or Aisha and Muhammad in the Pre-Paid Legal ranks were also previously either underemployed or unemployed and had never dreamed of becoming independent with their own home-based business. An average of $400 a month in extra income is not unusual among Inner Circle members who distribute the legal protection plan. You receive a check twice a week. Best of all, the risk is minimal. There is no inventory to buy, and the only investment you have to make is $65 for the start-up kit that explains the product and gives assistance with rules and regulations. Ongoing training is free.

Only 17.3 million households currently own a prepaid legal plan. Consider these facts: (1) Pre-Paid is already debt-free, with $500 million in assets and $17 million in cash; (2) the Inner Circle members' $1 million sales performance; and (3) Salomon Brothers' projected earnings growth rate of 36 percent for the company.

JUSTICE FOR ALL: POWER EMPOWERMENT
My enthusiasm for prepaid legal protection as a medium for creating wealth and power extends to its utility as a shield against government harassment. Up to this point, I have concentrated on money, the currency of power. And marketing Pre-Paid Legal Services, Inc., is definitely a way to empower

yourself by making money. However, legal protection is also essential to guarantee justice, the ultimate goal of the Inner Circle empowerment movement.

As we move to implement our empowerment agenda, we may need legal protection from either the wrath or the Constitutional ignorance of a local or state official who does not recognize our right to use legal money and tender in the payment of debts. Perhaps a mean-spirited tax consumer in an official position or one of the IRS agents profiled on a recent issue of *60 Minutes* will take a dislike to your race, gender, tone of voice, or the part in your hair.[15]

If you want more evidence of the kind of government tyranny that Americans face every day, write *60 Minutes* at CBS-TV in New York City for a transcript of its September 21, 1997, program or *Tony Brown's Journal* on PBS on the routine use of violence and persecution of taxpayers by IRS agents. As I have said, the state is your God, and this God-imposter is dangerously out of control. The *60 Minutes* exposé showed examples of outright persecution—driving families and businesses into bankruptcy and fearful citizens to personal ruin, and, in too many cases, suicide and jail because of personal vendettas.

But statistics show that legal action by citizens "leads to a high reversal rate for IRS penalties. Nearly 42% of the $13.2 billion in IRS penalties assessed against taxpayers were eliminated after taxpayers challenged the fines."[16]

## IT CAN HAPPEN TO YOU

The Clinton administration has quietly required banks to report "suspicious" transactions or series of transactions totaling $5,000 or more.[17] Under Part 103 of the Code of Federal Regulations, any would-be agent of Big Brother who works at a bank is required to file a Suspicious Activity Report (SAR) on the basis of any subjective impression that engenders suspicion. The law is so vague that any person deemed to be engaged in a transaction in which, in the judgment of the bank employee, he or she should not be engaged in, must be reported to the IRS. Anyone who unknowingly irritates a bank employee can now become an instant criminal.

Even worse than the 1996-enacted SAR, if that's possible, is a 1997 government regulation, Currency Transaction Report (CTR), that makes it a felony punishable by a five-year prison term and a $250,000 fine to purchase more than $3,000 in money orders or make transfers among bank accounts in a series totaling more than $10,000.[18] Everyone is required to file a CTR (IRS Form 4789) in the event they conduct the above transactions. But the bank teller, pawnbroker, credit card company, metals dealer, investment banker, loan company, or travel agent is not required to inform you that under this new law, one of a series of new government regulations, you are required to do so. In the event you fail to file IRS Form 4789, the bank teller or any of the aforementioned can report you and receive a $150,000 reward, at which time any funds you possess can be seized. And, of course, you can be convicted of a criminal felony.

Airports are potentially just as dangerous to law-abiding citizens as banks. According to a study published in the *Pittsburgh Press:* "Over 92 percent of all cash in circulation in the U.S. now shows some drug residue."[19] This incredible statistic has increased the risk to anyone carrying a large amount of cash, as in the case of a woman whom police arrested at a Houston airport because a drug-sniffing dog scratched at her luggage. The forty-nine-year-old woman was carrying $39,110 in cash from an insurance settlement and her life savings, which she had earned as a hotel maid and a hospital janitor. The police never charged her with a crime, but they would not return her money. Apparently, they assumed it was ill-gotten and therefore she would not protest.

It may come as a surprise to you that over two hundred

"civil asset forfeiture" laws enable police to confiscate your home, car, bank accounts, pocket money, and business without trial. It is happening to hundreds of thousands of Americans, Jarrett Wollstein writes in "The Looting of America," without an indictment, trial, or conviction. Any anonymous informant who reports an illegal transaction can cause the loss of your property—and "it is virtually impossible to get it back."[20]

Wollstein says that "civil asset forfeiture defines a new standard of justice in America; or more precisely, a new standard of injustice." Under those laws, the property is "guilty," therefore, the individual has no Constitutional rights.

> If government agents seize your property under civil asset forfeiture, you can forget about being innocent until proven guilty, due process of law, the right to an attorney, or even the right to trial. All of those rights only exist if you are charged with a criminal offense; that is, with an offense which could result in your imprisonment. . . . Seizure occurs when government takes away your property. Forfeiture is when legal title is permanently transferred to the state.[21]

The ability to hire a lawyer has become the litmus test for justice. The legal fees to defend your property will bankrupt the average person.

> You have to pay attorney fees—ranging from $5,000 to over $100,000—out of your own pocket. Even if you have it, the money you pay your attorney is also subject to seizure (either before or after the trial) if the government alleges that those funds were "tainted." And you may be forced to go through trial after trial . . . expect to spend years fighting government agencies and expect to be impoverished by legal fees.[22]

## DOCTORS AND VITAMIN LOVERS, BEWARE

President Clinton's "Health Security Act" makes it a federal crime for a doctor to accept money directly for 95 percent of all medical services. The penalty: confiscation of all of the doctor's assets, $50,000 fine, and fifteen years in prison. Doctors now need a full-time lawyer.

In a stunning development, the Food and Drug Administration (FDA) has announced a definition of "health fraud" that effectively abolished the First Amendment free speech rights of all Americans. The FDA said in an August 18, 1997, statement: "Health fraud has been defined by the agency as the promotion of unproven medical products." Promotion of "unproven" medical products is exactly what every health publisher, health food store, and innovative doctor in the United States does. The FDA now defines the mere dissemination of information as "health fraud," without any regard to the scientific evidence.

The FDA also defines as "health fraud" the promotion of any unapproved product, regardless of whether the promoter sells the product or not. This means that the FDA could arrest me for producing a TV program on a specific substance or for writing about a product. That includes any vitamin company, alternative doctor, Amway distributor, or health food store the FDA chooses to target. The FDA's definition of "health fraud" gives federal and state agencies the right to file criminal fraud charges against anyone involved with alternative medicine. This perverse definition of the law is of the same Orwellian style that corrupt totalitarian governments use to suppress free speech.

Prepaid legal protection, for the first time, gives citizens a shield against injustice, our own law firms to remind the errant government or police tyrant of Title 18, Section 241 of the United States Code (18 U.S.C. 241), "Conspiracy Against the Rights of Citizens." This law protects you against a conspiracy of two or more persons to "injure, oppress, threaten or intimidate any citizen" to the detriment of any Constitutional right. The penalty for this violation can be up to ten years' imprisonment or a $10,000 fine, or both. Under Title 18, Section 242 (18 U.S.C. 242), "Deprivation of Rights," you are protected from discrimination by reason of "being an alien, or by reasons of his color, or race. . . ."

## BLACKS, BEWARE

It is very apparent to me that Blacks who want to stop racially motivated attacks and also fight the tyranny of government confiscation of their income and savings should be extra careful. Challenging public officials to comply with the Constitution could be construed as confrontational behavior that would normally be excused if the antagonist were White. The same challenge coming from a Black can and, in some situations, will be perceived as an overt act of violence or a psychological threat.

I am Black and male, and I do not intend to shirk my Constitutional obligation to free America from the clutches of an emerging police state. I am armed with the Constitution and the Declaration of Independence and I am shielded by a legal protection service that has very well-qualified law firms standing by whenever I call. I plan to use these assets as I confront the government with the truths of Americanism.

Cowards and criminals in positions of authority select their victims carefully. They search out the powerless, the poor, and the poorly informed, as *60 Minutes* confirmed in the case of the IRS.

A recent incident that took place in New York City is another case in point. Four Black male teenagers were threatened by cops and placed under arrest. During a body search, one of the arresting officers discovered a Pre-Paid Legal Services membership card on one of the boys. Without any explanation, the youth was freed and told to go home. The other three were taken to jail to be branded as criminals and become statistics.

## ARTICLE I, SECTION 10

Get your Pre-Paid lawyer to read Article I, Section 10, of the United States Constitution. It prohibits the states from forcing people to use a paper currency or anything other than gold and silver coin as a medium of exchange in the payment of debts. Since this section of the Constitution has never been amended, every state may recognize paper money as being a lawful tender for the payment or receipt of debt—but *only* if the citizens don't object to its use.

Therefore, if anyone objects to any state doing so and asserts their right to be paid in gold or silver, that right is immediately invoked and any debt must be paid in gold or silver coin. Moreover, the debt must be forgiven altogether if it is not denominated in gold or silver coin. For instance, it is unconstitutional for a state or local official to collect taxes in unlawful money and you can't pay taxes in lawful money—gold and silver coin—because the Fed central bank does not provide it. Congress is not required to do so, but the states are prohibited from using paper scrip as "a tender in the payment of debts."[23]

After reading F. Tupper Saussy's book *The Miracle on Main Street,* a Baltimore mother and daughter told a Kmart cashier that their purchases of $82.10 was "an Article I, Section 10, no-tax sale." Saussy's book explained that Kmart is a corporation, a creature of the state, therefore bound by any Constitutional prohibitions against a state. Since no state could make anything but gold and silver coin as tender in payment of debts, Kmart was powerless to make anyone pay a state tax in something other than gold and silver coin. Because it is impossible to buy such coin in face amount equal to the sales tax, the Baltimore women chose not to voluntarily pay the tax in base-metal coin or paper. If there was no gold and silver coin to pay with, it was the state's fault for evading its requirement to "crush paper money," which was the intent of the Constitutional Convention of 1787.[24]

Compliance with this law is the responsibility of state and local governments, not Congress or the President. All public offices and courts are required by law to do business in "the money of account of the United States," which is gold and silver coin. Federal Reserve paper notes of debt are not the money of account of the United States. They are scrip issued by a privately owned bank called the "Federal" Reserve.

The women were arrested for shoplifting and released after they showed the police, the City Attorney, and a representative of the Department of Revenue page 31 of Saussy's book. It explained Article I, Section 10, and lawful money. Unanimously, all of the officials admitted that no law had been broken and released two of the most powerful people in America, who still have the option of suing the city of Baltimore for false arrest. One of the empowered women wrote Saussy: "This is about the most exciting thing that's ever happened to me in my life."

In fact, a retailer is only obligated to collect taxes "insofar as it can be done." That means it cannot be done if you refuse to pay because the government has not provided you with lawful money, i.e., gold and silver coin. According to Saussy, you can be exempted from the sales tax by simply filling out the tax-exempt sheet kept behind the counter by retailers: A1SEC10USC.[25]

A Kansas City municipal judge "was so impressed with the Constitutional solution to our economic woes" that he read "money rights" to anyone facing a fine in his court, Saussy reported. "It is clear by Article I, Section 10 of the *United States Constitution* and by Title 31 Section 371 of the United States Code," the judge said, "that this Court can only make gold and silver coin a tender payment of debts. However," Judge Moritz continued, "this Court will accept other forms of money such as Federal Reserve notes or personal checks if voluntarily tendered."[26]

## E=CLP+FSI: DEBT FREE

The preceding examples of government tyranny demonstrate why legal defense is the foundation of our freedom. The various marketing opportunities discussed in this chapter offer additional independence through debt elimination and wealth creation. You cannot be empowered—and in debt. Help yourself and others become free for the first time.

As I have previously explained, empowerment is the act of completely taking control of your life in all critical and vital areas of your existence. Legal protection is one of the first prerequisites to achieving empowerment and gaining control of your life. Financial independence is measured by your ability to create wealth, in the context of having totally eliminated all debt.

In fact, the first step to financial independence is to eliminate debt. The Debt-Free and Prosperous Living basic course is offered by Financial Independence Network Limited, Inc. (FINL), a twice-awarded Inc. 500 company. Its debt-elimination software will help you to work your way out of debt and provide you with a personalized debt-elimination plan. The software will help you operate on a cash basis and use the money you were previously spending to create wealth. It will also monitor every credit card, consumer loan, or mortgage you have. The FINL "mission" is to teach people the secrets of true financial freedom, and how to avoid the credit pitfalls that cause most people to fail financially. The debt-free strategy, utilizing only the money you already make, is basically a three-pronged approach: (1) Get completely out of debt, including your mortgage. (2) Operate 100 percent on cash, and *never* need credit again. (3) Safely and quickly build wealth so you can live off the interest.

The Inner Circle members market a complete, step-by-step manual and four-part audiocassette course that explains how to beat the moneymongers at their own game. You can become "un-vulnerable" to credit and mortgage companies, your boss, and even the economy, and you can do all this with the money you already make. By following the easy-to-understand, mathematical system, you'll wipe out all of your debt (including your mortgage) in about five to seven years.

## PROMOTIONAL TRAVEL AGENTS

Another viable opportunity for individuals is the home-based travel business, which can be established with a minimal investment. As part of the Inner Circle's Buy Freedom Travel program, promotional travel agents can earn lucrative commissions for their referrals of clients to hotels, cruises, tours, rental car agencies, theme parks, and other recreational venues, and receive special privileges reserved exclusively for traditional travel agents. This unique, flexible home-based business adventure also allows promotional agents to earn bonuses for agent referrals.

This program has eliminated most of the complex technical elements that the traditional travel agent was required to know. Professional training materials provide easy-to-use information and tips on how to make the business grow. Buy Freedom Travel allows entrepreneurs to work part-time from their homes and earn profits while having fun.

## TONY BROWN TOURS

Heritage as a dimension of empowerment also brings opportunities of cultural exchange and an income stream. Although tours are planned throughout the Caribbean and the world, Brazil, for example, with a population of 156 million people, 70 percent of whom are of African descent, offers one of the greatest income opportunities in the Americas. The tour will primarily focus on Salvador de Bahia, African history and Tony Brown's interpretation/angle on them with an additional/optional side trip to Rio de Janeiro.

The Tony Brown Tour has three levels of income-producing revenue streams: (1) If you have a travel agency, you can qualify as an exclusive distributor of the Tony Brown Tours in your designated area (our commission scale is very profitable) or you could just sell the tours as an add-on to your existing business. (2) If you are an individual who can organize groups, educational institutions, churches, sororities, etc., you can receive a commission based on your sales. (3) Importing and exporting to Brazil. The opportunities are in all products relating to African people, e. g., hair care, facial creams, clothes, music, etc. The Inner Circle can arrange the face-to-face meetings with Brazilian government officials and business leaders.

## STEP 3: START A ROOT ECONOMY AND A MONEY SYSTEM

Back in 1986, I started a nationwide self-empowerment campaign called Buy Freedom. We focused on the Black community because it is the most exploited and marginalized of America's population subgroups.

Blacks have been led to confuse their predicament—discrimination—with their problem—being powerless. Since the beginning of the eighteenth century, Blacks have been taught by illuminated spook White liberal racists and elitist Black Unaccountable Machine to shun wealth and self-empowerment.

The White "liberal" Illuminists, actually the Mongrelized Marxists and crony Capitalists in a "Negro Uplift Movement," programmed the Black community to fail. The Illuminati Capitalists such as Jacob Schiff and suspected Communists such as NAACP director Herbert Lehman, widely acknowledged as allies, were extremely careful never to promote empowerment for Blacks. As a result, Blacks' only avenue of self-assertion was to protest against the prevailing attitude of separatist Whites and to seek legislation against discrimination and other forms of injustice. Notwithstanding the virtues of desegregation, this approach could only fail to achieve socioeconomic equality because in the final analysis, socializing with White people and achieving civil rights legislation does not solve economic and spiritual problems. Pragmatism and money—power—do.

As a result of the propaganda and other manipulations of the Illuminati White American Establishment and its Black spooks, the Black community has by and large shunned the establishment of an alternative root economy that would recycle its enormous wealth, and instead has chosen continued statist victimization. That statist system under which it had been living was organized to fail economically, but to remain a perpetual source of social disruption necessary for the Hegelian process of keeping the nation in turmoil.

The liberal racist Illuminists who were the architects and overseers of the American economy recruited Black elitists in the early twentieth century as mental spook agenturs to shape Black opinion and mold a Black voting bloc to favor its so-called liberal causes. Freemason W.E.B. Du Bois was the chief propagandist in this assimilation conditioning process. These black conspirators equated racism with Capitalism, and self-empowerment was defined as segregationist, anti-White, nationalistic, and petit bourgeois. Many Blacks who advocated a sensible self-help philosophy were socially and politically excommunicated and became pariahs in the Black community. In this way, the Illuminati prevented Blacks from ever organizing and harnessing the enormous talent (capital) that they possessed, which would have resulted in phenomenal incomes for them instead of the Illuminati. The Black community is the victim of planned failure, and the plethora of unworkable and failed government promises, such as affirmative action and busing, have only been a smokescreen to hide this fact.

Black America possesses great wealth, and has learned to use its wealth to buy its freedom! It is the quintessential example of a community of interest that could become empowered if it developed a "root economy" and used its own money system.

Numbers do not lie. As already noted, Black America's annual income of $500 billion is the equivalent to the GDP of the tenth richest nation in the world. In New York alone, Blacks earn $50 billion a year. In 1995, the growth in buying power of Black households outpaced that of White households in several categories of consumer spending. For example, Blacks spent $10.8 billion on cars and trucks that year—a 163 percent increase over the $4.1 billion spent a year earlier. The increase among Whites was just 9 percent.

However, Blacks were organized historically by their elitist, Socialist leaders, mostly White, to boycott themselves. Although the income of Blacks is growing faster than that of any other group of Americans, they spend only 3 percent of their $500 billion income with one another. That is why the most successful economic boycott in history is the current one that Blacks wage against their own entrepreneurs. On average, other ethnic and racial groups recycle 80 percent of their income within their own community. In addition to recycling only 3 percent of its income, the Black community turns a dollar over less than once. Conversely, a dollar turns over from five to twelve times before it leaves a Jewish-American, Chinese-American, Indian-American, or numerous other ethnic communities.[27]

Blacks are rich enough to easily create, or buy, the jobs and businesses that affirmative action will never give them. It is not that affirmative action would not work if it were aimed at the poor, but it was designed as a Hegelian wedge used by the Illuminati Ruling Class Conspiracy to divide and conquer Blacks and Whites. It was intentionally not designed to attack the real source of Black America's predicament: the lack of skills among the poor that breeds social pathology. Instead, it was created to antagonize Whites and frustrate Blacks, while allowing a handful of Blacks to prosper and sympathetic Whites to believe something was being done.

## FREEDOMS AT LAST

After ten years of searching for a solution to this predicament, I am pleased to announce that I have come up with the missing ingredient and a universal model for the economic empowerment of any community of interest. It is a solution that not only will recycle the money of a community and solve its social and economic problems but will also give members of any community of interest—religious, ethnic, geographical, gender, whatever—control of their money and their lives.

The solution is the development of local money systems based on the two forms of real wealth of communities. *Social capital* is a community's skills, services, ability to help one another, and the goodwill it has for itself—its self-esteem. A community's *human capital* is measured in educational achievement and work experience. Together, these two forms of wealth allow a community to build its financial capital (usually earned income). Money is not essential to the operation of a root economy or the recycling and building of wealth. Money as wages is the by-product of social and human capital. However, a barter money system can facilitate the process by igniting the engine of social-capital building and human-capital development in a community. Communities of interest can use barter money to create their own economies, protect their families, rehabilitate their institutions, and employ the jobless. Such money systems will also offer real protection during the coming economic crash, whether it comes in 1998 or sometime later.

## USE A PRINTING PRESS TO RULE THE WORLD

Black America is rich, yet it is not using its money to buy its freedom! It is the quintessential example of a community of interest that could become empowered if it developed a root economy and used its own money system. Although this at first blush might seem to some like an unfeasible plan, they should understand that it is the knowledge of money and the use of money that drives the creation of wealth.

Take, for example, the hostile bid of $30 billion by a nearly unknown Hattiesburg, Mississippi, company, WorldCom, to acquire MCI Communications, the number two long-distance company in the United States. At the same time, WorldCom was busy offering $2.9 billion to acquire Brooks Fiber Properties and $1.4 billion for CompuServe. If all of these deals go through, WorldCom's stock will be worth $67 billion, compared with AT&T's $74 billion in stock shares.

How can an unknown company that has revenues of just $5.6 billion bid nearly $35 billion? Easy. Do what the private stockholders who own the U.S. government's central bank, the "Federal" Reserve, do. Create your own currency, or, in reality, scrip money. The Federal Reserve calls its scrip IOUs "dollars" and WorldCom names its scrip currency "WorldCom stock." During the first nine months of 1997, WorldCom "printed an astounding $45 billion to $50 billion," *Newsweek* reported in an article appropriately entitled "How WorldCom Uses Its Printing Press to Buy the World." The article also explained that "no one but the U.S. Treasury had peddled that much new paper during the same period.[28]

I also print a barter scrip that I use as money. I call it a "Freedom." And if Americans would accept my money as they do the dollar IOU of the power elite and WorldCom's stock— both backed only by the hope that someone else will accept them in a barter transaction—we the people, instead of the Illuminati Conspiracy, would control the world.

## FREEDOM MONEY

To help you understand what we currently call money, here is a paragraph from Andrew Gause's book *The Secret of Money:*

A Federal Reserve Note is not in itself money, but it is a promise to pay money. It is not the payment itself.

Imagine if you were able to convince everyone in your town to accept your personal checks for goods and services, and then you additionally convinced them that instead of cashing your checks they should just pass them on to others, who in turn would accept them as payment for goods and services. If you were able to do this, you wouldn't need to have any money in your checking account! Moreover, the amount of checks or "promises to pay" you could write would be virtually without limit. The Federal Reserve bank has no actual "money" in its account to back up the "notes" it writes, so it has, over the years, quietly removed the written promises to pay which used to appear on the face of each of their notes. Federal Reserve notes have replaced money as the circulating medium of exchange.[29]

I must admit that this definition of money leads to a slippery slope, but since that is the way the new money game is played, we cannot let the government and the Federal Reserve have all of the fun—and money. In the Inner Circle, we have created a barter money system called *Freedom*.

A Freedom note, just like the Federal Reserve note we call the dollar, is evidence of debt. However, it does not signify our indebtedness to the Illuminati Ruling Class Conspiracy, but rather to other members of our community. And its value is determined by our faith in one another. The Freedom money system uses a legal paper barter currency that represents our community's network of skills, where each person is a resource for the other and we depend on one another to create a higher standard of living. The Freedom money is also the currency that builds the social capital necessary for a self-empowerment economy.

Freedoms are scrip that enables us to perform barter transactions. Rather than conventional barter, which is a direct swap of items by two people, our system uses this scrip as a medium of exchange for goods and services. Unlike the Federal Reserve, this system is based on hourly units of labor, exchangeable as money in five denominations—one eighth, one quarter, one half, one, and two Freedoms. The One Freedom bill, which features the picture of abolitionist Frederick Douglass, is the equivalent of ten dollars in U.S. currency. The Freedom's aim is to help all people become self-employed and create work they enjoy by restructuring their community's economy to benefit them.

According to *The Wall Street Journal*:

> Local currency is legal, but the government stipulates that the notes must be smaller in size than dollar bills, issued in denominations valued at a minimum of $1 and reported as taxable income to the Internal Revenue Service. Prior to the Civil War, virtually the only currency in the U.S. was local, issued by banks. National currency came into being in 1863.[30]

By now you must realize that our trust is the only thing that keeps the U.S. dollar note of debt in circulation. The monetary value that backs the Freedom currency is the trust that we place in one another. "In Each Other We Trust," Freedom bills proclaim. The Freedom is *our* money. It is the only national paper currency that honors Blacks—Frederick Douglass, Madam C. J. Walker, Booker T. Washington, Marcus Garvey, and Harriet Tubman. And it is backed by the talents of people who know one another and by the faith that members of this empowerment-conscious community of interest have in one another.

When we pay each other for work done with Freedoms, we buy freedom, social justice, and equality. To do this, individuals simply have to work for one another and accept Freedoms as payment for their time and skills. As more and more people and businesses become participants and use the "Freedomlist" or *Tony Brown Online* computer service to find barter trades, Freedom money will move through the community's root economy as perfectly legal wages; payment for rent, meals, entertainment, and computer services; mortgage fees, etc.

The Freedom money system provides the structure for moving people from welfare dependency to jobs. It lets people who are time-rich but dollar-poor buy items they need to survive and move out of poverty. A case in point is child care for those families in which both parents work, or in which single mothers are being forced by the new law to work off their welfare benefits. Such people are often in desperate need of someone to take care of their children but usually cannot afford child care. The Freedom money system allows for child care on a barter basis.

Freedoms are paid to individuals and businesses that agree to accept Freedoms as part or whole payment for goods and services. People earn Freedoms by helping other people. This stimulates a community to meet its own needs.

A list of these Freedom businesses and workers—a yellow pages of Freedom products and services—is printed in the *Buy Freedom* newsletter and listed on the nationwide *Tony Brown Online* computer service. The Freedom system can increase the standard of living of all of its participants, and it can groom those who are the least employable to become self-employed and to develop good work habits.

With proper controls and checks on capital flow, Freedoms can grow the local gross domestic product (GDP) and achieve sustainable economic development. The Freedom money system can make the Black community economically independent and stem the tide of mounting social and economic crisis. This is a viable alternative to the poverty, transgenerational welfare, poor education, crime, and governmental and political paternalism that engulfs much of our community today in misplaced and destructive statist dependence, such as an allegiance to the

Hegelian wedge of affirmative action "entitlements." This community money system increases and recycles a group's wealth and its consumer power. The spin-off effect is enormously beneficial for consumers and entrepreneurs alike.

### FREEDOM BUSINESSES: ENGINES FOR GROWTH

Businesses have low sales when potential customers have few dollar notes because the dollar system does not use their full productive capacity. But when a Freedom money system is introduced as another way to earn income—especially for the time-rich-and-dollar-poor unemployed—the skills not employed by the dollar money system can earn barter cash instead. With Freedoms, everyone's productive potential is tapped, and more people have more income. Therefore, they can trade more. Increased trading means increased profits for businesses, employment for the idle, more home-based businesses, and extra income for the average person.

As a result of this economic expansion, Freedom businesses become the engines for recycling a larger percentage of the people's spending power within the community, because these firms dramatically and exponentially increase the number of people who trade within their community and the amount of money spent and retained there. The Freedom money network provides a sophisticated, community-sponsored marketing and advertising vehicle.

*Freedom Business Designation.* Being designated a Freedom Business allows companies to connect with a broader range of the community, and it sends a message to injustice-weary consumers, tired of being exploited by the Illuminati money system, that the merchant accepts Freedoms. That is a distinct competitive advantage over businesses that have not joined this community movement.

*A Promotion Coupon.* For a specific portion of the payment, the Freedom is used as a promotional coupon, which the participating merchant can also spend for other products and services. Freedoms also provide businesses and individual brokers with a splendid marketing tool for special and seasonal events such as Black History Month, Martin Luther King's birthday, Christmas, etc. The portion of a purchase accepted in Freedoms is always determined by the merchant. For example, a business may accept Freedoms as 50 percent or 25 percent of the purchase price. Each business also sets its own exchange rate and can change it at its own discretion. By accepting Freedoms—at first cautiously, setting a maximum that can be accepted at any one time as a portion of the price—businesses can use Freedoms to attract dollar-poor customers and "foot traffic" on slow days and/or during specified hours. As Freedoms prove their value, Freedom businesses will benefit more and more.

As you can see, a Freedom economy is a powerful tool for taking control of our own property and destiny. When we rely on ourselves and each other, we loosen the grip of the Illuminati Ruling Class Conspiracy on our communities and our nation.

## STEP 4: MAKE SURE EVERY HOME IN YOUR NETWORK HAS A COMPUTER

In this age of information technology, marketing networks, root economies, and local money systems are not enough to empower all Americans. We are already witnessing the effects of technological displacement of workers. To rebuild America's devastated and threatened real proximal communities—the ultimate objective of empowerment—we will have to ensure that there is a computer in every home and that every family is connected to a computer online network and a local intranet.

To empower real proximal communities, we must build in cyberspace a virtual community of opportunity for the members of our inner circles and the socially and economically disadvantaged. This model requires human-capital investment—education, technical training, and work experience. We must develop a cadre of highly trained cyberleaders who will help empower all members of the community in the field of information technology.

In the absence of technological justice, we will become a nation of information haves and have-nots, torn apart by class and race warfare and led by demagogues from all classes and races. Self-empowerment of individuals and communities through the planned use and egalitarian management of information technology is the only way to keep the technological displacement of workers from destroying our society. It is going to take virtual communities of newly trained cybercitizens to save our real proximal communities. And it is not the global village that will save America, but the intranets of local villages. For example, as *The Wall Street Journal* pointed out, "people have long envisioned the Internet as a massive electronic mall in the making—a place where people could buy and sell on-line 24 hours a day. It hasn't happened."[31]

My plan creates electronic markets in self-sufficient "local villages" where people do buy and sell online from one another, as well as from other communities around the world twenty-four hours a day. These electronic villages are created by dividing communities into clusters of dwellings, which are transformed into Mutual Help Organizations (MHOs). These MHOs are organized neighborhood self-empowerment associations, based on a communitarian ideal of Americans taking care of one another. A critical component of the MHO empowerment plan is the "intranets," computer networks electronically linking homes, businesses, schools, volunteer groups, charity agencies, and government offices to one another within a shared environment. Through networking over intranets, these MHOs will function as self-sufficient economic blocs and will improve the delivery of social services, provide technical job training and placement, facilitate the starting of home-based businesses, help fight crime, contribute to the improvement of education and computer skills, and link up to an online service for tasks as mundane but crucial as matchmaking (for the purpose of reducing the growth of female-headed homes and enhancing the stability of the family).

My plan is to train novice cybercitizens and network them into a cadre that will build a virtual community of opportunity in cyberspace. The Cyberspace Institute was created to meet today's economic and social challenges: displacement of workers by new technology, financial uncertainty, the breakdown of family life into single-parent homes, and the lack of computers in too many schools. We cannot take every youngster from poverty and into the middle class by way of Harvard, but we can take every youngster from poverty to the middle class by means of a computer. This is the human-capital aspect of self-empowerment.

## STEP 5: REACH OUT AND STOP CIVIL WAR II

I may be accused of being an alarmist for saying this, but it seems that America has hit its racial nadir and we are near the flashpoint for a race war. The origin of this Civil War II, like that of the American Civil War, would be economic.

Those who at their own peril dismiss Thomas Chittum's civil-war scenario would do well to read *The Transformation of War,* a book by Dr. Martin van Creveld of the Hebrew University in Israel. Creveld, who is regarded as a distinguished source in military circles, says pretty much the same thing as Chittum. He argues that America "has a tradition of internal violence second to none" and that "global expansion enabled Americans to raise their standard of living."[32] That is now over, and America has no new frontiers to conquer. Creveld says that "America's economic viability has been on the decline" since around 1970, because it can no longer "dominate the rest of the world."[33]

Many Whites now feel that the government has made them its new victim class and its instrument is affirmative action preferences for Blacks and Hispanics. They feel they must fight back to reclaim their rightful place. A wave of technological displacement by computers is fueling this perception of affirmative-action-led unemployment for Whites. Whether this fear is real or imagined, Thomas Chittum's book (discussed in Chapter 7) is a wake-up call to the potential for a premeditated race war. America is suffering from a declining industrial base and Blacks and Whites, encouraged by a phony government-sponsored race dialogue, blame one another for it.

American progress has been replaced with mounting social tensions and escapism, especially in the form of the neurotic use of drugs. And if the United States' economic decline is not halted, "the crime that is rampant in the streets of New York and Washington, D.C., may develop into low-intensity conflict by coalescing along racial, religious, social and political lines, and run completely out of control."[34] The match that could ignite this tinderbox of intra-group conflagration, the professor believes, is "economic decline."

"Across the nation, bombings and attempted bombings are soaring," *The New York Times* reported.[35] That same front page of one of America's most prestigious daily newspapers reported another aspect of the new American way of life: domestic terrorism by Ozzie-and-Harriet militias. This is another societal reaction to the destabilizing effects of the Illuminati Ruling Class Conspiracy's grip on the nation.

Violence, of course, is no lasting solution; violence breeds violence. Arming ourselves to kill one another or resorting to homegrown anarchy will only turn a solvable predicament into an irreparable national disaster. The change we need to bring about in this country must be accomplished nonviolently and in accordance with our laws. We must not blow up America in an effort to save her.

Rather than fight a race war, I believe that Whites and other Americans, out of desperation, will eventually join with Blacks in an empowerment movement to save themselves from the coming economic catastrophe and totalitarian oppression. Blacks and Whites must (1) recognize the common enemy and (2) agree on the common objective of eliminating it. All Americans, although of different descent, share a common destiny.

The government-imposed choice between forceful assimilation or hatred cannot be allowed to define the nature of race relations. The core of our relationships must be respect for individual choice, that is, toleration for the rights and preferences of everyone in this most pluralistic and multiethnic of all nations—in a word, Americanism. All Americans have the right to live in the neighborhood of their choice, marry the person of their choice, and worship the God of their choice. No other American, no matter how averse to that choice, has a right, other than through free speech, to act against it.

The Illuminati Ruling Class Conspiracy's strategy of divide and conquer now defines all Blacks as preference idiots and all Whites as bigots. Notwithstanding the legitimate differences over affirmative action, the majority of Whites sanction the principle of giving Blacks a hand up without giving them their jobs, and Blacks, many of whom shun any type of preference program, are seeking an opportunity to prove themselves as qualified for the task at hand. This is the common ground that my plan seizes.

We are all facing serious threats imposed on us because we are Americans: moral decay, economic bankruptcy, and oppressive government. The greatest single blow that can be struck at the Conspiracy is for Black Americans and White Americans to work together to eliminate the Illuminati central bank and the income tax and to expose Quigley's "Anglophile network." Every time Blacks and Whites join together, they are one more step closer to freedom. Americans can have differences and live in peace. We must. No other course is rational.

Start an anti–Civil War II campaign to counter the race-war fever that is building. Reach out to other ethnic groups, especially those who have a history of antagonism toward people with your ancestry, but leave assimilation at home. Let people choose their own friends. Focus on fighting the Conspiracy that is setting us up to kill one another and is destroying America.

## STEP 6: START A PUBLIC AWARENESS CAMPAIGN TO FIGHT THE DRUG WAR AGAINST U.S.

As I said in Chapter 8 about the drug war against America, the only surefire way to defy the Illuminati Ruling Class Conspiracy's plot to weaken the will of Americans and drain the country's resources with drugs is to empower people in order that they will be strong and assertive enough not to buy or use drugs. We must educate each other and our children about the evils of drugs and adopt the Ali Shuffle as our first defense against Illuminati mind control.

A national "Stop the Drug War Against U.S." campaign, supported by every community of interest through its MHOs, intranets, and Freedom businesses, will guarantee that we can defeat the Illuminati narco Goliath. Ours will be a conspiracy of pride, awareness, and faith in each other and God.

## STEP 7: JUSTICE: MAKE THE GOVERNMENT WORK FOR U.S.

Throughout this book and especially this chapter, we have been talking about empowerment as a way to fight the Illuminati Ruling Class Conspiracy. The final step in empowering ourselves is restoring our inalienable human rights and a government "of the people, by the people, and for the people."

With Conspiracy agenturs, many of whom are Rhodes Scholars, in control of the White House and both houses of Congress, all we do when we vote is choose between the evil alternatives presented by the Illuminati Establishment. When we empower ourselves, we do not have to continue to vote the political spooks of the central bank and the avatars of inflated scrip into office. The political agenda outlined below will give us power equal to that of those for whom we vote.

That agenda provides a litmus test for all political candidates. Before you vote, find out the positions of the candidates with respect to the issues described below. Using these guidelines, you can easily determine if you are dealing with a spook agentur or an American. Our strategy is nothing less than a quest to reclaim the lost promise of America.

Enactment of this political agenda is the first step toward neutralizing the Illuminati and putting the currency back under the control of the people. With the money where everyone can see it, ownership of the schools, the military, the Congress, the Presidency, the banks, and your income will be returned to you. Inflation will be nonexistent, your savings will be safe, and your children's future will be secure. Racial tensions will abate, and the potential of a civil war will be greatly diminished.

All we have to do is to insert the following measures into the political process:

1. Reinstatement of the gold standard for a U.S. currency that will be controlled by Congress.

    Demand that your state or local government not accept anything but gold and silver coin as "tender in payment of debts," in accordance with Article I, Section 10 of the United States Constitution, which stipulates that the States demand from Congress a legal tender that can only be gold and silver.

For low-cost legal insurance to protect you from the wrath of the government when you demand compliance with the Constitution, you can rely on Pre-Paid Legal Services, Inc. (see Step 2, pages 287–305). I will personally provide each of the Pre-Paid provider law firms nationwide with the necessary legal background on this issue.

2. Repeal of the nefarious Federal Reserve Act of 1913. Make the U.S. Treasury the central bank of the U.S. government, as it was previously.

3. Physical inventory and description of the gold in Fort Knox. See Chapter 5 for details on the possibility that the U.S. gold supply may be missing.

4. Elimination of Karl Marx's Illuminati-Communist income tax that was designed to destroy the middle class. A national sales tax that is adjusted to protect the poor should be instituted instead.

5. Removal of the Illuminati's Seal of the Devil from the U.S. dollar bill and the United States Seal, and the pagan symbols from the halls of Congress.

6. Public disclosure of membership in all secret societies by all elected and appointed officials, especially cops and judges. Bring the Illuminati and their agenturs out into the light and expose the illegal preference program that advances Freemasons in employment, politics, and business.

7. Restoration of the human rights granted by God as enunciated in the Declaration of Independence to replace the "entitlements" doled out by the government as a form of control. We should worship God, not welfare statism.

There is no chance that the current government of Illuminati statists will voluntarily invoke the gold standard to protect us against the Fed's inflationary money. There is equally little chance of eliminating the central bank or reducing its collection agency, the IRS, by assigning it to the task of managing a state-run national sales tax. However, if somehow miraculously we do enact these three simple steps alone, your property would become your own once again, your savings would be safe, and the size of government would be reduced and limited to serving the people rather than oppressing them. God would be back as the Divine inspiration of America. However, none of that is likely to happen without us.

## EMPOWERMENT BEGINS

Empowerment begins when you make the decision to stand up to the Illuminati Ruling Class Conspiracy. Start your own empowerment network or work with the Inner Circle. The Inner Circle is a community with no boundaries, no ethnic hang-ups, and no partisan politics. We're Team America, determined to save Americans. To reach us, call 212–575–0876 and select option 576; write to 1501 Broadway, Suite 412, New York, N.Y. 10036; direct e-mail to cyberspaceclub@bbs.tonybrown.com; fax 212–391–4607; or get our free *Tony Brown Online* start-up software to join us and network online (you need a computer and a modem). Or you can download the software at tonybrown.com on the World Wide Web.

Do not let ancestry or political differences keep us from uniting against a common enemy that robs us of our property, power, faith, and future. We did not all come over on the same ship, but we are all in the same boat. And it is time that we join together to chart a course for a glorious future.

# CODA: EMPOWERING THE SOUL

*What shall it profit a man, if he shall gain the whole world,*
*and lose his soul?*
—MARK 8:36

I know that when this book comes out, the cynical, the termi-
nally disillusioned, and the "illuminated" will say, "Who is this
guy—with his TV series, radio program, newspaper columns,
books, keynote speeches, and seminars—to point the finger at
certain members of the power elite as conspirators?" I answer
not to the critics or to the scandal-ridden sociopathic President
of the United States, Bill Clinton; I answer to God. It is my
faith in the truth of God that guides me in my work. And it is
my faith that empowers me to share the truth.

It was my belief in God that helped me discern the truth
about the Illuminati Ruling Class Conspiracy and its evil purpose. The knowledge that this book contains is illuminated by
faith. I do not claim to be a prophet or a messiah. I am not a

scholar of religion. In fact, I am not even conventionally religious; I simply love God.

I am very spiritual, and I embrace Jesus Christ and His teaching that He is "the way, the truth, and the life: no man cometh unto the Father but by me."[1] By that I believe He meant living our lives the way He lived His, following Him as a Divine role model for spiritual empowerment. In my own humanly imperfect way, I try to emulate Jesus' noble emotions, thoughts, and actions. This book is part of the treasure that I will take with me to my judgment day to offer as an acknowledgment of God's greatness. Every living day reminds me that life is God's gift to me. What I do with it is my gift to God.

Jesus, the Son of God, was neither a Christian nor did He organize a religion. To my knowledge, He never asked anyone to worship or glorify Him. However, He emphatically instructed humanity to glorify God. I try to do that with my life. This is my religion of God. May He be blessed.

The Bible predicted the Illuminati Ruling Class Conspiracy's rule as the Antichrist and a prerequisite for Christ's return and the establishment of His kingdom. And as I await the Second Coming, the Muslims await the Imam Mahdi; Jews await the Messiah; Buddhists, the Fifth Buddha; and Hindus, the return of Krishna. God loves all of His children equally. He allows differences in faith because He wants us to find our own way, with His help, of course. Because I have more faith in the spiritual nature of people than in religious doctrine, dogmatic Christians will summarily excommunicate me from their restricted version of Christianity for my inclusive vision of God.

It does not matter. I am at peace in my faith and in my opposition to evil. I witness God's truth; I do not judge the shortcomings of others. "Faith is never contrary to reason when based upon the truth," I once read.

## SPIRITUAL EMPOWERMENT

I have been labeled an out-of-the-box thinker. My friends tell me that I will die not knowing who I am. They mean that I do not acknowledge my celebrity and do not behave as a celebrity is expected to behave. They are right. I do not feel like a celebrity, nor any different from the average person. People who meet me for the first time are usually surprised that I am, as many comment, "down to earth."

I abhor elitism and phonyism. I know that they are symptons of an insecurity that is due to the absence of spiritual empowerment and it is the force that drives people who take themselves too seriously. They don't realize that love is the only thing you can receive by giving it away. But most of all, I do not feel special. I feel blessed, gifted, and humbled by God's charity. I am good at what I do, and that is my reward. Spiritually empowered people like myself, with liberated minds and souls, must be careful, however, because our inner power is perceived as a threat by the powerful and the powerless alike.

Throughout this book, I have explained and given examples of how the idea of elitism—of the chosen superior few— has powered the evil conspiracy to dominate the world. The first Illuminist was Lucifer, the second Nimrod. Adam Weishaupt followed in their footsteps when he founded the Illuminati in 1776. Illuminati elitism is based on race, class, intellect, wealth—whatever convenient excuse one has to justify following the innate, sinful human desire to feel superior to others.

Adam and Eve, our parents, who believed they could find happiness with reasoning and without faith in God, sowed the seeds of the spiritual darkness in which the human race now lives. In our fallen state, we can be convinced that becoming an intellectual or joining a secret society illuminates the soul. That is ignorance. And ignorance is sin. You can only become wise by loving God.

You can observe the struggle to find God everywhere and in everything. You can also find universal confirmation of the existence of the opposing supernatural force in the world. To begin with, Illuminati begins with "Ill," a prefix of negation—not wisdom. Statism, racism, Hegelianism, secret societies, Illuminism, Communism, Marxism, crony Capitalism, elitism, and conspiracy are merely appellations for principalities of evil in high places, as the Bible has instructed us all along. In life, just as in drama, the conflict between good and evil defines the narrative.

The struggle is and always has been truly *against* "evil in high places" and wicked "principalities" of the soul manifested in the flesh. The need to feel superior, to be mentally illuminated, in order to dominate others is in each of us. On the inner level, the Illuminati Conspiracy is us against ourselves, against humanity—against God's will.

It is an encouraging sign to see that even some politicians are troubled enough by their inner struggles to resign from a government that worships the state as God, enslaving the people into the servitude of the power elite and forcing the political leaders to become agents of the Devil. Many who remain in the political class suffer in public, trying to figure out how to serve God and our nation's Divine purpose in such an evil environment.

The signs of the corruption of our collective spirit and our institutions are manifold, beginning with the election in 1992 and the reelection in 1996 of a virtue-impaired national leader and someone whose moral fault line was already known to the electorate as a tawdry philanderer. Morality has become a vanishing isssue in American life as the nation identifies increasingly with the French norm of laissez-faire atheistic Freemasonry. In fact, only a few days after the allegations surfaced in the Lewinsky case, Clinton's job rating went up 12 percentage points. He received his best rating ever from the American public.

Power that controls others is an illusion, because it really makes little sense to empower yourself materially and starve yourself spiritually. That is not happiness. That is the Devil's plan to deceive and destroy you. The Great Deceiver makes fools rich at every opportunity.

To be empowered in the material world means, in part, knowing what empowerment is and how to attain it. Life is an opportunity to use your inherent wealth for good or evil. We serve God when we cleanse our wealth by helping others. We sin out of ignorance when we become greedy and selfish—when we fail to do the will of God by loving and helping others.

On the way to high self-esteem, straightening out the government, fixing the schools, making more money, and lifting the yoke of the Illuminati Ruling Class Conspiracy, there are two main lessons to be learned: (1) your wealth is worth far more than your money; and (2) spiritual empowerment is the only way to build wealth. In fact, faith in God and love for others, properly understood, is the only real foundation for wealth, which comprises financial capital, social capital, and human capital.

In short, life is an opportunity to find out that self-empowerment is a process of wealth creation—in the true sense of the word. The meaning of eternal life is discovering the meaning of God. That is wisdom. In turn, this higher consciousness makes life the opposite of evil. Even as the word evil is "live" spelled backward, an evil life is a life lived backward.

May you live in the light of truth. And may God grant you the words to speak his thoughts.

# NOTES

## INTRODUCTION

1. Rick Marin and T. Trent Gegax, "Conspiracy Mania Feeds Our Growing National Paranoia," *Newsweek,* December 30, 1996/February 6, 1997, p. 64.
2. Senator Patrick Moynihan on *Hardball* with Chris Matthews, CNBC-TV, December 15, 1997.
3. Judy Keen, "Hillary Clinton Suggests an Ongoing Conspiracy," *USA Today,* January 28, 1998, front page.
4. Associated Press, January 27, 1998.
5. Ibid.
6. Linda Massarella, "Bill Might Stray If Hill Were Gay, Says Morris," *New York Post,* January 28, 1998, p. 4.
7. Thomas C. McAuliffe, "Debt Bomb and the Savings Pool," unpublished, 1997, p. 42.

8. Carroll Quigley, *Tragedy and Hope: A History of the World in Our Time* (New York: Macmillan, 1966), p. 950.

9. Ibid., pp. 979–980.

10. Paul A. Fisher, *Behind the Lodge Door* (Rockford, Ill.: Tan Books and Publishers, Inc., 1988), p. 245.

11. Matthew 12:24.

12. Revelation 12:9.

13. John 12:31; 14:31; 16:11.

14. Salem Kirban, *Satan's Angels Exposed* (Huntington Valley, Pa.: Salem Kirban, Inc., 1980), p. 165.

15. Edith Starr Miller, *Occult Theocracy*, Vol. 1 (Hawthorne, Calif.: Christian Book Club of America, 1980), p. 32 (first published in 1933, recorded by A. C. De La Rive in *La Femme et l'Enfant dans la Franc-Maconnerie Universelle*, p. 558).

16. Ibid.

17. Ibid.

18. Scott Lively and Kevin Abrahams, *The Pink Swastika* (Keizer, Ore.: Founders Publishing Corporation, 1996), p. 215.

19. Miller, *Occult Theocracy*, p. 33.

20. Ibid., p. 32.

21. Ibid.

22. Ibid., p. 31.

23. Robert D. Novak, review of Ambrose Evans-Pritchard, *The Secret Life of Bill Clinton: The Unreported Stories* (Federalsburg, Md.: Regnery, 1997) in *American Spectator*, January 1998, p. 64.

24. Ibid., p. 65.

## 1: THE LOST SPIRIT OF AMERICANISM

1. Manly P. Hall, *The Lost Keys of Freemasonry* (Richmond: Macoy Publishing and Masonic Supply Co., 1976), pp. 47–48; first published in 1923.

2. Manly P. Hall, *The Secret Destiny of America* (Los Angeles: The Philosophical Research Society, 1958), p. 181.

3. David Nicholson, "Washington's Quandary," *Washington Post*, December 9, 1997, p. D2; review of *George Washington and Slavery* by Fritz Hirschfeld, University of Missouri, 1997.

4. "The 105th Congress," *New York Times*, January 7, 1997, p. B9; excerpts from Bonior's speech in Democratic response to vote.

5. "The 105th Congress," *New York Times,* January 8, 1997, p. B9; excerpts from Gingrich's remarks to House after reelection as Speaker.

6. Ibid.

7. Ibid.

8. Ibid.

9. Gary Allen, *None Dare Call It Conspiracy* (Rossmoor, Calif.: Concord Press, 1971), p. 9.

10. Quoted in Holly Skylar, ed., *Trilateralism* (Boston: South End Press, 1980), pp. 35–36.

11. Ann Gerhart and Annie Groer, "Pointed Paragraphs for Vernon Jordon," The Reliable Source, *Washington Post,* January 15, 1998, p. B3.

12. R. W. Apple, "Jordan Trades Stories with Clinton, and Offers Counsel," *New York Times,* January 25, 1998, p. 18.

13. Jacob Heilbrunn, "Are U. S. Ethnics Loyal?" *New York Post,* November 24, 1997, p. 31.

14. Quoted in ibid.

15. Des Griffin, *Fourth Reich of the Rich* (Clackamas, Ore.: Emissary Publications, 1976), p. 43.

16. Quoted in Don Bell, "Who Are Our Rulers?" *American Mercury,* September 1960, p. 136.

17. Quoted in David Halberstam, *The Best and the Brightest* (New York: Random House, 1972), p. 6.

18. *F.D.R.: His Personal Letters* (New York: Duell, Sloan and Pearce, 1950), p. 6.

19. Quoted in Wickliffe B. Vennard, Sr., *The Federal Reserve Hoax: The Age of Deception* (N.p., n.d.), pp. 147–148.

20. Marvin S. Antleman, *To Eliminate the Opiate* (New York: Zahavia, 1974), p. 94.

21. John Daniel, *Scarlet and the Beast: A History of the War Between English and French Freemasonry,* Vol. I (Tyler, Tex.: JKI Publishing, 1995), p. 190.

22. Ibid., p. 191.

23. Ibid., p. 348.

24. Norman Cohen, *Warrant for Genocide: The Myth of the Jewish World-Conspiracy and the Protocols of the Elders of Zion* (New York: Harper & Row, 1966), p. 65.

25. Daniel, *Scarlet and the Beast,* p. 762.

26. Ibid., p. 196.

27. Ibid., p. 347.

28. Revelation 2:9.

29. Daniel, *Scarlet and the Beast,* Vol. I, p. 204.

30. Ibid.

31. Ibid., p. 381.

32. Quoted in Richard Pipes, *Russia Under the Bolshevik Regime* (New York: Alfred A. Knopf, 1933), p. 257n.

33. Daniel, *Scarlet and the Beast,* Vol. II, p. 156.

34. W. Cleon Skousen, *The Naked Capitalist* (Salt Lake City, self-published, 1970), p. 8.

35. Tony Brown, *Black Lies, White Lies: The Truth According to Tony Brown* (New York: Morrow, 1995), pp. 132–133.

36. Edith Starr Miller, *Occult Theocracy,* Vol. I (Hawthorne, Calif.: Christian Book Club of America, 1980), p. 571 (first published in 1933, recorded by A. C. De La Rive in *La Femme et l'Enfant dans la Franc-Maconnerie Universelle,* p. 558).

37. Ibid., p. 466.

38. Carroll Quigley, *Tragedy and Hope: A History of the World in Our Time* (New York: Macmillan, 1966), p. 950.

39. Antleman, *To Eliminate the Opiate,* pp. 87–88.

40. Ibid., p. 116

41. Brown, *Black Lies, White Lies,* p. 77.

42. Adam Parfrey and Jim Redden, "Patriot Games," *Village Voice,* October 11, 1994, p. 26.

## 2: THE RULING CLASS

1. Carroll Quigley, *Tragedy and Hope: A History of the World in Our Time* (New York: Macmillan, 1966), p. 950.

2. Ibid., p. 945.

3. Richard Robertiello and Diana Hoguet, *The WASP Mystique* (New York: Donald I. Fine, 1987), pp. 20, 183.

4. Ibid., p. 183.

5. Ibid.

6. A. Ralph Epperson, *Clinton's Conspiracy* (N.c.: n.p., 1992), p. 12.

7. Ibid., p. 27.

8. Quigley, *Tragedy and Hope,* p. 950.

9. Phillip Knightley, *The Master Spy* (New York: Alfred A. Knopf, 1989), p. 142.

10. Robert Dreyfuss, *Hostage to Khomeini* (New York: New Benjamin Franklin House, 1980), pp. 217–219.

11. John Daniel, *Scarlet and the Beast: A History of the War Between English and French Freemasonry,* Vol. I (Tyler, Tex.: JKI Publishing, 1995), p. 519.

12. Ibid., p. 945.

13. Ibid., pp. 800–801.

14. Roger Morris, *Partners in Power* (New York: Henry Holt and Co., 1996), p. 102.

15. Ibid., pp. 102–103.

16. Ibid., p. 103.

17. Terry Reed and John Cummings, *Compromised: Clinton, Bush and the CIA* (New York: SPI Books/Shapolsky, 1994), p. 235.

18. Daniel, *Scarlet and the Beast,* Vol. I, p. 801.

19. Ibid.

20. Eustace Mullins, *The Secrets of the Federal Reserve: The London Connection* (Staunton, Va.: Bankers Research Institute, 1993), p. 63.

21. Karl E. Meyer, "The Opium War's Secret History," *New York Times,* June 28, 1997, p. 20.

22. Adam Smith, *Wealth of Nations,* representative selections (New York: Bobbs-Merrill, 1961).

23. Lyndon LaRouche, *Dope, Inc.* (Washington, D.C.: Executive Intelligence, 1992), p. 118.

24. Eustace Mullins, *The World Order: Our Secret Rulers,* election ed. (Staunton, Va.: Ezra Pound Institute of Civilization, n.d.), p. 54.

25. LaRouche, *Dope, Inc.,* p. xii.

26. Ibid., p. 653.

27. Jack Beeching, *The Chinese Opium Wars* (New York: Harvest Books, 1995), p. 258.

28. LaRouche, *Dope, Inc.,* p. 125.

29. Meyer, "The Opium War's Secret History," p. 20.

30. LaRouche, *Dope, Inc.,* p. 127.

31. Howard Brett, *Boston: A Social History* (New York: Hawthorn Books, 1973); quoted in LaRouche, *Dope, Inc.,* p. 127.

32. John Coleman, *Conspirators' Hierarchy: The Story of the Committee of Three Hundred* (Carson City, Nev.: America West Publishers, 1992), p. 137.

33. LaRouche, *Dope, Inc.,* p. 125.

34. Meyer, "The Opium War's Secret History," p. 20.

35. James M. Cornelius (1980 U.S. Census Bureau), *The English Americans* (New York: Chelsea House Publishers, 1980), p. 10.

36. Robertiello and Hoguet, *WASP Mystique,* p. 172.

37. Ibid.

38. Ibid., p. 38.

39. Ibid., p. 19.

40. Quoted in E. C. Knuth, *The Empire of the City: The Jekyll Hyde Nature of the British Government* (Milwaukee, Wisc.: E. C. Knuth, 1946), p. 5.

41. Ibid., p. 63.

42. Ibid., p. 64.

43. Ibid.

44. Quoted in ibid. p. 32.

45. Coleman, *Conspirators' Hierarchy,* p. 178.

46. Ibid., p. 123.

47. Ibid., p. 179.

48. Rod Nordland, "The Diana File," *Newsweek,* October 20, 1997, p. 38.

49. Julian Nundy, "Fiat Sought in Diana Crash," *USA Today,* September 18, 1997, p. 1.

50. Nordland, *Newsweek,* October 20, 1997, p. 34.

51. Ibid., p. 35.

52. William Neuman, "Police Nix Theory That Fotog's Car Caused Death," *New York Post,* September 15, 1997, p. 5.

53. Ibid.

54. LaRouche, *Dope, Inc.,* p. 454.

55. Ibid., p. 455.

56. Eustace Mullins, *The Curse of Canaan: A Demonology of History* (Staunton, Va.: Revelation Books, 1987), p. 8.

57. Ibid., p. 7.

58. Ibid., p. 28.

59. L. A. Waddell, *The Phoenician Origin of the Britons, Scots and Anglo-Saxons* (Hawthorne, Calif.: Christian Book Club of America, 1983); quoted in Jim Goad, *The Redneck Manifesto* (New York: Simon & Schuster, 1997), p. 42.

60. Mullins, *Curse of Canaan,* p. 26.

61. Ibid.

62. Ibid., p. 78.

63. Ibid.

64. Ibid., p. 79.

65. Ibid.

66. Emanuel M. Josephson, *The Strange Death of Franklin D. Roosevelt* (New York: Chedney Press, 1948), p. 44.

67. Mullins, *Curse of Canaan,* p. 80.

68. Josephson, *Strange Death of Franklin D. Roosevelt*, p. 12.

69. "Finds Touch of Africa in 28 Million Whites," *Sunday News*, June 15, 1958, p. 72.

70. Robertiello and Hoguet, *WASP Mystique*, p. 183.

71. Quoted in Sidney Zion, "Don't Tell Me Brits Were Benign," *New York Daily News*, July 10, 1997, p. 43.

72. Mullins, *World Order*, p. 54.

73. Zion, "Don't Tell Me Brits Were Benign," p. 43.

74. LaRouche, *Dope, Inc.*, p. 263.

75. Daniel, *Scarlet and the Beast*, Vol. I, p. 581.

76. Jim Shaw and Tom C. McKenney, *The Deadly Deception* (Lafayette, La.: Huntington House, 1988), p. 143.

77. Robert Keith Spenser, *The Cult of the All-Seeing Eye* (N.C.: Monte Cristo Press, 1964), p. 32.

78. David L. Carrico, *The Occult Meaning of the Great Seal of the United States.* 1965. Rev. ed. (Evansville, Ind.: Followers of Jesus Christ Ministries, 1995), p. 52.

79. Spenser, *Cult of the All-Seeing Eye*, pp. 23–24.

80. Carrico, *Occult Meaning of the Great Seal of the United States*, p. 53.

81. Quoted in Richard J. Whalen, *Founding Father* (New York: New American Library, 1964), p. 182.

82. Knuth, *Empire of the City*, p. 62.

83. Quigley, *Tragedy and Hope*, p. 950.

84. Quigley quoted in Roger Morris, *Partners in Power*, p. 65.

85. Ibid.

86. Quoted in Gary Allen, *Ted Kennedy, in over His Head* (Atlanta/Los Angeles: '76 Press, 1980), p. 15.

87. Quoted in *The Wall Street Journal*, April 30, 1980.

88. Quoted in ibid.

89. Bill Moyers, "The World of David Rockefeller," *Bill Moyers' Journal*, WNET/Thirteen, New York, February 7, 1980.

90. Barry Goldwater, *With No Apologies: The Personal and Political Memoirs of a United States Senator* (New York: Morrow, 1979), n.p.

91. Quoted in Daniel Brandt, "Clinton, Quigley, and Conspiracy: What's Going On Here?" E-text (gopher://conch.aa.msen.com:70/00/vendor/. . .piracy/a-albionic/up-dates/update.010895).

92. *Los Angeles Times*, January 23, 1977, p. 1.

93. Jeff Gerth, "The First Friend," *Washington Post*, July 14, 1996, p. 1.

94. Quoted in ibid.

95. Marcy Gordon, "Huang Phoned Foreign Employer During Period of Intelligence Meetings," *New York Daily News,* January 10, 1997, p. 22.

96. *Human Events,* December 27, 1996, p. 1.

97. Quin Hillyer, "A Nugget amid an Implausible Tale," *Wall Street Journal,* November 25, 1997, p. A22.

98. Ibid.

99. Novak, review of *The Secret Life of Bill Clinton* in *American Spectator,* p. 64.

100. Ambrose Evans-Pritchard, *The Secret Life of Bill Clinton* (Federalsburg, Md.: Regnery Publishing, 1997), p. 66.

101. Ibid., p. 58.

102. Michael Kellett, *One More Link* (Columbia, Md.: CLS Publishing, 1996), p. 43.

103. Evans-Pritchard, *Secret Life of Bill Clinton,* p. 363.

104. Ibid., p. 362.

105. Ibid., p. 359.

106. Thomas Galvin and William Goldschlag, "Bill's Cousin Kissing Kin?" *Daily News,* January 24, 1998, p. 5.

107. Richard L. Berke, "Differences Between President and Top House Democrat Deepen After a Speech by Gephardt," *New York Times,* December 5, 1997, p. A28.

108. Ibid.

109. Kenneth R. Timmerman, "While America Sleeps," *American Spectator,* June 1997, p. 34.

110. Ibid.

111. Ibid.

112. Ibid.

113. Marlette, *Newsweek,* June 9, 1997, p. 27.

114. Christopher Ruddy, "Experts Differ on Ron Brown Head Wound," *Pittsburgh Tribune-Review,* December 3, 1997, p. 1.

115. Ibid.

116. Robert Hare, *Without Conscience* (New York: Simon & Schuster, 1994).

117. Kellett, *One More Link.*

118. Ibid., p. 62.

119. Ibid., p. 57.

120. Antony Sutton, *Trilaterals over America* (Boring, Ore.: CPA Book Publishers, 1995), p. 27.

121. C. Wright Mills, *The Power Elite* (London/New York: Oxford University Press, 1956), p. 4.

122. LaRouche, *Dope, Inc.,* pp. 655–656.

123. James Perloff, *The Shadows of Power* (Appleton, Wisc.: Western Island, 1988), p. 5.

124. George Stephanopoulos, "Why We Should Kill Saddam," *Newsweek,* December 1, 1997, p. 34.

125. Ibid.

126. Ibid.

127. Ibid.

128. Carroll Quigley, *The Anglo-American Establishment: From Rhodes to Cliveden* (New York: Books in Focus, 1981), p. 33.

129. James Brooke, "Denver Police Say Skinheads Beat Up Black at a 7-Eleven," *New York Times,* November 29, 1997, p. 8.

130. Daniel, *Scarlet and the Beast,* Vol. I, p. 439.

131. Ibid., p. 437.

132. Ibid., p. 439.

133. Myra MacPherson, "McNamara's 'Other' Crimes: The Stories You Haven't Heard," *Washington Monthly,* June 1995, p. 28.

134. Ibid.

135. Ibid.

136. Quigley, *Tragedy and Hope,* p. 56.

## 3: THE ILLUMINATI RULING CLASS CONSPIRACY

1. Edith Starr Miller, *Occult Theocrasy,* Vol. I (Hawthorne, Calif.: Christian Book Club of America, 1980), pp. 363–364 (first published in 1933, recorded by A. C. De La Rive in *La Femme et l'Enfant dans la Franc-Maconnerie Universelle,* p. 558).

2. Albert Pike, *Morals and Dogma of the Ancient and Accepted Scottish Rite of Freemasonry* (Richmond: L. H. Jenkins, Inc., Edition Book Manufacturers, 1949), p. 744; reprint of 1906 edition.

3. Benjamin Disraeli, *Coningsby* (New York: Penguin, 1983), p. 233; reprint of 1844 edition.

4. Ephesians 5:11.

5. Theodore J. Forstmann, "Statism: The Opiate of the Elites," *IMPRIMIS,* Vol. 26, No. 5 (May 1977), p. 2.

6. Quoted in ibid.

7. Revelation 22:16.

8. Ezekiel 28:12.

9. Ephesians 2:2.

10. Genesis 3:5.

11. Ezekiel 28:15.

12. John Robison, *Proofs of a Conspiracy,* Americanist Classics edition (Belmont, Mass.: Western Island, 1967), p. 57.

13. Ibid.

14. Ibid.

15. Gerald B. Winrod, *Adam Weishaupt: A Human Devil* (N.C.: privately published, n.d.), p. 32.

16. Robison, *Proofs of a Conspiracy,* Introduction.

17. David A. Carrico, *The Occult Meaning of the Great Seal of the United States,* 1965, rev. ed. (Evansville, Ind.: Followers of Jesus Christ Ministries, 1995), p. 60.

18. Ibid., p. 6.

19. Winrod, *Adam Weishaupt,* p. 8.

20. Ibid., p. 36.

21. Quoted in ibid., p. 32.

22. Ibid., p. 16.

23. Ibid., p. 41.

24. Ibid.

25. Ibid., p. 30.

26. Quoted in ibid., p. 31.

27. David Allen Rivera, *Final Warning: A History of the New World Order* (Harrisburg, Penn.: Rivera Enterprises, 1984), p. 21.

28. Winrod, *Adam Weishaupt,* p. 18.

29. Robison, *Proofs of a Conspiracy,* Introduction.

30. John Daniel, *Scarlet and the Beast: A History of the War Between English and French Freemasonry,* Vol. I (Tyler, Tex.: JKI Publishing, 1995), p. 717.

31. Ibid., p. 165.

32. Auset Bakhufu, *The Six Black Presidents* (Washington, D.C.: PIK2 Publications, 1993), p. 16.

33. Barbara Murray, "Clearing the Heirs," *U.S. News and World Report,* December 22, 1997, p. 54.

34. Ibid.

35. Daniel, *Scarlet and the Beast,* Vol. I, p. 163.

36. Ibid., p. 165.

37. Ibid., p. 168.

38. Ibid., p. 712.

39. Ibid., p. 174.

40. Ibid., p. 710.
41. Revelation 13:16–17.
42. Daniel, *Scarlet and the Beast,* Vol. I, p. 711.
43. Ed Decker, *Freemasonry: Satan's Door to America;* quoted in Daniel, *Scarlet and the Beast,* Vol. I, p. 707.
44. Lyndon LaRouche, *Dope, Inc.* (Washington, D.C.: Executive Intelligence, Inc., 1992), p. 263.
45. Ibid.
46. Daniel, *Scarlet and the Beast,* Vol. II, p. 125.
47. Ibid.
48. Ibid.
49. Carroll Quigley, *Tragedy and Hope: A History of the World in Our Time* (New York: Macmillan, 1966), p. 131.
50. Des Griffin, *Fourth Reich of the Rich* (Clackamas, Ore.: Emissary Publications, 1976), p. 43.
51. "Fabian Socialism," *The New Encyclopaedia Britannica,* 1973 ed., Vol. 20 (Chicago/London/Toronto: Encyclopaedia Britannica, 1979), pp. 750–751.
52. Forstmann, "Statism," p. 2.
53. Ibid.
54. Ibid., pp. 2–3.
55. Robison, *Proofs of a Conspiracy,* Introduction.
56. Ibid.

## 4: THE THREAT OF SECRET SOCIETIES AND PAGANISM AT WORK

1. William Guy Carr, *Pawns in the Game* (N.c., privately printed, U.S.A., 1956), p. xvi.
2. David Carrico, "Freemasonry and the Twentieth Century Occult Revival," in *The Dark Side of Freemasonry,* ed. Ed Decker (Lafayette, La.: Huntington House Publishers, 1994), p. 196.
3. Ibid., p. 212.
4. Jim Shaw, quoted in John Daniel, *Scarlet and the Beast: A History of the War Between English and French Freemasonry,* Vol. II (Tyler, Tex.: JKI Publishing, 1995), p. 110.
5. Arthur Edward Waite, *A New Encyclopedia of Freemasonry* (New York: Random House, Wings Books, 1970), p. 417.
6. Tom C. McKenney, *Please Tell Me . . . Questions People Ask About*

*Freemasonry—and the Answers* (Lafayette, La.: Huntington House Publishers, 1994), p. 33.

7. John J. Robinson, *Born in Blood: The Lost Secrets of Freemasonry* (New York: M. Evans, 1989), p. 311.

8. McKenney, *Please Tell Me,* p. 201.

9. Ibid., p. 202.

10. Ibid., p. 203.

11. Daniel, *Scarlet and the Beast,* Vol. I, p. 8.

12. Carr, *Pawns in the Game,* p. xviii.

13. William Guy Carr, *The Red Fog over America* (New York: n.p., n.d.), p. 233.

14. Cardinal Caro y Rodriguez, *The Mystery of Freemasonry Unveiled* (Hawthorne, Calif.: Christian Book Club of America, 1925/1980); quoted in Carr, *Red Fog over America,* p. 224.

15. Ibid.

16. Warren Weston, *Father of Lies* (London: n.p., 1930s), p. 245.

17. Edith Starr Miller, *Occult Theocrasy,* Vol. 1 (Hawthorne, Calif.: Christian Book Club of America, 1980), pp. 363–364 (first published in 1933, recorded by A.C. De La Rive in *La Femme et l'Enfant dans la Franc-Maconnerie Universelle,* p. 558).

18. Ibid.

19. Lyndon LaRouche, *Dope, Inc.* (Washington, D.C.: Executive Intelligence, Inc., 1992), pp. 419–420.

20. Ibid., p. 420.

21. Jim Shaw and Tom C. McKenney, *The Deadly Deception* (Lafayette: La.: Huntington House, 1988), p. 89.

22. Shaw, quoted in Daniel, *Scarlet and the Beast,* Vol. I, p. 230.

23. Shaw and McKenney, *Deadly Deception,* pp. 157–158.

24. McKenney, *Please Tell Me,* p. 139.

25. Daniel, *Scarlet and the Beast,* Vol. II, p. 48.

26. Weston, *Father of Lies,* pp. 243–245.

27. Oswald Wirth, *The Ideal Initiate,* quoted in Daniel, *Scarlet and the Beast,* Vol. II, p. 111.

28. Vicomte Leon de Poncins, *Freemasonry and the Vatican* (N.c.: n.p., 1968); quoting Wirth in *L'Idéal Initiatique,* pp. 10–11, quoted in Daniel, *Scarlet and the Beast.*

29. Benjamin L. Cook, *Freemasonry Condemned from Its Own Sources,* (Palmdale, Calif.: Omni Publications, 1991), p. 82.

30. Ibid., p. 83.

31. Daniel, *Scarlet and the Beast,* Vol. II, p. 37.

32. Quoted in Miller, *Occult Theocrasy,* Vol. I, pp. 220–221.

33. Daniel, *Scarlet and the Beast,* Vol. I, p. 411.

34. Nigel Davies, *Human Sacrifices in History and Today* (New York: Morrow, 1981), p. 13.

35. Miller, *Occult Theocracy,* pp. 220–221.

36. Ibid., p. 32.

37. Ibid., p. 31.

38. Eliphas Levi, *The Book of Splendors* (Wellingborough, England: Aquarian Press, 1973), p. 119.

39. Daniel, *Scarlet and the Beast,* Vol. II, p. 48.

40. Quoted in J. A. Rogers, *The Five Negro Presidents* (St. Petersburg, Fla.: Helga Rogers, 1965/1993), p. 6.

41. Brian Blomquist, "Starr Probe of Bill's Sex Life," *New York Post,* June 26, 1997, p. 4.

42. Cited in Daniel, *Scarlet and the Beast,* Vol. I, p. 249.

43. Ibid., p. 836.

44. Jeffrey Hadden, *Pulpit Helps* (survey), December 1987 edition; quoted in Daniel, *Scarlet and the Beast,* Vol. I, p. 255.

45. Ibid., p. 255.

46. Ibid.

47. Peter Lalonde, *"American Health Magazine:* Metaphysics Belief on Rise," *The Omega-Letter,* Vol. I, No. 12 (December 1986), p. 12.

48. I Corinthians 15:17.

49. II Thessalonians 2:1, 3.

50. Paul A. Fisher, *Behind the Lodge Door* (Rockford, Ill.: Tan Books and Publishers, 1988), p. 244.

51. Ibid.

52. Ibid.

53. "Senate Mud Balls," *Wall Street Journal,* April 15, 1987; editorial.

54. Blair Dorminey, "Iced Because He's a Mason," *Washington Times,* April 16, 1987; commentary.

55. Fisher, *Behind the Lodge Door,* p. 243.

56. Ibid.

57. Ibid., p. 111.

58. Ibid., p. 116.

59. David Johnson, "FBI's Chief Tries to Influence Reno," *New York Times,* December 2, 1997, p. 1.

60. Shaw and McKenney, *Deadly Deception,* p. 140.

61. *World Book Encyclopedia,* Vol. 13 (Chicago: World Book, 1969), p. 210.

62. Robinson, *Born in Blood,* p. 329.

63. Shaw and McKenney, *Deadly Deception,* p. 29.

64. A. Ralph Epperson, *The Unseen Hand: An Introduction to the Conspiratorial View of History* (Tucson, Ariz.: Publius Press, 1985), pp. 162–163.

65. Ibid., p. 160.

66. Daniel, *Scarlet and the Beast,* Vol II, p. 66.

67. Fisher, *Behind the Lodge Door,* pp. 95–97.

68. William J. Whalen, *Christianity and American Freemasonry* (Huntington, Ind.: Our Sunday Visitor, 1987), pp. 23–25.

69. Ibid.

70. Quoted in Delmar Duane Darrah, *History and Evolution of Freemasonry* (Chicago: Charles T. Powers, 1979), p. 319.

71. Albert G. Mackey, "Legend of the Craft," *Mackey's Encyclopedia of Freemasonry,* Vol. I (Richmond: Macoy Publishers and Masonic Supply Co., 1946).

72. William Josiah Sutton, *The Antichrist 666* (New York: TEACH Services, Inc., 1980), p. 42.

73. Daniel, *Scarlet and the Beast,* Vol. I, p. 855.

74. Sutton, *Antichrist 666,* p. 27.

75. Robert Graves, *Mammon and the Black Goddess* (London: n.p., 1964), p. 162.

76. Ean Begg, *The Cult of the Black Virgin* (New York: Penguin, 1985), p. 127.

77. Ibid., p. xiii.

78. Ibid., p. 1.

79. *The New Catholic Encyclopedia,* Vol 7 (New York: McGraw-Hill, 1977), p. 2053.

80. Russell Tardo, *Easter Errors* (Arabi, La.: Faithful Word Publications, 1994), p. 4.

81. Albert J. Dager, *Facts and Fallacies of the Resurrection* (Redmond, Wash.: Sword Publisher, 1984), p. 3.

82. Daniel, *Scarlet and the Beast,* Vol. II, p. 122.

83. Tardo, *Easter Errors,* p. 9.

## 5: Karl Marx's Trojan Horse: The Fed

1. *The Writings of Thomas Jefferson,* Vol. 7 (Washington, D.C.: Committee of Congress, 1861), p. 685; autobiographical and other writings.
2. Andrew Gause, *The Secret World of Money* (Hilton Head, S.C.: SDL Press, 1996), pp. 92–93.
3. Eustace Mullins, *The Secrets of the Federal Reserve: The London Connection* (Staunton, Va.: Bankers Research Institute, 1993), p. 5.
4. Quoted in Hamish McRae and Francis Cairncross, *Capitol City* (London: Methuen, 1991), p. 63.
5. Gause, *Secret World of Money,* p. 90.
6. Ibid., p. 110.
7. Ibid., p. 109.
8. Mullins, *Secrets of the Federal Reserve,* p. 63.
9. McRae and Cairncross, *Capital City,* p. 1.
10. Ibid., p. 225.
11. Mullins, *Secrets of the Federal Reserve,* p. 64.
12. Ibid.
13. McRae and Cairncross, *Capital City.*
14. Mullins, *Secrets of the Federal Reserve,* p. 68.
15. Antony Sutton, *America's Secret Establishment: An Introduction to the Order of Skull and Bones* (Billings, Mont.: Liberty House Press, 1986), p. 11.
16. "The Money Masters: How International Bankers Gained Control of America" (video transcript), *Monetary Reform* No. 5 (Summer 1997), p. 20.
17. Quoted in ibid.
18. Quoted in Gause, *Secret World of Money,* pp. 78–79.
19. Ibid., pp. 92–93.
20. Quoted in Bill Lerach, "Plundering America: How the Abuse of Corporate Power Threatens to Destroy Your Life Savings, and What You Can Do About It," unpublished, 1997, p. 1.
21. Ernie Ross, "The Impossible Task of the Fed," in *Bankers and Regulations* (Irvington-on-Hudson, N.Y.: Foundation for Economic Education, 1993), pp. 15–17.
22. Quoted in Richard Wurmbrand, *Was Karl Marx a Satanist?* (Glendale, Calif.: Diane Books Publishing, 1976), p. 25.
23. Ibid.

24. Carroll Quigley, *Tragedy and Hope: A History of the World in Our Time* (New York: Macmillan, 1966), p. 5; Rabbi Marvin S. Antleman, *To Eliminate the Opiate* (New York: Zahavia, 1974), p. 26.
25. Gary Allen, "The Conspiracy: Planning for Economic Collapse," *American Opinion,* May 1968, p. 33.
26. A Ralph Epperson, *The Unseen Hand: An Introduction to the Conspiratorial View of History* (Tucson, Ariz.: Publius Press, 1985), p. 111.
27. John Maynard Keynes, *The Economic Consequences of the Peace;* quoted in Epperson, *Unseen Hand,* p. 57.
28. Ibid.

### 6: STATISM: THE RELIGION OF OPPRESSION AND THE SCIENCE OF CONTROL

1. Antony Sutton, *The Secret Cult of the Order* (Bullsbrook, Western Australia: Veritas Publishing Company PTY. Ltd., 1983), p. 85.
2. Ibid., p. 118.
3. Antony Sutton, *America's Secret Establishment: An Introduction to the Order of Skull and Bones* (Billings, Mont.: Liberty House Press, 1986), p. 119.
4. Thomas Jefferson to Samuel Kercheval, 1816, in *Thomas Jefferson on Politics and Government: Quotations from the Writings of Thomas Jefferson,* ed. Eyler Robert Coates, Sr., Online Library of Electronic Text, University of Virginia.
5. John Kenneth Galbraith, *Consumer Reports,* February 1979, p. 95.
6. *Wall Street Journal,* September 12, 1996, p. 1.
7. Alan Greenspan, "Gold and Economic Freedom," in Ayn Rand, *Capitalism: The Unknown Ideal* (New York: Signet Books, 1967), p. 96.
8. Ibid.
9. Ibid., pp. 97–98.
10. Ibid., pp. 100–101.
11. Larry Parks, *FedWATCH,* Foundation for the Advancement of Monetary Education, April 14, 1997, p. 1.
12. Ibid.
13. Greenspan, "Gold and Economic Freedom," in Rand, *Capitalism: The Unknown Ideal,* p. 99.
14. John Daniel, *Scarlet and the Beast: A History of the War Between English and French Freemasonry,* Vol. I (Tyler, Tex.: JKI Publishing, 1995), p. 92.
15. Ibid.

16. Ibid., p. 94.
17. Ibid.
18. Ibid., p. 84.
19. Antony C. Sutton and Patrick M. Wood, *Trilaterals over Washington* (Scottsdale, Ariz.: The August Corp., 1978), pp. 116–117.
20. Ibid., pp. 146–174.
21. A. Ralph Epperson, *The Unseen Hand: An Introduction to the Conspiratorial View of History* (Tucson, Ariz.: Publius Press, 1985), p. 57.
22. "Too Many Jobs?" *Time,* September 16, 1996, p. 68.
23. Ibid.
24. Robert Eisner, "The Fed Should Keep Its Head," *New York Times,* September, 19, 1996, p. A27.
25. Leonard C. Lewin, *Report from Iron Mountain on the Possibility and Desirability of Peace* (New York: Dial Press, 1967).
26. Robert Samuelson, "Confederacy of Dunces," *Newsweek,* September 23, 1996, p. 65.
27. Sybil Leek and Bert R. Sugar, *The Assassination Chain* (Los Angeles: Pinnacle Books, 1976), p. 268.
28. Theodore J. Forstmann, "Statism: The Opiate of the Elites," *IMPRIMIS,* Vol. 26, No. 5 (May 1977), p. 2.
29. Ibid.
30. David Boaz, *Libertarianism* (New York: The Free Press, 1977), p. 60.

## 7: The Illuminati-Sponsored American Race War

1. William Guy Carr, *Pawns in the Game* (N.c.: privately printed, U.S.A., 1956), Glossary.
2. Gerald Suster, *Hitler: Black Magician* (London: Skoob Books Publishing, 1996), p. 159.
3. Quoted in ibid.
4. Devlin Barrett, "Hugs for Louima Cop at Scandal Precinct," *New York Post,* December 13, 1997, p. 7.
5. "Lynching Termed a Type of Dixie Sex Perversion," *Baltimore Afro-American,* March 16, 1935, n.p.
6. Ralph Ginzburg, *One Hundred Years of Slavery* (Baltimore: Black Classic Press, 1962), p. 12.
7. Tony Brown, *Black Lies, White Lies: The Truth According to Tony Brown* (New York: Morrow, 1995), p. 76.
8. James H. Jones, *Bad Blood* (New York: The Free Press, 1981/1993), p. 27.

9. Quoted in ibid. p. 163.

10. Ibid., p. 164.

11. Ibid.

12. "Another Version of the Tuskegee Experiment" (#2012), *Tony Brown's Journal,* No. 2012, PBS, May 30, 1997.

13. Kenneth O'Reilly, *Racial Matters: The FBI's Secret File on Black America, 1960–1972* (New York: The Free Press, 1989), p. 275.

14. Ibid., p. 122.

15. Ibid., p. 269.

16. Stephen G. Thompkins, "Top Spy Feared Current Below Surface Unrest," *Memphis Commercial Appeal,* March 21, 1993, p. A8.

17. Stephen G. Thompkins, "Army Feared King, Secretly Watched Him," *Memphis Commercial Appeal,* March 21, 1993, p. A7.

18. Ibid., p. A8.

19. Ibid.

20. Ibid., p. A9.

21. Quoted in ibid., p. A8.

22. Brown, *Black Lies, White Lies,* p. 87

23. Ibid., p. 86.

24. Ibid., p. 87.

25. "Ex-Army Agents Discuss 1968 Monitoring of King," *Washington Post,* December 1, 1997, p. A14.

26. Ibid.

27. William F. Pepper, *Orders to Kill: The Truth Behind the Murder of Dr. Martin Luther King* (New York: Carroll and Graf Publishers, 1995); dust jacket.

28. David Saltonstall, "Mystery Man: New Trail in King Slay," *New York Daily News,* April 6, 1997, p. 18.

29. Kevin Sack, "Son of Dr. King Asserts LBJ Role in Plot," *New York Times,* June 19, 1997, p. 12.

30. David J. Garrow, "The Assassin's Name Is James Earl Ray," *New York Times,* April 2, 1997, p. A21.

31. Ibid.

32. Reported on "Who Killed Malcolm?" *Tony Brown's Journal,* No. 1603, PBS, February 5, 1993.

33. Ibid.

34. Ibid.

35. Ibid.

36. Ibid.

37. "Malcolm X Shot to Death at Rally Here," *New York Times*, February 22, 1965, p. 1; early edition.
38. Ibid.
39. "Malcolm X Slain," *New York Daily News*, February 22, 1965, p. 1.
40. "Who Killed Malcolm?" *Tony Brown's Journal*, No. 1603.
41. Ibid.
42. Abigail Thernstron, "Going Toe to Toe with Bill," *Newsweek*, December 15, 1997, p. 35.
43. Antony Sutton, *America's Secret Establishment: An Introduction to the Order of Skull and Bones* (Billings, Mont.: Liberty House Press, 1986), p. 118.
44. Tom Wicker, "The Coming Race War in America: A Wake-up Call," *Washington Monthly*, March 1977, p. 57; book review.
45. Thomas W. Chittum, *Civil War II: The Coming Breakup of America* (Show Low, Ariz.: American Eagle Publications, 1996); back cover.
46. Virginia Breen and Jere Hestur, "Khalid Blasts Black Pols," *New York Daily News*, March 30, 1994, p. 26.
47. Chittum, *Civil War II*, p. 1.
48. Ibid.
49. Ibid., p. 2.
50. Peter Baker, "Race Forum in Fairfax Finally Hits a Nerve," *Washington Post*, December 18, 1997, p. 1.
51. Chittum, *Civil War II*, p. 19.
52. Ibid.
53. Gore Vidal, *The Decline and Fall of the American Empire* (Berkeley, Calif.: Odonian Press, 1992), pp. 50, 57; and Peter Brimelow, *Alien Nation* (New York: Random House, 1995), p. 35.
54. Jack Miles, "Book Review," *Atlantic Monthly*, April 1995, p. 136.
55. Chittum, *Civil War II*, p. 114.
56. Ibid., p. 108.
57. Ibid.
58. Charles Krauthammer, "Quebec and the Death of Diversity," *Time*, November 13, 1995, p. 124.
59. Ed Koch, "Since You Asked . . . ," *New York Post*, December 12, 1997, p. 35.
60. Ibid.

## 8: The Drug War Against U.S.

1. John Daniel, *Scarlet and the Beast: A History of the War Between English and French Freemasonry,* Vol. III (Tyler, Tex.: JKI Publishing, 1995), p. 135.

2. George Orwell, *1984* (New York: Harcourt Brace Jovanovich, 1977), p. 142.

3. Daniel, *Scarlet and the Beast,* Vol. III, p. 52.

4. Ibid., p. 153.

5. Ibid.

6. Ibid., pp. 153–154.

7. Jack Beeching, *The Chinese Opium Wars* (New York: Harvest Books, 1975), p. 258.

8. "Chronicle of HK's Major Historical Events," Xinhua News Agency, June 30, 1997, E-text.

9. Lyndon LaRouche, *Dope, Inc.* (Washington, D.C.: Executive Intelligence, Inc., 1992), p. 134.

10. Ibid., p. 114.

11. Eustace Mullins, *The World Order: Our Secret Rulers,* election edition, (Staunton, Va.: Ezra Pound Institute of Civilization, 1992), p. 54.

12. LaRouche, *Dope, Inc.,* p. 283.

13. Harry Anslinger, quoted in Alfred W. McCoy, *The Politics of Heroin in Southwest Asia* (New York: Harper & Row, 1972); quoted in LaRouche, *Dope, Inc.,* p. 277.

14. Quoted in Mohammed Hassanein Heikal, *The Cairo Documents* (Garden City, N.Y.: Doubleday, 1973), pp. 306–307.

15. LaRouche, *Dope, Inc.,* p. 653.

16. Ibid.

17. *San Jose Mercury News,* May 16, 1975, reported in LaRouche, *Dope, Inc.,* p. 653.

18. Jonathan Vankin, *Conspiracies, Cover-ups and Crimes: Political Manipulation and Mind Control in America* (New York: Paragon House, 1991), E-text.

19. Ibid.

20. Ibid.

21. LaRouche, *Dope, Inc.,* p. 482.

22. Vankin, *Conspiracies, Cover-ups and Crimes.*

23. Ibid.

24. Ibid.

25. Gary Webb, "Dark Alliance," *San Jose Mercury News,* August 18–20, 1996.

26. Cinque Henderson, "Myths of the Unloved," *The New Republic,* August 25, 1997, p. 14.

27. "The CIA Drug Conspiracy That Wasn't," *Tampa Tribune,* May 26, 1997, p. 12.

28. Jack E. White, "Dividing Line," *Time,* September 30, 1996, p. 59.

29. Quoted in "CIA Drug Conspiracy That Wasn't," p. 12.

30. "CIA Ally Indicted in Drug Trafficking," *Washington Post,* November 24, 1996, p. A15.

31. "Report: Venezuelan Official Indicted," UPI, November 23, 1996.

32. "CIA Ally Indicted in Drug Trafficking," p. A15.

33. Walter Pincus, "Inspectors General Find No Ties Between CIA, L.A. Drug Dealers," *Washington Post,* December 19, 1997, p. A2.

34. Ibid.

35. Associated Press, "Reno Seals Report on CIA-Crack Claims," *Los Angeles Times,* January 24, 1998, p. A15.

36. Claude Lewis, "Even if the CIA Flooded Inner Cities with Crack, Blacks Didn't 'Say No,' " *Philadelphia Inquirer,* September 25, 1996, p. A23.

37. Vankin, *Conspiracies, Cover-ups and Crimes.*

38. William Brian Key, *Media Sexploitation* (Scarborough, Ont.: Prince Hall, 1976), p. 137.

39. Daniel, *Scarlet and the Beast,* Vol. I, p. 40.

40. Quoted in Mark Spaulding, *The Heartbeat of the Dragon: The Occult Roots of Rock and Roll* (Sterling Heights, Mich.: Light Warrior Press, 1992), p. 69.

41. William Josiah Sutton, *The Illuminati 666* (New York: TEACH Services, 1980), p. 129.

42. Daniel, *Scarlet and the Beast,* Vol. III, p. 17.

43. Spaulding, *Heartbeat of the Dragon,* p. 63.

44. William and Sharon Schnoebelen, *Lucifer Dethroned* (Chino, Calif.: Chick Publications, 1993), p. 39.

45. Daniel, *Scarlet and the Beast,* Vol. I, p. 40.

46. Jeff Godwin, *The Devil's Disciples* (Chino, Calif.: Chick Publications, 1993), p. 134.

47. Ibid.

48. *Newsweek,* November 17, 1997, p. 29.

49. Dean Grace, *Guide to Masonic "Handshakes" in the Movies* (N.c.: n.p., December 1995), p. 30.

50. John O'Toole, "Those Sexy Ice Cubes Are Back," *Advertising Age,* October 2, 1989, p. 26.
51. Ibid.
52. "Washington Whispers," *U. S. News & World Report,* January 5, 1998, p. 12.
53. Janet Weeks, "Controversial Japanese Cartoon Coming to USA," *USA Today,* December 31, 1997, p. D1.
54. "Why Are Kids Killing?" *People,* June 23, 1997, p. 46.
55. Edith Starr Miller, *Occult Theocrasy,* Vol. I (Hawthorne, Calif.: Christian Book Club of America, 1980), p. 581 (first published in 1933, recorded by A. C. De La Rive in *La Femme et l'Enfant dans la Franc-Maçonnerie Universelle,* p. 558).
56. Ibid.

## 9: The Choice: Good Versus Evil

1. Time/CNN poll, Reuters, *San Francisco Chronicle,* January 24, 1998, p. 2.
2. Zev ben Shimon Halevi, *Kaballah and Exodus* (York Beach, Me.: Samuel Weiser, 1988), Preface.
3. Florence Scovel Shinn, *The Game of Life and How to Play It* (Marina del Rey, Calif.: De Vorss, 1925), p. 7.
4. John Horgan, *The End of Science* (New York: Addison Wesley, 1996), p. 94.
5. Ephesians 6:11.
6. General Douglas MacArthur, broadcast to the American people following the surrender ceremony aboard the U.S.S. *Missouri,* September 2, 1945.
7. Ephesians 6:13.

## 10: The Coming Crash: Chaos and Opportunity

1. Ericka Cheetham, *The Final Prophecies of Nostradamus* (New York: Putnam, 1989), p. 424.
2. R. E. Search, *Lincoln Money Martyred* (Palmdale, Calif.: Omni Publications, 1989), p. 3; reprint of 1935 edition.
3. Ibid.
4. Ibid.
5. Peter McAlpine, *The Occult Technology of Power: The Initiation of the Son of a Finance Capitalist into the Arcane Secrets of Political and*

*Economic Power* (Port Townsend, Wash.: Alpine Enterprises, 1974); reprinted from Alpine Enterprises E-text edition, p. 6.

6. Ibid., p. 7.

7. Ibid.

8. Tony Brown, *Black Lies, White Lies: The Truth According to Tony Brown* (New York: Morrow, 1995), p. 29.

9. "The Puzzling Failure of Economics," *Economist,* August 23, 1997, p. 11.

10. McAlpine, *Occult Technology of Power,* p. 7.

11. Ibid.

12. Ibid.

13. Thomas C. McAuliffe, 'Debt Bomb and the Savings Pool," unpublished, 1997, p. 42.

14. Frank Swoboda, "Report Finds No Solace in Recovering Economy," *Washington Post,* September 8, 1996, p. F11.

15. Richard Wolfe, "Cities Report More Hunger, Homelessness," *USA Today,* December 15, 1997, p. A1.

16. Lester Thurow, speech, Milton S. Eisenhower Symposium, Johns Hopkins University, Baltimore, October 18, 1988.

17. Ibid.

18. Stephen Leeb, "Biggest Economic Megatrends of 1997," *Special Reports from the Editors of Personal Finance* (McLean, Va.: KCI Communications, 1997), p. 1–1.

19. Ibid.

20. Ibid.

21. Leeb, "The Inflation of '97 and the Crash of '98," *Personal Finance,* July 1997, p. 1.

22. Ibid.

23. Ibid., p. 3.

24. Ibid.

25. "America's Economy: Crash or Boom?" *Tony Brown's Journal,* No. 2013, PBS, June 13, 1997.

26. Leeb, "Inflation of '97 and the Crash of '98," p. 4.

27. "Government Is Prepared for Market Crash," *New York Post,* July 21, 1997, p. 26.

28. Dyan Machan, "Volcker Blows Off Steam," *Forbes,* August 11, 1997, p. 56.

29. Ibid., p. 58.

30. Ibid.

31. "Bracing for an Apocalypse," Street News, *Business Week,* November 18, 1996, p. 10.

32. "America's Economy: Crash or Boom?" *Tony Brown's Journal*, No. 2013.

33. Ibid.

34. Ibid.

35. Machan, "Volcker Blows Off Steam," p. 58.

36. Leeb, "Inflation of '97 and the Crash of '98," p. 4.

37. Ibid., p. 5.

38. Leeb, "Special Mid-Year Forecast," *Personal Finance,* July 1997, pp. 7–20.

39. Leeb, "Why Gold Prices May Rise Steeply in 1998," *Personal Finance,* July 1997, p. 5.

40. Charles Cerami, "Although Luster has Dulled, Gold Remains Store of Value," *Insight on the News,* August 18, 1997, p. 23.

41. Ibid., p. 22.

42. Leeb, "Why Gold Prices May Rise Steeply in 1998," p. 5.

43. William F. Buckley, Jr., "Balancing Budget Bill: Numbers Don't Add Up," *New York Post,* August 11, 1997, p. 21.

44. Allan Sloan, "The Surplus Shell Game," *Newsweek,* January 19, 1998, p. 28.

45. "The Surplus Mirage," The Concord Coalition, *New York Times,* January 25, 1998, p. 23.

46. *Wall Street Journal,* August 8, 1997.

47. Jill Dutt, "Dow Tumbles 157 Points; Bond Market Jitters over Growth, Drop in Dollar Spill Over to Stocks," *Washington Post,* August 8, 1997, p. F1.

48. Jonathan Fuerbringer, "Selloff on Wall Street: Stocks, Bonds and Dollar All Drop," *New York Times,* August 8, 1997; Features section.

49. Beth Piskora, "What If Wall Street Crashed in '97?" *New York Post,* August 10, 1997, p. 1.

50. David Smith, "Brace Yourself for the Crash," *London Sunday Times,* July 27, 1977, n.p.

51. Piskora, "What If Wall Street Crashed in '97?" p. 1.

## 11: THE SEVEN STEPS TO EMPOWERMENT

1. Robert Uhlig, "Millennium Bug Warning for Airlines," *The Electronic Telegraph,* January 15, 1998, Issue 965.

2. Andrea Rock and Tripp Reynolds, "The Year 2000 Bug and You," *Money*, February 1998, p. 48.

3. Amy Harmon, "Software Jobs Go Begging, Threatening Technology Boom," *New York Times*, January 13, 1998, p. A1.

4. Rock and Reynolds, "The Year 2000 Bug and You."

5. Ibid.

6. David E. Kalish (Associated Press), "2000 Glitch Already Here," *Albany Times Union*, January 25, 1998, p. B1.

7. Ibid.

8. "Debt Load Growing for College Graduates," *New York Times*, October 24, 1997, p. A10.

9. Katie Hafner and Michael Meyer, "Help Really Wanted: A Nerd Shortage Has Companies Scrambling to Lure High Tech Workers—and Growing Their Own," *Newsweek*, December 8, 1997, p. 94.

10. Michael S. Clouse, *Business Is Booming* (Charlottesville, Va.: Upline Press, 1996), p. 18.

11. "Pre-Paid Legal Services, Inc.—Redefining the Legal Industry," Salomon Brothers, May 29, 1997, p. 1.

12. Ira Breskin, "Pre-Paid Meets Rising Need for Legal Advice and Services," *Investor's Business Daily*, September 16, 1997, p. A27.

13. "Prepaid Legal Services," *Essence*, January 1997, p. 36.

14. Ibid.

15. *60 Minutes*, CBS-TV, September 21, 1997.

16. Sandra Block and Carl Weiser, "IRS Accused of Abuse As Hearing Looms," *USA Today*, September 22, 1997, p. 1A.

17. *Strategic Weekly Briefings*, October 24, 1997, p. 3.

18. Robert Huddleston, "Another Government Assault," E-mail: cab-hop@highfiber.com, December 3, 1997.

19. Quoted in Jarrett Wollstein, "The Looting of America," *A-albionic Research Weekly, Update*, July 17, 1995, p. 1.

20. Ibid.

21. Ibid., p. 2.

22. Ibid., p. 3.

23. F. Tupper Saussy, *The Miracle on Main Street: Saving Yourself and America from Financial Ruin* (Sewanee, Tenn.: Spencer Judd, Publishers, 1980), pp. 105–106.

24. Ibid., pp. 91–92.

25. Ibid., p. 91.

26. Ibid., p. 93.

27. Tony Brown, *Black Lies, White Lies: The Truth According to Tony Brown* (New York: Morrow, 1995).

28. Allan Sloan, "How WorldCom Uses Its Printing Press to Buy the World," *Newsweek,* October 20, 1997, p. 46.

29. Andrew Gause, *The Secret World of Money* (Hilton Head, S.C.: SDL Press, 1996), p. 4.

30. Ellen Graham, "Community Groups Print Local (and Legal) Currencies," *Wall Street Journal,* June 27, 1996, p. B1.

31. Ibid.

32. Martin van Creveld, *The Transformation of War* (New York: The Free Press, 1991), p. 195.

33. Ibid.

34. Ibid.

35. Timothy Egan, "Terrorism Now Going Homespun As Bombings in the U.S. Spread," *New York Times,* August 21, 1996, p. 1.

### 12: CODA: EMPOWERING THE SOUL

1. John 14:16.

# BIBLIOGRAPHY

Allen, Gary. *None Dare Call It Conspiracy*. Rossmoor, Calif.: Concord Press, 1971.

———. *Ted Kennedy, in over His Head*. Atlanta/Los Angeles: '76 Press, 1980.

Antleman, Marvin S. *To Eliminate the Opiate*. New York: Zahavia, 1974.

Bakhufu, Auset. *The Six Black Presidents*. Washington, D.C.: PIK2 Publications, 1993.

Breeching, Jack. *The Chinese Opium Wars*. New York: Harvest Books, 1975.

Begg, Ean. *The Cult of the Black Virgin*. New York: Penguin, 1985.

Boaz, David. *Libertarianism*. New York: The Free Press, 1977.

Bork, Robert. *Slouching Towards Gomorrah*. New York: Regan Books, 1996.

Brett, Howard. *Boston: A Social History*. New York: Hawthorn Books, 1973.

Brimelow, Peter. *Alien Nation*. New York: Random House, 1995.

Brown, Tony. *Black Lies, White Lies: The Truth According to Tony Brown.* New York: William Morrow, 1995.

Carr, William Guy. *The Red Fog over America.* New York: n.d.

———. *Pawns in the Game.* Privately printed, 1956.

Carrico, David L. *Lucifer-Eliphas Levi-Albert Pike and the Masonic Lodge.* Evansville, Ind.: Followers of Jesus Christ Ministries, 1991.

———. "Freemasonry and the Twentieth Century Occult Revival." In *The Dark Side of Freemasonry,* edited by Ed Decker. Lafayette, La.: Huntington House Publishers, 1994.

———. *The Occult Meaning of the Great Seal of the United States.* 1965. Rev. ed. Evansville, Ind.: Followers of Jesus Christ Ministries, 1995.

Cheetham, Ericka. *The Final Prophecies of Nostradamus.* New York: Putnam, 1989.

Chittum, Thomas W. *Civil War II: The Coming Breakup of America.* Show Low, Ariz.: American Eagle Publications, Inc., 1996.

Cohen, Norman. *Warrant for Genocide: The Myth of the Jewish World-Conspiracy and the Protocols of the Elders of Zion.* New York: Harper & Row, 1966.

Coleman, John. *Conspirators' Hierarchy: The Story of the Committee of 300.* Carson City, Nev.: America West Publishers, 1992.

Cook, Benjamin L., *Freemasonry Condemned from Its Own Sources.* Palmdale, Calif.: Omni Publications, 1991.

Cornelius, James M. *The English Americans.* New York: Chelsea House Publishers, 1980.

Creveld, Martin van. *The Transformation of War.* New York: The Free Press, 1991.

Dager, Albert J. *Facts and Fallacies of the Resurrection.* Redmond, Wash.: Sword Publisher, 1984.

Daniel, John. *Scarlet and the Beast: A History of the War Between English and French Freemasonry.* Vol. 1. Tyler, Tex.: JKI Publishing, 1995.

Darrah, Delmar Duane. *History and Evolution of Freemasonry.* Chicago: Charles T. Powers, 1979.

Davies, Nigel. *Numan Sacrifices in History and Today.* New York: William Morrow, 1981.

Decker, Ed. *Freemasonry: Satan's Door to America.* In John Daniel, *Scarlet and the Beast,* vol. 1. Tyler, Tex.: JKI Publishing, 1995.

Disraeli, Benjamin. *Coningsby.* 1884. Reprint. New York: Penguin, 1983.

Dreyfuss, Robert, *Hostage to Khomeini.* New York: New Benjamin Franklin House, 1980.

Epperson, A. Ralph. *The Unseen Hand: An Introduction to the Conspiratorial View of History*. Tucson, Ariz.: Publius Press, 1985.

———. *Clinton's Conspiracy*. N.p., 1992.

Evans-Pritchard, Ambrose. *The Secret Life of Bill Clinton*. Federalsburg, Md.: Regnery Publishing, 1997.

*F.D.R.: His Personal Letters*. New York: Duell, Sloan and Pearce, 1950.

Fisher, Paul A. *Behind the Lodge Door*. Rockford, Ill.: Tan Books and Publishers, Inc., 1988.

Gause, Andrew. *The Secret World of Money*. Hilton Head, S.C.: SDL Press, 1996.

Ginzburg, Ralph. *100 Years of Slavery*. Baltimore: Black Classic Press, 1962.

Goad, Jim. *The Redneck Manifesto*. New York: Simon & Schuster, 1997.

Goldwater, Barry. *With No Apologies: The Personal and Political Memoirs of a United States Senator*. New York: William Morrow, 1979.

Graves, Robert. *Mammon and the Black Goddess*. London: n.p., 1964.

Griffin, Des. *Fourth Reich of the Rich*. Clackamas, Ore.: Emissary Publications, 1976.

Halberstam, David. *The Best and the Brightest*. New York: Random House, 1972.

Halevi, Zev ben Shimon. *Kaballah and Exodus*. York Beach, Me.: Samuel Weiser, Inc., 1988.

Hall, P. Manly. *The Secret Destiny of America*. Los Angeles: The Philosophical Research Society, Inc., 1958.

———. *The Lost Keys of Freemasonry*. 1923. Reprint. Richmond: Macoy Publishing and Masonic Supply Co., 1976.

Hare, Dr. Robert. *Without Conscience*. New York: Simon & Schuster, 1994.

Heikal, Mohammad Hassanein. *The Cairo Documents*. Garden City, N.Y.: Doubleday, 1973.

Horgan, John. *The End of Science*. New York: Addison Wesley, 1996.

Jones, James H. *Bad Blood*. New York: The Free Press, 1981/1993.

Josephson, Emanuel M. *The Strange Death of Franklin D. Roosevelt*. New York: Chedney Press, 1948.

Kellett, Michael. *One More Link*. Columbia, Md.: CLS Publishing, 1996.

Kershaw, Peter. *Economic Solutions*. N.p., n.d.

Keynes, John Maynard. *The Economic Consequences of the Peace*. New York: Harcourt, Brace and Howe, 1920.

Kirban, Salem. *Satan's Angels Exposed*. Huntington Valley, Pa.: Salem Kirban, Inc., 1980.

Knightley, Phillip. *The Master Spy*. New York: Alfred A. Knopf, 1989.

Knuth, E. C. *The Empire of the City: The Jekyll Hyde Nature of the British Government*. Milwaukee, Wisc.: E. C. Knuth, 1946.

LaRouche, Lyndon. *Dope, Inc.* Washington, D.C.: Executive Intelligence, Inc., 1992.

Leek, Sybil, and Bert R. Sugar. *The Assassination Chain*. Los Angeles: Pinnacle Books, 1976.

Lerach, Bill. "Plundering America: How the Abuse of Corporate Power Threatens to Destroy Your Life Savings, and What You Can Do About It." 1997.

Levi, Eliphas. *The Book of Splendors*. Wellingborough, England.: Aquarian Press, 1973.

Lewin, Leonard C. *Report from Iron Mountain on the Possibility and Desirability of Peace*. New York: The Dial Press, 1967.

Lively, Scott, and Kevin Abrahams. *The Pink Swastika*. Keizer, Ore.: Founders Publishing Corporation, 1996.

McAlpine, Peter. *The Occult Technology of Power: The Initiation of the Son of a Finance Capitalist into the Arcane Secrets of Political and Economic Power*. Port Townsend, Wash.: Loompanics Unlimited, 1974.

McAuliffe, Thomas C. "Debt Bomb and the Savings Pool." 1997.

Mackey, Albert G. "Legend of the Craft." In *Mackey's Encyclopedia of Freemasonry,* Vol. 1. Richmond: Macoy Publishers and Masonic Supply Co., 1946.

McCoy, Alfred W. *The Politics of Heroin in Southwest Asia*. New York: Harper & Row, 1972.

McKenney, Tom C. *Please Tell Me . . . Questions People Ask About Freemasonry—and the Answers*. Lafayette, La.: Huntington House Publishers, 1994.

McMaster, R. E. *No Time for Slaves*. N.p., n.d.

McRae, Hamish, and Francis Cairncross. *Capital City*. London: Eyre Methuen, 1991.

Miller, Edith Starr. *Occult Theocracy*. 1933. Reprint. Hawthorne, Calif.: Christian Book Club of America, 1980.

Mills, C. Wright. *The Power Elite*. London/New York: Oxford University Press, 1956.

Morris, Roger. *Partners in Power*. New York: Henry Holt and Co., 1996.

Mullins, Eustace. *The Curse of Canaan: A Demonology of History*. Staunton, Va.: Revelation Books, 1987.

———. *The World Order: Our Secret Rulers*. Election ed. Staunton, Va.: Ezra Pound Institute of Civilization, 1992.

———. *The Secret of the Federal Reserve: The London Connection*. Staunton, Va.: Bankers Research Institute, 1993.

*New Catholic Encyclopedia, The*. Vol. 7. New York: McGraw-Hill, 1977.

*New Encyclopaedia Britannica, The*. Vol. 20. 1973 ed. Chicago/London/Toronto: Encyclopaedia Britannica, Inc., 1979.

O'Reilly, Kenneth. *Racial Matters: The FBI's Secret File on Black America, 1960–1972*. New York: The Free Press, 1989.

Orwell, George. *1984*. New York: Harcourt Brace Jovanovich, 1977.

Pepper, William F. *Orders to Kill: The Truth Behind the Murder of Dr. Martin Luther King*. New York: Carroll & Graf Publishers, Inc., 1995.

Perloff, James. *The Shadows of Power*. Appleton, Wisc.: Western Island, 1988.

Pike, Albert. *Morals and Dogma of the Anient and Accepted Scottish Rite of Freemasonry*. 1906. Reprint. Richmond: L. H. Jenkins, Inc., Edition Book Manufacturers, 1949.

Pipes, Richard. *Russia Under the Bolshevik Regime*. New York: Alfred A. Knopf, 1933.

Poncins, Leon de. *Freemasonry and the Vatican*. N.p., 1968.

Quigley, Carroll. *Tragedy and Hope: A History of the World in Our Time*. New York: Macmillan, 1966.

———. *The Anglo-American Establishment: From Rhodes to Cliveden*. New York: Books in Focus, 1981.

Rand, Ayn. *Capitalism: The Unknown Ideal*. New York: Signet Books, 1967.

Reed, Terry, and John Cummings. *Compromised: Clinton, Bush and the CIA*. New York: S. P. I. Books/Shapolsky Publishers, Inc., 1994.

Rivera, David Allen. *Final Warning: A History of the New World Order*. Harrisburg, Pa.: Rivera Enterprises, 1984.

Robertiello, Richard, and Diana Hoguet. *The WASP Mystique*. New York: Donald I. Fine, Inc., 1987.

Robinson, John J. *Born in Blood: The Lost Secrets of Freemasonry*. New York: M. Evans, 1989.

Robison, John. *Proofs of a Conspiracy*. 1798. Reprint. Americanist Classics ed. Belmont, Mass.: Western Island, 1967.

Rodriques, Cardinal Caro y. *The Mystery of Freemasonry Unveiled*. Hawthorne, Calif.: Christian Book Club of America, 1925/1980.

Rogers, J. A. *The Five Negro Presidents*. St. Petersburg. Fla.: Helga Rogers, 1965/1993.

Ross, Ernie. "The Impossible Task of the Fed." In *Bankers and Regulations*. Irvington-on-Hudson, N.Y.: Foundation for Economic Education, 1993.

Saussy, F. Tupper. *The Miracle on Main Street: Saving Yourself and America from Financial Ruin*. Sewanee, Tenn.: Spencer Judd Publishers, 1980.

Schnoebelen, William, and Sharon Schnoebelen. *Lucifer Dethroned*. Chino, Calif.: Chick Publications, 1993.

Search, R. E. *Lincoln Money Martyred*. 1935. Reprint. Palmdale, Calif.: Omni Publications, 1989.

Shaw, Jim, and Tom McKenney. *The Deadly Deception*. Lafayette, La.: Huntington House, Inc., 1988.

Shinn, Florence Scovel. *The Game of Life and How to Play It*. Marina del Rey, Calif.: DeVorss & Company, 1925.

Skousen, W. Cleon. *The Naked Capitalist*. Salt Lake City, self-published, 1970.

Skylar, Holly, ed. *Trilateralism*. Boston: South End Press, 1980.

Smith, Adam. *Wealth of Nations*. New York: Bobbs-Merrill, 1961.

Spaulding, Mark. *The Heartbeat of the Dragon: The Occult Roots of Rock and Roll*. Sterling Heights, Mich.: Light Warrior Press, 1992.

Spenser, Robert Keith. *The Cult of the All-Seeing Eye*. N.c.: Monte Cristo Press, 1964.

Suster, Gerald. *Hitler: Black Magician*. London: Skoob Books Publishing, 1996.

Sutton, Antony C. *The Secret Cult of the Order*. Bulls Brook, Western Australia: Veritas Publishing Company PTY. Ltd., 1983.

———. *America's Secret Establishment: An Introduction to the Order of Skull and Bones*. Billings, Mont.: Liberty House Press, 1986.

———. *Trilaterals over America*. Boring, Ore.: CPA Book Publishers, 1995.

Sutton, William Josiah. *The Illuminati 666*. New York: TEACH Services, Inc., 1980.

Tardo, Russell. *Easter Errors*. Los Angeles: Faithful Word Publications, 1994.

Vankin, Jonathan. *Conspiracies, Cover-ups and Crimes: Political Ma-*

*nipulation and Mind Control in America.* New York: Paragon House, 1991.

Vennard, Wickliffe B., Sr. *The Federal Reserve Hoax: The Age of Deception.* N.p., n.d.

Vidal, Gore. *The Decline and Fall of the American Empire.* Berkeley, Calif.: Odonian Press, 1992.

Waddell, L. A. *The Phoenician Origin of the Britons, Scots & Anglo-Saxons.* Hawthorne, Calif.: Christian Book Club of America, 1983.

Waite, Arthur Edward. *A New Encyclopedia of Freemasonry.* New York: Random House, Wings Books, 1970.

*Webster's New International Dictionary.* 2nd ed. (unabridged). Cambridge, Mass.: The Riverside Press, 1959.

Weston, Warren. *Father of Lies.* London: n.p., n.d.

Whalen, Richard J. *The Founding Father.* New York: The New American Library, 1964.

———. *Christianity and American Freemasonry.* Huntington, Ind.: Our Sunday Visitor, 1987.

Winrod, Gerald B. *Adam Weishaupt: A Human Devil.* Privately published, n.d.

Wirth, Oswald. *L-Ideal Initiatique.* N.p., n.d.

*World Book Encyclopedia.* Vol. 13. Chicago: The World Book, 1969.

*Writings of Jefferson, The.* Vol. 7. Washington, D.C.: Committee of Congress, 1861.

Wurmbrand, Richard. *Was Karl Marx a Satanist?* Glendale, Calif.: Diane Books Publishing, 1976.

## YEAR 2000 (Y2K) PROBLEM ARTICLES

Barr, Stephen, and Rajiv Chandrasekaran. "Defense Audit Highlights Issues with Year-2000 Computer Glitch." *The Washington Post,* January 12, 1998, p. A15.

Bloomberg Wire Service. "First Call Bit by Year 2000 Bug." *New York Post,* January 14, 1998, p. 34.

Brock, Fred. "Can You Crush the Millennium Bug?" *The New York Times,* January 18, 1998, p. B10.

Chandrasekaran, Rajiv. "U.S. to Train Workers for Tech Jobs." *The Washington Post,* January 12, 1998, p. A1.

Gross, Neil. "Year 2000: The Meter's Running." *Business Week,* December 29, 1997, p. 41.

# BIBLIOGRAPHY

Hafner, Katie, and Michael Meyer. "Help Really Wanted." *Newsweek,* December 8, 1997, p. 94.

Harmon, Amy. "Software Jobs Go Begging, Threatening Technology Boom." *The New York Times,* January 13, 1998, p. A1.

Koprowski, Gene. "Raiders Search for New Talent." *Insight,* December 15, 1997, p. 40.

Myerson, Allen R. "Need Programmers? Surf Aboard." *The New York Times,* January 18, 1998, World sect., p. 4.

Rock, Andrea, and Tripp Reynolds. *Money,* February 1998, p. 48.

"Wall Street May Take Dec. 31, 1999, Off to Prepare for 2000." *Dallas Morning News,* New York Times Service, January 19, 1998, p. D5.

Zuckerman, M. J., and Anthony DeBarros. "Avoiding Digital Disaster." *USA Today,* December 17, 1997, p. A1.

# INDEX

# INDEX

# INNER CIRCLE APPLICATION

## Tony Brown's Inner Circle Empowerment Program
## E=CLP + FSI

**Tony Brown Online Computer Network**

Internet
(50 million users)

Networking
Downline Org.

MLM Training
(Audio/Video)

Cyberspace Cadet
Training Corps
(Wealth Cleansing

**Super-marketing**
**Network Marketing**
**INNER CIRCLE OPPORTUNITIES**

Information: 1. *Empower the People* (book)
Products: 2. Wittnauer Watches
3. Laundry Cleaning Disc
4. Inner Circle Computers
Services: 5. Prepaid Legal Services
6. Debt-Elimination System
7. Promotional Travel Agent
8. Y2K Computer Training
9. Tony Brown Tours

Empowerment
Opportunity

Seminars/MLM
Training

The Cyberspace
Institute

Infomercials

Tony Brown
Syndicated

Radio/Speeches
(Lead Generation
System)

Individuals can either apply to Tony Brown's Inner Circle as independent distributors or agree to network with distributor-members as consumers of Inner Circle products. The Inner Circle has two main objectives: (1) Create wealth and (2) Cleanse wealth by helping others develop twenty-first-century computer skills.

*Send application to:*
*Tony Brown Enterprises, Inc.*
*1501 Broadway*
*Suite 412*
*New York, NY 10036*

*To sign up with Tony Brown Online, use your modem and dial 212-869-5555 or . . . download our installation software from our website: http://www.tonybrown.com*
*To order our software, phone 212-575-0876 or fax 212-391-4607*
*E-mail mail@tbol.net*

*CHECK AS MANY AS APPLY        (COPY AND MAIL)*
❑ I have read the rules and conditions and I want to become a member of Tony Brown's Inner Circle as an independent distributor of at least one Inner Circle product.
❑ I will support this empowerment program by purchasing the Inner Circle products. If it is possible, I will also use *Tony Brown Online* to network with other Inner Circle members.
❑ I want to become a member of *Tony Brown Online*. Please send me the software.
*PLEASE PRINT*

Name: _____

Address:_____

City: _____ State _____ Zip Code _____

Phone: (   ) _____ Fax: (   ) _____

E-mail: _____ www: _____